Salish Solutions

Uniquely Northwest Diversity

Jay Miller, PhD, ed

© 2020

contents

contents

3 preface

4 Salish Language Family Chart > Coastal & Interior
5 Salishan Family
6   Changers > $duk^wib\partial\textit{ł}$ $sg^w\partial dili\check{c}$ 11 k'^{w}i'ʔat   12 Misp^h

20 Upper Skagit Villages June Collins   23 map   24 Martin Sampson 11 tribes = 24
      1 *kiki'alus* 2 *dəq^{w}ə́čabš* 3 *čubə'abš* 4 *bəskik^{w}ig^{w}ilc* 5 *sbaliuq^w* 6 *bəsk'əwix^w*
      7 *sak^{w}bix^w* 8 *dx^{w}a'ha* 9 *sk^{w}idabix^w* 10 *sx^{w}adabš* 11 *sabš*

38 Swinomish Story Pole Martin Sampson intro 41 Deception Pass Maiden 43 Boy and
      Magic Robe 45 Sun, Moon and Stars 48 Mink and the Fox 50 Hail 51 Grizzly Bear
      and Rattlesnake 51 Blackfish 53 Mt Goat &animal powers 55 Nookachamis

56 Slox̱ house interior 57 text 60 update

61 SSP Texts >> Doctor training   76 Memories 89 Revenge Murder 95 Windstorm

106 Jacob Wahalchu Quest

108 Arthur Ballard, Auburn's Collector of Indian Myths by Charlotte Widrig

111 Names 112 *k^{w}əskadəb*

122 House 118 *ləx̱albid*

133 Map of Habitats & Elevations Trade
134 Totemic Plateau

140 Six Northwest Language Families

145 Five Chehalis Ages

149 time line

157 finale

158 bib

162 index 166

Unique to the Northwest, the Salish(an) Language Family emerged in estuaries of the Fraser River, followed ancestral offshoot Kootenay upriver into the British Columbia Interior along Fraser tributaries and then down the Columbia into what is now central Washington. Along the way, communities also adapted to local resources at a wide range of elevations topping the Cascade Mountains. Each community relied on combinations of locale, talent, history, and ecology; gender balance, and contingencies, as well illustrated by the woman leader and training academy at Minter near the Tacoma Narrows.

Overlaying these geological and ecological conditions are strong cultural traditions involving successive epochs or ages of this world produced by a variety of culture heroes called Changers, variously, by region, known as *duk^{w}ibəɬ* in central Puget Sound, *sg^{w}ədilič* in northern Puget Sound, *Misp^h*, along the Chehalis River and Pacific Coast, X̱als along the Fraser, and others.

Relying on the wealth of details provided by a century of ethnography, we look specifically at the Skagit, in the Salish homeland, to consider the map and work of June Collins from the University of Chicago, of leader Martin Sampson and his mother Susie Sampson Peters, and their close kin Vi Hilbert, especially in terms of their shared ancestral community of slox, which serves as a critique of prior work. Vi's son Ron, interviewing family elders, sketched the interior of their grandfather's house and Vi later provided more kinship and census data on this village. Skagit "tribes" are comprised of *kiki'alus, dəq^{w}ə́čabš, čubə'abš, bəskik^{w}ig^{w}ilc, sbaliuq^w, bəsk'əwix^w, sak^{w}bix^w, dx^{w}a'ha, sk^{w}idabix^w, sx^{w}adabš,* and *sabš.*

Martin summaries family and tribal components of the Swinomish community as portrayed on there story pole, newly made and standing at its major intersection, with sections of the original one preserved in the community building. Martin is careful to note family descendants and ancestral spirits, along with there carved and painted graphic images.

Susie Sampson Peter provided long taped interviews to Leon Metcalf, a family ally, transcribed by Vi with advice from Martin and brother Al. Herein she is concerned with her training to become a native doctor healer, varied memories, revenge murder of her male line for malpractice, and the preparations or lack of them confronting a huge windstorm as often happens in January, such as when a vital Seattle bridge blew down.

To contrast with Susie's questing we turn to Edward Curtis's account from aged Suquamish leader Jacob Wahalchu set against familiar Seattle land- and water-scapes. Remaining in south Puget Sound, we pay homage to Arthur Ballard, a friend of Leon Metcalf who taped him, in an illustrated newspaper article.

The continuing importance of inherited ancestral names, based in idealized cedar plank houses, is next studied, particularly *k^{w}əskadəb* and *ləx̱albid*. A map of elevations, habitats, and traditional trade goods prepares us to move into the Salishan Plateau represented by tribes now enrolled at Colville, where spirit animal locations in stories have a totemic reflection within localized families.

We end in southwest Washington among Tsamosan branch of Coast Salish, considering first their language diversity and then their sequential five ages now represented in a 40-foot mural in the hallway of their tribal hotel, Eagle's Landing across the street from their casino.

An overall historic time line precedes the final bibliography.

Salish chart
Salishan Language Family
Coast

Nuxalk (Bella Coola)

Central
  Comox
  Pentlatch
  Sechelt(Shishahl)-Sliammon
  Squamish
  Halkomelem (dialect chains -)
    Island (həl̓q̓əmin̓əm') **Cowichan-Chemainus-Nanaimo**
    Delta (hən̓q̓əmin̓əm') **Musqueam**(xʷməθk̓ʷəy̓əm)**-Tsawwasen-Katzie**
    Upriver (hɛlq̓əmɛyləm) **Matsqui-Sumas-Chilliwack–Chehalis-Tait**

Straits
  Lummi-Samish-Semiahmoo-Songish-Saanich-Sooke(T'Sou-ke)
  Klallam (S'Klallam)

Nooksack

Lushootseed (Puget)
  North (dxʷləšutsid) **Skagit-Duxwaha-Sauk-Suiattle-Swinomish-Stillaguamish-
    Snohomish-Skykomish**
  South (Whulshootseed, (t)xʷəlšutsid) **Suquamish-Snoqualmi-
    Duwamish(Muckleshoot)-Puyallup-Steilacoom-Nisqually-
    Sahewamish(Squaxin)**

Twana-Skokomish

Tsamosan
  Quinault
  Chehalis
  Cowlitz (sƛ̓púlmixq)

Tillamook-Siletz

Interior

with dialect chains (-)	**North**
South	**Secwepemc (Shuswap)**
Coeur d'Alene	**Nlaka'pamux (Thompson)**
Flathead(Selish)-Kalispel-Spokan	**Stl'atl'imc–Lillooet (Lil'wat)**
Lakes-Colvile-Sanpoil-Nespelem-Okanagan	
Columbia(Snkʸuse)-Wenatchee(Pskʷaws)-Entiat-Chelan-Methow	

Salishan Family

The Salishan Language Family is localized in the Northwest from the Pacific shore to western Montana and British Columbia, Canada and is characterized by divisions, branches, and dialect chains, with no obvious links with the dozen or so major linguistic stocks (Algic, Iroquoian, Uto-Aztecan, for example) across the continent. Its name has been applied to its international waterway now called the Salish Sea along Washington and British Columbia.

The Salishan Family has 23 interlinked languages, separated by the Cascade Mountains, divided into Coast (16 members) and Interior (7 members), with coastal branches, from the north, of Nuxalk (Bella Coola), Central, Tsamosan, and Tillamook. Central Coast Salishan includes Comox, Sechelt, Pentlatch (dormant), Squamish, Nooksak, Halkomelem (including Chilliwack, Musqueam, Cowichan), Straits (including intergrading Sooke, Saanich, Songhees, Lummi, Samish, Semiahmoo, and, more apart, Klallam), Twana of Hood Canal, and Lushootseed of Puget Sound. Tsamosan, once called Olympic, includes Upper Cowlitz, Upper (including Satsop) and Lower Chehalis, and Quinault.

Interior Salishan consists, from the north, of St'at'imcets (Lillooet), of Nlakapamuxcin (Thompson) and of Sexwepemxcin (Shuswap), and of Mid-Columbia dialect chains with "upriver" Methow-Okanogan-Nespelem-Sanpoil-Colvile-Lakes and "downriver" Chelan-Entiat-Psk^{w}aws (Wenatchi)-Snk^{y}use (Columbian), of Kalispel-Spokan-Selish (Flathead), and of Coeur d'Alene.

Over a century ago, some Central speakers shifted from nasals to orals (M > B, N > D), such as Lushootseeds, Twana, and neighboring Chimakum and southern Nootkans (Makah and Ditidat, though still called Nitinat in English). This seems to have been a counter-response to territorial aggression by nasal-using Straits Salish speakers such as Lummi, Klallam, and Samish (Duwaha, Nuwaha, dxwa'ha) who left the Gulf islands to occupy disease-depopulated mainland sites, displaced Nooksacks. Thus, any consistently snowcapped mountain is now called *taq^{w}oba*, in Lushootseed, which is the source for what the settlers heard as *takoma* (Tacoma) and applied to Mt. Rainier and a nearby city.

Tribal communities are distinguished by their habitats, especially elevations. Chehalis and Cowlitz relied on extensive prairies, abounding in camas gardens, with upriver access to the Cascades. Quinault are on the Pacific seashore with access to the Olympic Mountains upriver, as Tillamook are on the Oregon coast. Klallam are on the US side of the Strait of Juan de Fuca, with Sooke, Saanich, Songhees across on the Canadian side. Lummi and Samish were on the Gulf islands, without rivers and therefore relying on reef nets to catch salmon migrating through on their way to their spawning rivers.

Among Lushootseeds along Puget Sound, Suquamish are on west side creeks with access to the Olympics, along with Twana on huge Hood Canal. Also on the lowlands are Duwamish, Snohomish, Lower Skagit, Stillaguamish, and Swinomish, with access to nearby islands. The Snohomish River forks into the Snoqualmie and Skykomish Rivers, derived from the word meaning 'uprivers'. In the foothills and mountains are Snoqualmie, Skagit, and, especially high, Sauk-Suiattle, with a mountain pass giving access to Lake Chelan. Skagit have another pass into Chelan.

In the Interior, tribes have namesake rivers, tributary to either the Fraser, such as Lillooet, Thompson, and Shuswap, or the Columbia. Snk^{y}use lived on a wide plain within the Big Bend of the Columbia. Psk^waws were in the Cascades and foothills along Wenatchi Lake and river. Chelan, Coeur d'Alene, and Lakes lived along big lakes, with high falls at Chelan and lower falls on the Spokan blocking salmon runs. Entiat means 'grass in the water' and is where trees and woody debris logjamed, providing fuel for cooking and heating.

Changers, now regarded as a lone figure, functioned as teams in the past, variously known as *Duk^wibəł* in Puget Sound, *Misp^h* along the Pacific coast, Coyote (as *snklip* or *smiyaw*) on the Plateau, as well as regionally Bluejay or *sg^wədilič* partnered with Fire, Knife, and Baby (initiate).

duk^wibəł
Changer

duk^wibəł was the name of the great and mighty man who created the world. He started his wonderful task away over in the East and gradually worked towards the West, creating everything as he went along. He carried with him a great variety of languages and as he created each group of people, he gave them a language, being careful to select the best languages he had.

While working his way West, he reached Puget Sound country and decided that he would go no farther West or North. In his hand he still had a great number of languages left and at a loss to know what to do with them he scattered them all around him and to the North, and that is the very reason why there are so many different languages among the Indians of the Sound country and the North.

After duk^wibəł had scattered the languages about in this wasteful fashion, the different tribes of Indians found that they could not understand one another; they were not satisfied with the way in which duk^wibəł had created the world – they found that the sky was much too low to suit their convenience, for the taller people would very often bump their heads on the sky. Also, people got into the habit of climbing trees and making their way into the next world, which was not as it should be.

The wiser Indians of the different tribes held a meeting and it was agreed that the people should try to shove the sky up higher and it would be possible to do this if all [2] the people would shove at the same time. How could they make them all understand just when they were to shove? duk^wibəł had given animals, birds, insects, people all a different language and it would be difficult to make them all understand just when they were to shove. Finally, one of the wiser men thought of the word "yəhaw'" which means to proceed [in this case *lift together*] and so these wise men who were attending the meeting scattered the news among the different tribes and the date for the lifting of the sky was set.

In the meantime everybody was busy making poles with which to lift the sky. You will see a bundle of these sticks or poles carved on the big story pole [in Everett, WN] – they are carefully wrapped in matting and tied with Indian packing straps so that they may be preserved for a long time. You can only see the ends of the sticks protruding from the matting.

On the day set for the lifting of the sky, all the people braced their poles against the sky and the command "yəhaw'" was given and everybody lifted as hard as they could and they succeeded in raising the sky a little bit; after the second "yəhaw'" the sky was raised a little higher and after the fourth attempt they raised the sky up to its present position.

Now it happened that just as the people had been ready to shove the sky up, three hunters who had been chasing four elk for several hours came to where heaven and earth nearly met and the elk jumped into the next world, and, of course, the hunters and the elk were raised with it.

To this very day, you can see them in the sky at night; the three hunters form the handle of the dipper – the one in the center is leading his dog, the tiny star so close to him – and the four elk form the rest of the dipper. Then, too, you have noticed the skatefish formation of stars in the sky; two canoes with three Indians in each canoe and a little fish happened to be making their way into the sky when the people shoved the sky up and so they have had to remain there ever since. All the Indians know that the hunters and the little dog, the elk, the little fish, the fisherman in the canoes were on earth once upon a time and all tribes have the same names for these stars.

From the time the people moved the sky, there was no more jumping into the next world, and the people were content and happy. Although they could not yet understand the language of all the different tribes, they were happy because they had been able to use the wonderful word "yəhaw'" and in that way they had been able to accomplish what they had set out to do.

<h2 style="text-align:center">sg^wədilič</h2>

According to June Collins (1974: 157-159):

There [are] an important group of spirits which animated material objects. One of the best known and most widely possessed of these was *sg^wədilič*, which enlivened objects. At least four different types of objects were listed by informants [instructors] as variants of *sg^wədilič*; I do not know exactly how these were related to one another. These are as follows: *s.xpayaxubiq^w*, boards of cedar; *t'əqt'əqacabiuq^w*, an object of vine maple boughs covered with [158] cedar bark in the shape of a twisted doughnut large enough to be held by eight men; *čáju?*, painted ducks of cedar; and *k^wastəd*, goat hair.

It is certain that the kind of *sg^wədilič* called *čáju?* was associated with ducks in that people who owned him could bring ducks down out of the air and in that his symbol was a wooden duck. I am not certain that the other three variants were also associated with ducks. For this reason I have called this spirit "guarding power" elsewhere (Collins 1952: 297ff), since it did guard the house and any specific object placed near it. When the pre-White house still stood, the owner might keep his objects symbolizing *sg^wədilič* on display, tied to the middle of one of the house posts.

John Fornsby said:

sg^wədilič is a powerful thing. He is all head and no body. He knows what people are thinking about, *sg^wədilič* is *s.tubš* [man]. There is no *sɬadəy?* [woman] *sg^wədilič*. He is just like a person. He knows what a man is thinking about. He beats *x^wda?əb*. [He can overcome *x^wda?əb* in curing the sick.] Some fellows dream about *sg^wədilič* and make it. If you just dream it, it is no good. If you find it living [as living trees] in the daytime or nighttime to help you, then it is powerful.

Changers

In speaking about woodworking, he said also that *sg^wədilič* is helpful in learning this craft.

There is [an epic] which tells of the arrival of *sg^wədilič* and his brothers to the Skagit valley. They are described as naming what they found, introducing fish, and instructing the Indians in basic kinds of knowledge. Lucy Williams told the following version of this myth. The chief characters, Raven, Mink, Coyote, and *duk^wbəł* of the other Upper Skagit myths of transformers are found widely distributed in Puget Sound and in the case of the first three, far beyond this area. In contrast, the myth of *sg^wədilič* has not been reported from other areas and may have originated in the Skagit valley.

A long time ago when first the world was made, *sg^wədilič* was the oldest of four brothers who first came this way. His two younger brothers were Knife and Fire. He also had a Baby brother, the youngest who had the most power. They walked on the right side of the river, going up river. They named the creeks, lakes, mountains, and places where there are going to be tribes. The younger brother is Knife; he has more power than the two older ones. If somebody cuts him up, he puts himself together; he has a strong *s.qalalitut*. [159]

They named the mountains, lakes, creeks, *sg^wədilič* put little fish in every creek. He named the tribes. He did that a long time ago. He was human at that time. Knife was human; Fire was human. This was the first time Indians learned to have a knife, to have fire, to have power [guardian spirits], *sg^wədilič* taught Indians how to prepare deer meat and salmon. His brother taught them to have a knife, to cut fish. The third brother taught them how to make fire to cook their fish. The youngest one taught Indians to have a power [guardian spirit].

Well, they were coming way up to Skagit Falls. The oldest, *sg^wədilič*, gave everything a name on the Skagit; the people had the knife and fire now. After the *sg^wədilič* had finished his job, he said, "I'm going to be here now, right in Skagit Falls. I'm going to dive now." He dove right in the middle of the falls. He was going to be *sg^wədilič* then. He told his brothers, "Well, I'm through now. They [the Indians] are going to find me. I'm going to be power now."

Brother Knife kept on walking with his other two brothers, going in different tribes in Okanogan. They crossed the Cascades. Knife is the leader now. He was going to show Indians how to use the knife over there, The Fire brother worked to show Indians how to build fire. The youngest brother told the Indians, "You are going to have power before you find your food. You are going to have power; that's where you earn your living." Knife said, "I'm going to be right here; my job is done."

There were just two left. Fire was the leader now. They got way back to Okanogan and saw other Indians. They taught them to have fire and to have the knife. The Indians were able to grab red hot rocks and play with them. Their hands never burned because they had power. They burned pitch and hit themselves in the face. When they started powwowing [singing their guardian spirit songs] they couldn't stop. The Indians burned pitch and threw it in their faces. This was the only thing to wake them up [bringing them out of the spirit possession]. They taught them how to have power. Fire was going to stay there. Next to Naches was the place where Fire stopped.

Now just the Baby was left, the youngest one. The Indians got strong power. If you cut them up, they could patch themselves together. They couldn't die. The youngest one taught them. The Indians were strong; they couldn't die when you hurt them. If you cut them, they patch themselves together. If they started powwowing [singing their song] they can't stop. The Indians burned pitch and threw it in the singer's face. This was the only way to wake them [bring them out of the spirit possession]. The power got in them and they wanted to sing all the time. Where the youngest one stopped was the *wišəb* [Wishram] tribe.

According to Sally Snyder, also from Lucy Williams:

MX (73)   Upper Skagit

This is how these Indians came to have Indian power. There were four boys who were brothers from way, way off someplace. The oldest brother was *Sg*ʷ*ədilič*, the head of the power, and he would work hard for the Indians here. The brother of all the powers was walking up this way on the other side of the river. He made one man and one woman and put them down. After that he told them to look on the mountain. They twisted and looked. Deer meat came down, and this power showed them and he said, "This is your food right here."

The youngest brother of the powers was Knife *sduuk*ʷ power. Knife showed the people how to cut and cook meat. Fire, his brother, showed them how to burn. He showed them the Indian matches, dry roots of willow – real, real dry. He took a stick with a hole and twisted another stick in this hole and made the roots bum. He showed them how to make fire and to cook the meat. Then *Sg*ʷ*ədilič* showed the man and woman all the berries on the mountain.   "This is food to eat. You are going to get it." *Sg*ʷ*ədilič* told the Indians this; this that he made at this one little village. Next, the fire was burning. And he told the Indians to look at the river. Soon, all the fish came in and lay down by the Indians. "That's for you to eat, too. But you can't get them for nothing. You have to work hard and be clean. That's what you are going to tell your children." The *Sg*ʷ*ədilič* said, "You feed from the river. You are going to get the trouts and bring them home. After you have children you have to be clean and wash up, and get the power. You can't have anything in the stomach. And go way up in the mountains and lie down and stay for maybe ten days or even more." This was same for the woman; to be clean and go out and learn to make blankets and baskets easy.

That power came and put the two people in one village to be raised there and to teach them [taught] by Knife and Fire.

The fourth brother was *Swa'dx*, who was an Okanagon. He was a power and song belonging to the Okanagon, and the youngest brother (?). He was just watching all this time because he was working for other people, the Okanagon. All of this story goes to Skagit Falls – all the same story to each them the same. They made for the people the meat and berries and fish. The first food was made by the Skagit.

The *Sg*ʷ*ədilič* sat down in the river facing down(stream) after the end of his job. It's a rock now, called *Sk*ʷ*dələb*. His brother is *x*ʷ*skedəb*, named after a large rock in the middle of the Skagit at its head. *Sg*ʷ*ədilič* is *Sk*ʷ*dələb*'s power. And he sang his power song after he sat down, and told the people, "You'll hear me before daylight. Those that are raised here and (are) clean will find me, and will be (have) a strong power and (it will) be easy to get fish, easy to get meat, easy to get food." The people camped there and heard the song early in the morning, about three o'clock. He was singing the song when they dived.

And most significantly, delivered in Lushootseed by Isadore Tom to his cousin Vi Anderson Hilbert:

This sg^wədilič was a gift from the creator when the earth was first created.
There was not just one kind of *sg^wədilič*. When an individual received the power of the sg^wədilič he was shown. He learned which kind he would use if or when he used it.
My respected older cousin pətius [Isadore Tom] told me. There are five kinds of *sg^wədilič*. We could name them all:

Vine maple	= t'əqt'əqac
Cedar tree [power board type]	= x̱əpayac
Cedar sapling	= stidg^wəd
Cedar bark [pounded then twisted into shape]	= sła?g^wac
Rock	= č'əƛ̓a?ak^wbix^w

A long time ago there were those possessing the *sg^wədilič* power who left the *sg^wədilič* at home when they went to do their work. They just used their song because the spirit power of the sg^wədilič, the strength, is carried through the song. It is his song that the owner of the *sg^wədilič* sings. Then the sick person is helped, the lost is found, the thief is identified. This is the work of the owner of the *sg^wədilič* power.

Long ago, when one possessing the power of the *sg^wədilič* became old, the *sg^wədilič* was taken, carried away to be hid sometimes in an old dead hollow cedar tree. They are deposited there, not to be removed by anyone. They are finished, *sg^wədilič* is put to rest. This is all concerning the *sg^wədilič*.

Vi (taq^wšəblu) Hilbert 2/18/79

To uphold these responsibilities of k'^wi'?at = 'sacred, holy', there were strict rules:

Respect (Hold sacred) All of the Earth —
?əsk'^wi'?a(t)tx^w ti?ə? bəəəək'^w swatix^wtəd
Respect (Hold Sacred) All of the Spirits —
?əsk'^wi'?a(t)tx^w k^wi tul'al sqəlalitut
Remember (Hold sacred) The Creator — Esteem ?əshig^wəd Honor ?əstəłildx^w
?əsk'^wi'?a(t)tx^w k^wi x̱ax̱a? šəq si'ab Remember ?əslax̱ədx^w
Be Honest —
x^wi k^w(i)adsubədčəb (Don't You Dare Lie!)
Be Generous —

Changers

ləskʷaxʷad kʷ(i)adiišəd (Be Helpful to Your People in Any Way You Can!)

Be Compassionate —

əsušəbid kʷ(i)adiišəd (Feel Forgiveness/Pity for Others!)

Be Clean —

əsc'akʷ čəxʷ (You Will Be Washed)

əsc'akʷ tulal bəkʷ sa (sč'iq'ʷil i dᶻək'ʷadad)

(Keep Washing Away All Badness (Dirt and Sin-Crime))

Be Industrious —

čəxʷa ck'ʷaqid łuləyayus (And You Will Work Always, Don't Be Lazy!)

As a lesson, negative examples are used because they are contrary and reinforce our teachings.

Missing Misp[h]:
Restor(y)ing the Transformer of
Tsamosans of coastal Washington

Abstract

Virtually unknown among Northwest Changer ~ Transformers is Misp[h] of the Tsamosans in southwest Washington. As twins born miraculously to a murderous mother, they destroy her ogress sisters, save nebulously-formed children, and decree skills, foods, and customs at specific places and times. Their living embodiment is a duck -- once call old squaw (old sqwawk), now longtail – with appropriately complex changes in bright plumage by season and gender.

Introduction

The major loss, academically, from the life-long institutionalization of Thelma Adamson after her fieldwork among Tsamosan Salishan speakers of Southwestern Washington has been the continuing failure to recognize *Misp[h]* as a major transformer in the oral literature of the Tsamosan Coast Salish of Southwestern Washington. As a graduate student, Adamson spent 1926 collecting folklore among the Upper Chehalis at Oakville, followed by a concern with ethnography in 1927, when her mentor Franz Boas joined her to conduct linguistic research at the same community. Her dissertation, completed, approved, but never filed in May of 1929, was a study of transformers and tricksters among Coast Salish. Her supporting folklore collection was published, through the efforts of Ruth Benedict, in 1934 and reissued in 2009.

Salish oral literature is particularly well known because of the sustained efforts of linguists and storytellers concerned with recording in these natives languages, as well as the interest of internationally known scholars and folklorists (Walls 1987), such as Franz Boas, Melville Jacobs (1959, 1960), Del Hymes, Dale Kinkade, Arthur Ballard (see all), June Collins (1952b), and Vi Hilbert (Miller and Hilbert 1993, 1996, 2004), as well as popular collections (Matson 1968, 1972), culminating in a recent Salish compendium (Thompson and Egesdal 2008) and the Adamson reprinting.

This reissue makes more available the epic of *Misp[h]* and his brother Kumol told by Lucy Heck (pp. 329-432), a noblewoman from the Lower Chehalis of Grays Harbor. Earlier, among Quinault, Livingston Farrand heard versions of *Misp[h]* from Bob Pope in 1902. Ronald Olson learned it from Billy Mason, Bob Pope, John Dixon, and Jonah Cole in 1926.

The earliest reference found so far appears in a letter, dated 20 July 1855, from James Swan at Shoalwater to George Gibbs, who asked for word lists of various native languages of the Northwest. Swan's source seems to have been Old Toke, a Chinook leader living at Tokeland on Willapa Bay, now the location of the tiny Shoalwater Bay reservation. The six page letter includes stories of Thunderbird, the *Smisspee* (duck), the winds, and customs and religious beliefs of Indians from Columbia River to Nisqually. *Smisspee* is obviously Misp[h], as explained in this extracted quote from page 2:

Changers Misp[h]

The Smisspee is a small duck of the Sheldrake species and the only tradition about it that I have heard is that it was formerly a man or as the Indians express it they were "ankartz Tillikums" [*ahnkutty tilakums*, past people]. This bird came to the ?ema? [Nemah] River in this bay when a great many Indians lived and seeing the river full of salmon asked why they did not catch them. The Indians replied they did not know what salmon were, and were afraid of them. The Smisspee then showed them how to make nets and spears and they took immense quantities of fish. And from this bird all Indians learned to catch fish.

Edmond Meany (1905: 6) of the University of Washington visited local reservations to make notes and write a series of newspaper articles, that for the Chehalis includes a version by the famous Secena, who worked with Franz Boas in 1927:

After some persuasion, See-see-nah told legends and stories of the old life, which I was very glad to write down with the aid of the two interpreters.
Long ago, before the whites came, his people owned all the prairies and land around the Chehalis river. *Misp* and his older brother, *Kom-mol-owish*, taught the Indians how to make fire by spinning one dry piece of wood on another. They also taught the people how to use fish and roots for food. Then they used flint and bluestone for arrowheads and axes.

Quinault creation, according to a cultural and economic overview by Justine James and Leilani Chubby (2002: 99), involved three distinct epochs, each with its own reformer. At the beginning was Xwani Xwani [X^{w}ani X^{w}ani], then came the protean Animal People, and third, setting the stage for the time of human people, was Misp[h] -- the culture hero ~ transformer ~ reformer.

Misp[h] and his twin, in particular, did much to form present Grays Harbor, and coastal Washington state. He was a key ancestral figure for Tsamosans. While other regional reformers are well known, such as *Kw'ati* of the Quileute and Makah, *Misp[h]* is not. In part this is a consequence of the fate of Thelma Adamson. Thus, Misp[h] has remained unheralded for seventy-five years.

Such great epics of Native American can easily be misunderstood by mainstream readers because they teach by negative examples, rather than extolling the rewards of virtue or financial success. Presenting these stories in English voids many of their nuances. The idioms used in the native language explicitly indicate what is real and what is not, what is worthwhile and what is greedy, or what is good for everyone and what is selfish. By the end of these epics morality, decency, and community values are instituted, not always in the easiest or safest manner.

Only at the end of each epic are Misp[h] and his brother identified with their duck avatar – the immature male in winter plumage most like a "long-tailed", once also known (among 20 local names) as "old squaw," though "old squawk" is more appropriate since its species Latin name *Clangula hyemalis* refers to its noisy clanging in winter. Though attributed by whites to the female, it is the male which is the most noisy. This species is remarkably apt for a transformer since it is so changeable, going through two complete annual bright plumage changes, unlike the bright and dull ones of most birds, as well as gestational ones. It can also dive to 200 feet deep. Its diet is also human like, relying on mollusks, crustaceans, insects, and aquatic plants.

To aid in following the epic versions, a generalized condensation of versions follows:

An industrious young man (Wildcat) camps alone, either drying fish or making a canoe. He soon becomes backlogged, while continuing to gain more materials. One day, while he is away, his work is done for him. After several days of this unknown help, he hides to see who is doing it. A young woman appears who then marries him. They live together until the fishing season or canoe is done and then go back to his home town. Before they get there, she lets down her hair to hide her face and, once inside, sits backward looking at the wall. She lives quietly in the house, tormented by Bluejay who wants to see her face and hear her laugh. When she can endure no more, she hides her husband, pulls back her hair to reveal a frightful face and laughs five times, killing more people each time until everyone is dead, even her disobedient husband. She eats all of them, but saves her husband's genitals in a basket above her bed. She becomes pregnant and has twins. The oldest one is Misp[h], the other Kəmol.

The twins grow quickly and precociously. When their mother leaves for the day, they do everything she had forbidden them to do, finding their father's parts in the basket and his former town littered with gnawed bones. Alarmed, they go home to burn down their own house and flee. The mother sees the smoke and ash, including a bit retaining the design on the side of her cherished basket. Angry, she rushes home, finds the smoldering ruins, and chases after her sons.

They trick and kill her, then move on. Along the way they meet and kill her four sisters, each of whom kills children (unformed souls/spirits) in a special way before eating them. Each aunt is gutted and the more recently dead children are revived and given professions that are thereafter passed down family lines. They go from town to town around the Olympic Peninsula, decreeing livelihoods and abilities specific to each community. Near the end, the brother is killed and revived as a duck, while Misp[h] becomes a stone at the mouth of the Columbia River. Their spirits return as ducks in the late Summer.

Since the motivation of Misp[h] and his twin is to make the world ready for today, the epic by Lucy Heyden Heck is summarized next because it is the most detailed one known and would have been the basis for Adamson to properly highlight the importance of Misp[h]'s role among the Coast Salish.

The Reformer Twins
paraphrase of Lucy Heck to Thelma Adamson (1934: 329-342)

Chief Woodpecker lived in a town of twelve houses at present Humptulips City. He was a skilled carpenter who built all the houses and many of the canoes. His son worked with him, so as to master woodworking. When it came time, the son was sent alone into the forest to make his first canoe, and his father insisted that no one was to help the boy. He had to succeed on his own.

The boy selected a cedar tree, felled it, and began shaping it until dusk when he returned to his camp for the night. The next day he shaped the inside. When he came back on the third day, he found a big camas bulb inside the canoe form. It was tied with a long black hair. Surprised and suspicious, he hid the bulb in nearby brush. The fourth day, two bulbs were in the canoe, each tied with a long hair. On the fifth day, there were three bulbs, and on the sixth, four camas and elk marrow used for a protective greasing (sun block) of the face. When he returned the seventh day to rough out the canoe, nothing was there. Instead, he worked for a while until he became sleepy and took a nap inside the canoe.

He dreamed a pretty girl with very long hair was sitting beside him, asking why he did not eat the camas she brought to him. She pledged her love to this boy of royal blood. When he awoke, she was actually sitting there and they agreed to marry. She said she lived upriver, but would move to his town as long as it was after dark because she was very bashful.

Just outside the town, the girl unbraided her hair so it hung over her face. Inside the house, she sat with her face to the wall. At bed time, she slept beside her husband in the chief's section. The next morning, she again sat facing the wall with her hair down, weaving a basket. She ate her meal of camas in the same position. Ever nosey, Bluejay began to mutter about this overly modest behavior. When he got no response, he kept insisting to see her face and hear her laughter. He kept this up for five long days.

The fifth morning, the wife asked her husband to go with her far beyond the prairie while she dug camas. Instead, when they got there, she dug a very deep hole and told her husband to hide inside it. She stuffed his ears and nose with fine cedar bark, covered him with a box, and left him in supposed safety. Too curious, the husband raised the edge of the box, waiting to hear her laugh.

Back at the house, the girl began to dress up, braid her hair, and grease and paint her face. Then she went to Bluejay and said they would now laugh. She clapped her hands together and shouted. Bluejay fell over dead. As she continued laughing out loud, everyone in the house died, their eyes bulging out and tongues lolling. She went house to house in the town, shouting and killing. Then she started at one end and ate everyone up.

When she went to find her husband, he was dead. She wept. Then she took his torso, put it in a basket, and hung it over their bed at home. During the night, the basket shook. The next morning, the girl was pregnant with twins, who were born five days later. The elder was Misp[h] and the younger was Kmol. Two days after birth, they were walking and using bows and arrows. She favored Misp[h] and always threatened to eat Kmol if he cried. After five days, they were men. Each day their mother left to dig camas, warning them not to look in her basket nor go downriver.

They became suspicious and looked in the basket, identifying their father's remains. They went downriver and found his village, littered with skeletons. They knew the worse and decided to flee from home. They burned their house and walked away, with Misp[h] behind his brother in front. Their mother sensed something was wrong, then saw ashes in the air. One cinder showed the design pattern of her basket, and then she realized her home had burned up. She raced after her sons, singing a song to weaken them. They prepared for her attack by climbing to the top of a tree covered in loose bark, praying to the tree to hold on tightly to its own bark. The tree gave them special words (*dicta*) to grip onto its trunk. When their mother saw them in the tree, she spoke softly and nicely to lure them down. Instead they suggested she climb up, telling her the special words. She did not always remember them so she only got up slowly. Near the top, *Misp[h]* pushed the bark with his foot and it fell off and crushed their mother.

They climbed down and went on, knowing they had four aunts who were cannibals like their mother. A prairie, named Seated Children, near Humptulip City had a stepped slope filled with children, who were known as "Always Tears" because they were crying, dirty, and fearful. At the bottom were two trees leaning together with a swing between them. Further out was a huge bloody rock. Those children warned the twins that the woman who lived on the prairie would eat them.

They greeted their aunt, and she asked after their mother. They said she was slowed by a heavy pack and would be along soon. Their aunt tried to get Kmol to swing, but Misp[h] took his place, teaching the children instead to chorus "Go and Come Back". Misp[h] jumped off the swing beyond the rock and survived. He told his aunt it was her turn to swing, urging the children to sing "Go and Never Come Back". She hit the rock and died as her belly burst open. The twins revived the most recently dead children, but those longest dead stayed dead. The uneaten children were washed, dressed, and painted. They were told they would live there to become very old. Those who revived would live to middle age, while those (pre-souls) who stayed dead became stillborns.

The twins went on until they came to a prairie where they saw a pile of dirt covered in clam shells, shaped like a seated child. Five wide seats behind this figure were filled with children. The men greeted their aunt, and she asked after their mother. They said she would be along. The children explained that each was sent to fetch a stick standing near the figure without laughing, but he or she always failed, was dashed against the rock, and eaten. Misp[h] fetched the stick soberly, then said it was the aunt's turn. She laughed, so he grabbed her by the heels and dashed her against the rock so that she burst open and children's bodies tumbled out. The most recent victims revived fully after they were washed and cleaned, but those longer dead were slower to recover. Some never did. These children founded royal-blooded families.

At the next prairie, children were speared as each came to sit on a large fungus. Misp[h] sat but was not harmed, so it was the third aunt's turn. He speared her heart and threw her against a rock so her belly burst open. Again, the most recent meals were revived, but those longer dead were less lucky. These children became spirit helpers for hunting (Hunt power).

The twins went on to the prairie at Carlyle, where they met the fifth aunt, who killed children with a boy's game of see-saw that had a flat rock at either end. The aunt and Misp[h] got on the teeter-tauter. He jumped off when she was on the high end and she burst on the rock below. Victims were cleaned up and revived, founding a community of hunters, both men and skilled women.

At the mouth of the Humptulips, where they decreed the building of fish traps, the twins resolved to right the wrongs of the world. They went westward, coming to a house where people were shooting arrows inside. It was raining and no one there knew how to fix leaks in the roof. Instead, they shot arrows at the drips to try to stop them. Bluejay spoke for the household, explaining their tactic. The twins went up on the roof and saw that the shingles were placed the wrong way, so they set them right and the leaking stopped. All subsequent roofs were built this way.

They went toward the shore and came upon a house where Bluejay and his wife were cohabitating on the roof, so the Twins decreed modesty in the future. Further up the beach, clams were stuck on sticks to cook in the sunlight. Instead, the twins taught people there to cut out the clams from the shell and cook them on sticks over an open fire.

They went on and, at the surf, met a man walking upside-down carrying firewood between his legs. They set him upright and instructed everyone to carry firewood on the right shoulder. Farther up the coast they came to a house where they heard groaning, "Ouch, my head; Ouch, my hand." A man was splitting wood by driving the wedge into the log with his head. Instead, Misp[h] made him a stone mallet and gave instructions still followed to split wood. People there tried to cook their food by dancing on it. The brothers told them to get their nets to catch salmon, but the people instead got digging sticks for clamming.

At Corner Creek, they met a man sharpening the edges of three big clam shells and singing about how he would deal with the reformers. Instead, Misp[h] stuck the shells in his head and butt, turning him into a deer to be hunted to feed people. At Copalis, they met a man being dragged into the sea by his own head lice. The twins washed his hair in urine and rinsed it in fresh water, killing the lice. Then they carved him a comb that was made of wood, and taught him to comb, oil, and braid his hair. Finally, they called for people to bring out their salmon nets, but instead they got their clamming sticks. Ever after, they have clammed there.

At the Rocks, Wolves were eating raw crabs. Misp[h] tried to reform them into proper people who cooked their food, but they asked to remain as they were and so became five brothers consisting of four Wolves and a Dog. At Moclips, they taught proper sex technique to the people (especially modesty and respect by girls). At Rock Creek, they found a deeply sleeping man and attached clam shells to his front teeth. He became *X^wani X^wani* [active in a later age]. At Taholah, they called for people to bring out their fish gear and they did. As a reward, the twins taught them to make tight basket traps. Farther on they found empty houses, and following the stream [Raft Creek] there came to a suspicious whirlpool. They heated rocks in a fire and dropped them into the water until it began to boil. A huge black being with an enormous mouth floated up and they cut it open, finding whole families, canoes, and houses. Those most recently killed could be revived. Among them were Bluejay and X^wani X^wani, who decided to repopulate that locale using skin rubbed off Misp^h and himself. They blew on the exfoliate pellets and they became people, gifted with a special fish trap.

They went on and shouted for people to build fish traps because they already had fire, good houses, and tools. But they were dirty, so the twins taught them to bathe and groom. At Quileute, they shouted for fish traps but instead people launched canoes and ran out trolling lines, as they still do. Feeling threatened, the twins ran away and decreed the Quileutes would be mean. At Ozette, they also called for fishtraps, but some went into the hills to hunt and others went out to troll. They did everything properly.

They went on, calling for fish traps at each town, but some just went out to sea, others embraced warfare, and some developed other skills. At one town, they cleared away rocks creating a whirlpool and so killed a monster.

When they got along the Columbia River, at Clatsop, they called for fish traps but instead people caught crabs. Clatsops were confirmed in their royal blood. At Astoria, people came out with their nets and received runs of huge Chinook salmon. Across the river, people were drying sturgeon heads on warm rocks, but the twins instead taught them to smoke sturgeon. Further on they met people who did not know how to eat, putting food into every body orifice but the mouth. They were taught to chew and swallow, as well as drink. They then had to teach them how to sleep and to use a net.

At the next town, people packed everything they had and then went to sleep, thinking that was how things could be moved. Instead, the twins taught them to pack things up and move them by canoe. At Fort Columbia, everyone had a huge snake as a pet. If they did not feed these serpents enough, they ate children. Misp^h, instead, arranged to kill all the snakes and burn them up on a high hill, where the place where he sat to rest is now marked by a rock shaped like a duck.

At Chinook City, the town was infested with woodrats, who ate people alive. The twins set fire to the area, killing all the rats and enabling people to set out their nets. At Ilwako, people had their nets and used them well. At Nasell, they called for nets, but instead people went out to hunt or to hook sturgeon. They had no fires and had to be taught to use firesticks and to cook. At Nemah, people went out to hunt or built small salmon traps. At Bay Center, people brought out herring traps. Then the twins went across the bay and met people spearing salmon.

At Westport, people got crabs and clams, and the twins decreed "A whale will always wash ashore here; you are good people [and deserve it]". Further on, people at Ts'e'tc hunted elk and were decreed to have royal blood to establish the chiefly families of the Harbor people. At Mulla, people hooked sturgeon. At Hoquiam, people hooked sturgeon and set out herring traps. At James Rock, people had herring traps and boxy canoes. Instead they were taught to make proper canoes. At Owl, people ate gophers and changed into these night birds. At Chinoose Creek, people kept their herring traps and sturgeon hooks. At Cold Water, people caught only silver salmon.

Finally, they returned to the Humptulips, where they started and decided that they would finish by becoming a kind of duck that arrived in the middle of the fishing season. Before they came, salmon had to be prepared in a very strict manner, using a sharpened clam shell to gut the fish and separate head and tails from the body. After these ducks arrived, people could prepare fish in whatever manner was convenient. These are river ducks that are always in pairs, like the twins, that go north in the spring and arrive back in the fall.

Conclusions

Restored to the scholarly record, Misp[h] and his twin transformed the Tsamosan world to be as it is today. Their living embodiment is the longtailed [old sqwawk] duck, which breeds in the high arctic, and visits coastal waters. Its very changeability makes it an apt representative of Transformers ~ Changers who prepared the world for the humans were "coming soon".

Appendix A: Roster of Old Squawk Duck Names (Terres 1980:197)

Calloo	John Connelly	Old Wife	Scoldenore	Swallow-tailed duck
Cockawee	Long-tailed	Old Molly	Scolder	Uncle Huldy
Coween	Old Billy	Old Injun*	South Southerly	Winter Duck
Hound*	Old Granny	Quandy	Squeaking Duck	

*Hound references its baying cry
*Old Injun for its travcl singlc filc

Clangula hyemalis   Clangula clang, noise   Hyemalis of Winter

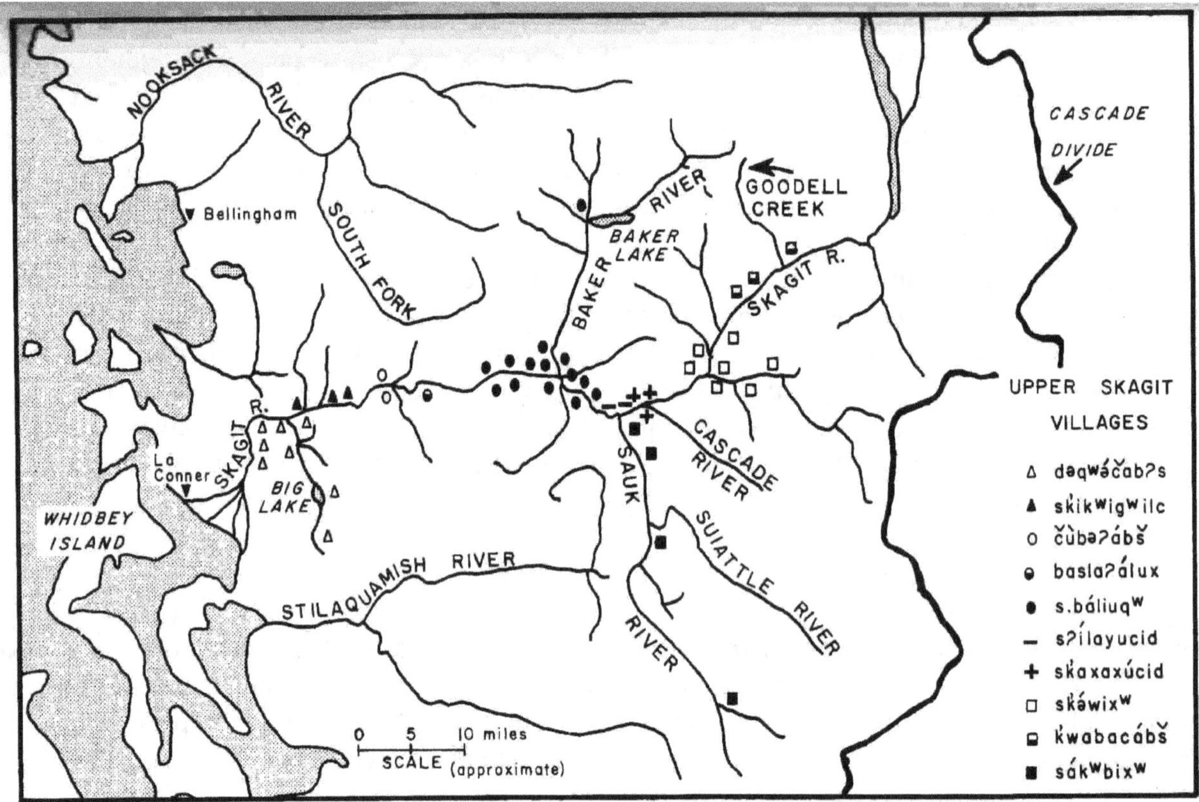

MAP 2. Upper Skagit villages

Upper Skagit villages, like others in the Puget Sound region, might extend some miles along the river with several separate living sites within them. Houses on a tributary entering the river were sometimes regarded as belonging to the same village as the houses on the main river near the mouth of the tributary. [16 Valley of the Spirits]

The location of Upper Skagit winter houses changed from time to time as the river cut new channels and deserted old beds. When this happened, the planks which formed the walls were removed and taken to the new site. The family graveyard, which was usually located near the house, was also moved. The preparations required for this event and the potlatch which had to be given in honor of the dead are described in Chapter 8.

The village closest to the delta of the Skagit was *dəqwə́čabš* ("people of the *dəqwə́č* River") which included sites extending from the present town of Mount Vernon to below Sedro Woolley (see Map 2). The first Upper Skagit houses which would appear on going upriver were five small wooden houses at *susutiya*, a summer fishing site on the west side of the Skagit River at the present town of Mount Vernon. Joseph Campbell, one of my informants, was born in the village. Still at Mount Vernon, north of the town and west of the cemetery, was *calgahabš*, with one large winter house. South of the present town of Burlington and on the south bank of the Skagit and east of the railroad bridge was the village of *swiwishəb* with one large winter house.

Between Burlington and Sedro Woolley on the south bank of the Skagit and east of the mouth of Nookachamps Creek was a summer fishing village called *scacuks* with five small houses. One large winter house named *wac'al'al* ("high ground") was located on Nookachamps Creek which entered the Skagit below Burlington and was a famous fishing site for suckers and silver salmon. The creek flowed from Big Lake, which had one large winter house called *culacabš*. Lake McMurray, further south than Big Lake, had a summer village, *kabalah*. A few people lived here during the entire year. One large winter house, *sq'əx^{w}šəd*, was located at Clear Lake, which also drained into the Skagit River.

Upriver from *dəq^{w}ə́čabš* was the extended village of *skik^{w}g^{w}ilc* ("big rocks"). One large winter house, *kakawacid*, was situated at Sterling, and three small winter houses, *wawalah*, east of Sedro Woolley at Skiyou {= ghost} Slough. At Minkler near Ross Island in the Skagit River and west of Hamilton were three large winter houses also called *kakawacid*.

Beyond this village was *čubə'abš* ("people who climb the bank," i.e., residents who move to avoid the periodic high waters at this place in the river) with two large winter houses, one, *tacic*, at Lyman, and one, *skwəb*, at the mouth of Day Creek. The next [18] extended village west of Hamilton, basta^alux, consisted of one large winter house, *slux^w ~ slox^w*.

The largest extended village on the Skagit River was *s.baliuq^w*, which reached from Birdsview to Faber's Ferry. At Birdsview there was one house, *litt'skay'dap*, on the north side of the river. One small house was located at the mouth of Finney Creek to the east and a similar house at the west. Two small winter houses were located at the mouth of Finney Creek, one on each side. Both were called *dakwikəb*. A large winter house, *bius*, stood at Cape Horn on the south side of the Skagit River. Two small winter houses, *sp'adak'*, were slightly to the south and west of Concrete at The Dalles. There is a famous folk tale about a blind man and his daughter who lived here. A deep pool near The Dalles is said to be the abode of a guardian spirit *tiyutəbaxəd* who conveys wealth. Five small winter houses, *dx^{w}qəlb*, were at Concrete west of the mouth of Baker River and one large winter house, *qəlbucid*, east of the mouth of the same river. One small winter house was located at Baker Lake connected by a tributary to Baker River. Before any of my informants were born, a large winter house had existed on the south side of the Skagit across from the Baker River at Concrete. This was also called *dx^{w}qəlb*.

Two small winter houses, *hahilwaykid*, were located, one on each side, at the mouth of Jackman Creek which is east of Concrete. At Van Horn, east of Jackman Creek, on the north side of the Skagit was one large winter house. Four small summer houses were on the south side of the Skagit. Both of these Van Horn sites were called *stayucid*. On the north side of the Skagit, east of Van Horn, there was one large winter house and three small summer houses. This site was called *q^{w}əq'^{w}q^{w}əq'^{w}* ("white") because of a rock slide with rocks in it. Alice Campbell, one of my informants, was born here.

The extended village *s'ilayucid* came next on the river, including one small winter house, *ĵijəq'šəd* ("foot of the mountain stuck in the river"), at the town of Sauk west of Rockport and two large winter houses, *'aytalushay*, one to the west and one to the east of the town of Rockport.

The village of *sk'axaxucid* included three winter houses: *sq'ix^{w}ucid*, at the bend in the river on the north side of the Skagit west of Rockport; *puk^{w}alicu*, near the mouth of Rocky Creek; and *saxipəp*, across the river from Rocky Creek on the south bank [19] of the Skagit. The first house on this site was 120 feet long and 40 feet wide. It was the largest house in Upper Skagit territory and could hold all of the Upper Skagit in meetings. The famous chief and religious leader of the last century, *sƛ'ababtikəd*, lived in this house.

Upriver from *sk'axaxucid* was the extended village of *bəsq'ix^wix^w*. Near Marblemount there was a winter house *ĵidsud* in which a number of different families resided. At *bəsq'ix^wix^w* about one mile west of Marblemount on the Cascade River, a tributary of the Skagit, were a winter house on the north side of the river and a summer house on the south side. The winter house was 120 feet long and 40 feet wide. At one time twenty families lived in it. One summer house, *cəq'cəd*, was on the south side of the Cascade River at Boulder Creek, and a large summer house, *sk'əčay*, on the north side of the Cascade River to the west side of Monogram Creek. Two small winter houses with two families in each house stood a mile below Diobsud Creek on the west side of the Skagit above Marblemount. A large winter house holding ten families was situated on the south side of the Skagit across from the mouth of Bacon Creek.

The last village upriver on the Skagit itself and deep in the Cascade Mountains was *k'wabacabš*, consisting of *t'skwab*, a large winter house at Portage, west of Damnation Creek on the north side of the Skagil; one small winter house with three families to the east of Thornton Creek on the north side of the Skagit; and one large winter house, *dawaylib* ({*x̱^wləb*} = "thread" or *t'əbiłəd* = "rope") at Newhalem on the north bank of the Skagit.

One of the principal tributaries of the Skagit River is the Sauk. It enters the Skagit east of Rockport. The extended village here was *sak^wbix^w* ("people of digging roots"). A winter house large enough to hold gatherings of all the people living on the Sauk River had stood here before the lifetime of my informants. Alice Campbell's mother had told her about this house, which was at [he mouth of the Sauk on the south bank of the Skagit. Sauk Prairie, one of the places where the Upper Skagit semicultivated wild roots, was up the Sauk beyond its confluence with the Suiattle. There were four winter houses here. One summer house was at Bedal near the joining of the North and South Forks of the Sauk River. The Upper Skagit, before the 1890 period, did not have winter houses on the Suiattle which is a tributary of the Sauk. They did [20] camp along the Suiattle during the summer. When they came to live on the Suiattle they called it *s'uyaƛ'bix^w*.

The villages on the Sauk were said not to have known how to make canoes. Some men in these villages crossed rivers by walking along "paths" in the river bed, carrying large boulders to help them keep their footing. This lack of knowledge was regarded as a sign of inland inferiority by people from other villages. It may mean that some of the ancestors of the Sauk villagers entered Skagit territory from a northern mountain route and were land travelers, not canoe users.

People of the extended village of *duwaha*, although it was located on the Samish River, had close affinities with the Upper Skagit. They had two large winter houses, *baslatlaus*, at Bayview on Padilla Bay, one large winter house at Belfast, and another, *stiksabš*, at the southern tip of Samish Lake. These people, as I have already pointed out, should not be confused with the Samish who spoke a dialect of the Straits language. The people of *duwaha* or the Upper Samish instead spoke the Upper Skagit-Nisqually group of languages. Mention has been made here of the Upper Skagit making portage into Upper Samish territory as one usual route to salt water. In the duwaha locale there were two large prairie areas, one at Warner's Prairie and one at German Prairie where both Upper Skagit and *duwaha* women went to get roots.

From this list of villages, part of the pattern of the seasonal round of activities can be identified. Other than the winter houses at Sauk, the permanent winter houses were nearly all situated at fishing sites near the mouth of tributaries of the Skagit with a few on the main branches of the river and a few on lakes linked by rivers or creeks to the Skagit. Small wooden houses were built at sites where the fishing was particularly good, to house the visiting relatives who came when the fish were running.

PART III
Individual History of the Eleven Tribes

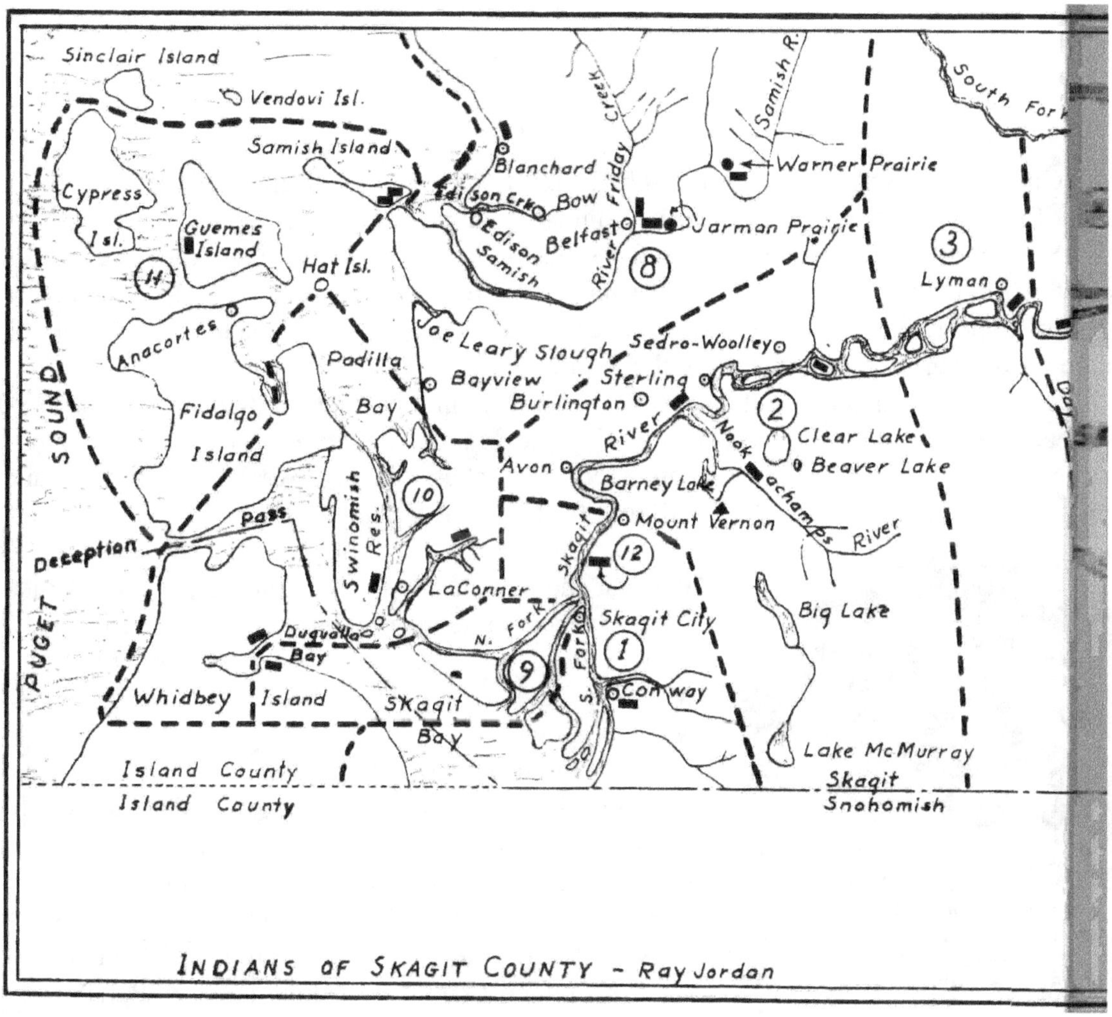

Skagit Martin S

1. *Kik-i-allus*
kiki'alus

Sd-zo-mahtl, who signed the treaty of 1855, was chief of the Kik-i-allus tribe which occupied the valley of the Skagit River from its mouth to Mount Vernon (excepting the North Fork of the Skagit from its mouth to Dry Slough, which was Squin-ah-mish territory) and the area from Brann's Camp to Crescent Harbor in Whidbey Island. This tribe also had holdings in Snohomish County.

Their main village was near Conway where there were four long houses at the time the land was settled by the pioneers.

John Lyons, a direct descendant of Patch-kanam, headed the tribe in 1916 when a suit concerning treaty rights was started against the United States Government. The late Alfanso Sampson, another direct descendant of Patch-kanam, is the most recent chief, having been elected to succeed Charles O'Brien in 1950.

2. Noo-qua-cha-mish
dəqʷə́čabš

Ch-Iah-ben, Spik-cum, Be-bash-chad, and Scha-ha-lab-ki were among the many noted leaders of the Noo-qua-cha-mish at the beginning of the history chronicled here.

Spik-cum was a great orator, and Be-bash-chad was a Medicine Man. Scha-ha-lab-ki was noted for having eleven wives. He has been described as being short, dark and bushy-headed in appearance. Scha-ha-lab-ki never claimed to be a chief. He said that [b] he just became wealthy and wealth brought in the women.

This tribe occupied the Skagit Valley from Mount Vernon to Lyman, including Big Lake and Clear Lake and the area west to the Olympic Marsh. At the time of the Treaty they still inhabited the lakes, the Nookachamps River, and the villages from Mount Vernon to just below Lyman.

Jim Thompson, whose Indian name is unknown, lived at the site of Mount Vernon, and when he died at a very advanced age, his only neighbors, the pioneers, buried him in their own cemetery. His great-grandniece, Lucy McLeod Gates (Mrs. Dave Gates) also rests in the Mount Vernon cemetery.

This tribe is rich in legend and lore. The use of the "Squa-de-lich" (*sgʷədilič* = magic cedar board shields) came to us from them. It was to them, too, that the "Star Child" came. This beautiful, enriching story has been handed down for untold generations around the long house fires; it is an example of the heights that ancient Indian culture attained. The story is told below in Part V.

Big Rock or "Yud-was-ta" where the mother of Star Child alighted from the Land of the Stars. Her rope should be coiled on the summit.   — Ray Jordan

The "Star Child" alighted from the sky on top of the huge rock, now known as Big Rock, across the highway from the Big Rock Service Station at the fork of the Big Lake and Mount Vernon roads. The big rock, sacred to the Noo-qua-cha-mish, was known as "Yud-was-ta," {yədwas-ta} meaning "heart" or "of the heart." It is said to have a huge pile of cedar sapling rope, by means of which the "Star Child" descended, coiled at the top. [20]
Big Rock or "Yud-was-ta" where the mother of Star Child alighted from the Land of the Stars. Her rope should be coiled on the summit. — Ray Jordan

One important village of the Noo-qua-cha-mish which existed during the life span of Indians now living was called "Whats-al-ul," {x^{w}ac'al'al = high house} meaning "elevated house" or "house on elevated ground." It was situated on the pleasant little bench on the Nookachamps River just above where it enters Barney Lake. Legend has it that this village was once wiped out by a war party of Skagits from Ut-sa-laddy, the surprise being so complete that only one young woman and her little brother-in-law escaped.

Another village occupied a spot on the Skagit River on the opposite side from where the Nookachamps enters. Big Lake also had an Indian settlement at the time of the Treaty of 1855.

The point of the little island north of the mouth of Dead Man's Slough above Sedro Woolley is the site of another village, "Whuid-zaub," known within the memory of living settlers. This place was the home of the sub-chief, Pol-queet-sa, known to many white settlers in the early days, and it is thought to be the birthplace of Joseph Sampson, the father of the [b] writer. The writer remembers living here as a child of six for a time before the family moved to LaConner.

In regard to the Indian population of Skagit County, Mrs. Harry Moses (Jessie) states that in her time every favorable bar on the river from Mount Vernon to Newhalem was occupied by Indian settlements, ranging from one habitation to villages in size.

Ch-lah-ben, their chief, signed the Point Elliott (Muckilteo) Treaty of 1855. George Washington, his nephew, was leader in 1916. The other direct descendants of Chief Ch-lah-ben are the children of Gardner Goodrich and Jennie, his second wife who was the granddaughter of Ch-lah-ben.

3. *Cho-bah-ah-bish*
čubə'abš

The principal village of the Cho-bah-ah-bish band was on the Skagit River near the mouth of a slough a short distance above Lyman on the Shoemaker Jim allotment.

Shoemaker Jim refused to move away from his home, the land of his wife's ancestors, when the white man who secured a deed for the land ordered him off. Friendly white men, among them steamboat Captain F.A. Dyer, took the case to court and won the homestead for the Indian. All expenses were paid by the white men.

Grave of Shoemaker Jim in the white men's cemetery at Lyman, next to the plot of Captain F. A. Dyer, the white man who befriended him. — Ray Jordan

The large cedar long house, once a familiar sight to living Indians, is gone now. Only a hoary old orchard in a pleasant little meadow marks the lonely spot where happy Indian children once played.

Descendants of Shoemaker Jim are four grandchildren, Dorothy Smith of Warm Springs, Oregon, and Henry, Donald and Willie Shoemaker of LaConner and Nooksack.

The story of the origin of Shoemaker Jim's white man's name is interesting. According to old settlers Jim was skillful with his hands and somehow became adept at repairing shoes. Because of this he was known far and wide as "shoemaker" Jim, and the nickname became permanent. Old-timers speak kindly of him and his family, [21] and fondly reminisce about the *Grave of Shoemaker Jim in the white men's cemetery at Lyman, next to the plot of Captain F. A. Dyer, the white man who befriended him. — Ray Jordan* time that he faithfully ferried school children across the sloughs with his canoe for weeks after a flood had washed out the bridges on the old upriver road. Today he sleeps in the Lyman cemetery in the family plot adjoining that of his friend and benefactor, Captain Dyer.

Twik-kadim was the leader of this band before and at the time of the Point Elliott Treaty of 1855. However, the authority to sign the Treaty was delegated to the Noo-qua-cha-mish chief, Ch-lah-ben. These two bands were closely affiliated by intermarriage and location.

The leader of the tribe from 1916 to 1938 was Jimmy Charles, since succeeded by his son, Ray Charles of LaConner.

4. *Me-sek-wi-guilse*
bəskikʷigʷilc

The Me-sek-wi-guilse tribe owned and occupied for four generations before the Treaty of 1855 the area from Lyman to Birdsview and the part of Whidbey Island from Sneatlum Point to Holmes Harbor between the lands of the Skagit to the north and the Snohomish to the south. Sd'zek-du-num signed the Treaty. [b]

At that time the tribe had a village on the site of the present day Hamilton, but encroachment by the whites forced them to move to the bend of the river below Hamilton.

Susan Sampson, aged 21. The picture was taken in 1884 or 1885. — Collection of Martin Sampson

26

Another thriving village was located about one mile above Birdsview on the north side of the river opposite the Charles von Pressentin claim. A large number of Indians were living here in their native-built cedar plank houses when the Pressentins came in 1877, and continued to inhabit this place for many years afterward. Also, Cape Horn on the south side of the river was the location of a large long house, and an early type tree, or platform burial ground. Living settlers remember the carved figures on the cedar slab grave markers in this cemetery.

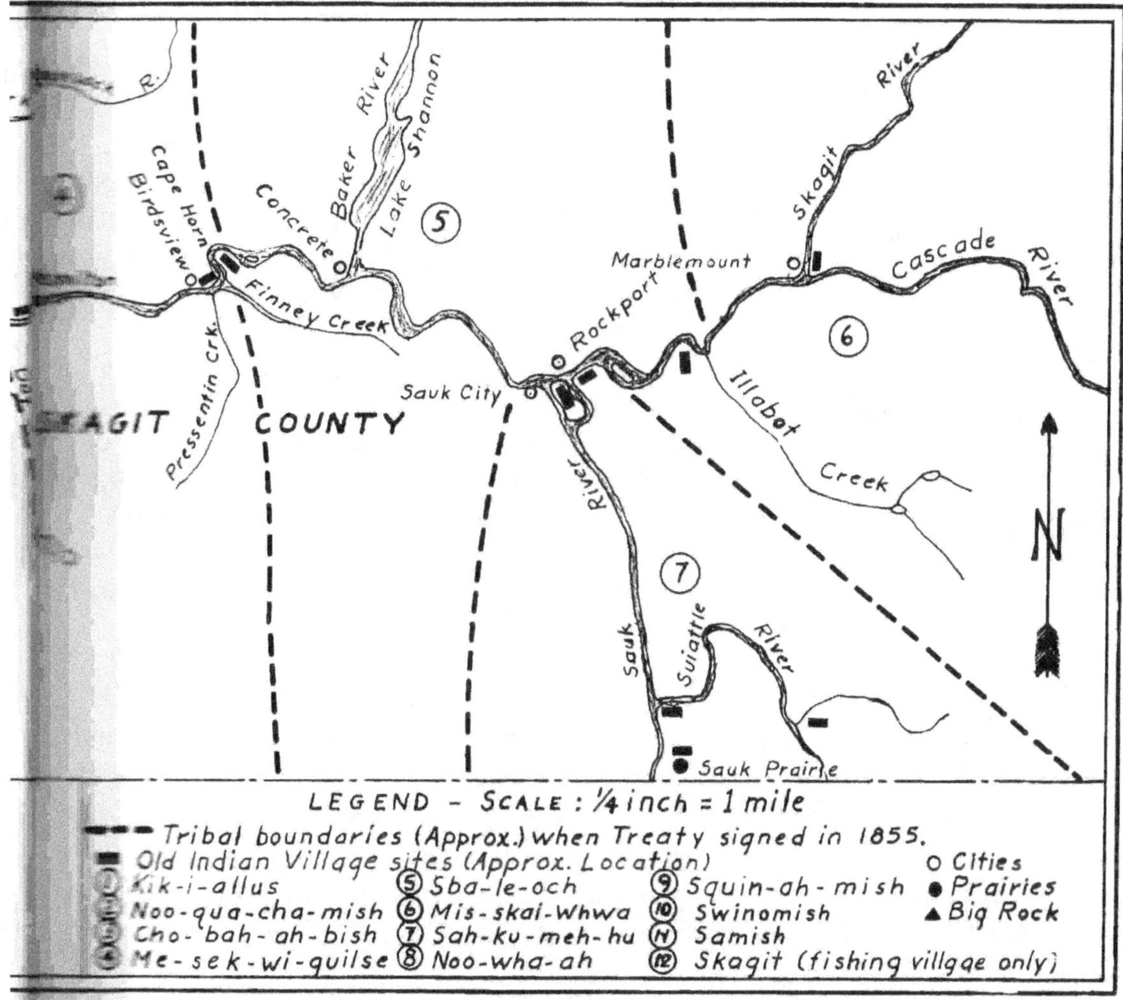

Glieu (Ca-caly-u), son of Da-sil-tud and a Chelan mother, had a son named Tul-la-had-bid. During the Leschi up rising Tul-la-had-bid was called upon by the Federal Government to defend the settlers. He answered the call with ten men. When he arrived at Brown's Point near Tacoma he was told by a cousin that the Indians were at peace, and that a police force was pursuing Leschi and a few of his relatives who were with him, so Tul-la-had-bid returned home with his troop.

The sons of Tul-la-had-bid were well known to the pioneers of the Hamilton to Utsaladdy area. Doctor Dick (Yallu-hut-su) lived all his life at Hamilton. Susan Williams, his granddaughter, has four sons, all of whom attended the public schools.

Tul-la-had-bid's youngest son, Doctor Bailey (Sba-qua-blth) was also a Medicine Man. Doctor Bailey's daughter, Susan Sampson Peter of the Swinomish Reservation, was the mother of the writer. A great-grandson, Benedict M. Sampson (son of the writer) graduated from the University of Washington in electrical engineering, was a captain in the United States Air Force when he retired, and is now employed in technical work. [22]

Susan Sampson Peter at about 74. The picture was taken in 1937. Mrs. Peter was the tribal historian of the Swinomish Reservation. — Collection of Martin Sampson

Susan Sampson Peter at about 74. The picture was taken in 1937. Mrs. Peter was the tribal historian of the Swinomish Reservation. — Collection of Martin Sampson

During the trouble with the surveyors in the Baker River district Bailey was sent to Olympia from Skagit City with a letter to the Governor. He and his men traveled day and night to deliver the message and returned with the answer to the citizens of Skagit City. All that Bailey knew about the contents of the letter was that it was very important. Soon afterward a company of soldiers went up the Skagit River to protect the settlers. What happened then is told in the next section below.

Bailey's Indian name, "Sba-qua-bith," translated from the Skagit to English would be "Fields." "Ba-quab" {baq^{w}ab} means field or prairie, and "Sha-qua-bith" means "of the fields or prairies." An older brother of Bailey was Charles Sieous, and the youngest child of Tul-la-had-bid, Bailey's sister, was named Sally.

5. *Sba-le-och* 6. *Mis-skai-whwa* 7. *Sah-ku-meh-hu*
sbaliuq^w bəsk'əwix^w sak^{w}bix^w

The history of these three tribes intermingles somewhat. The Sba-le-och held and occupied the Skagit River valley from Birdsview to the vicinity of Illabot Creek, and also the Baker River Valley and the Baker Lake area. At the time of the Point Elliott (Muckilteo) Treaty of January 22, 1855, Sta-ba-but-kin {sƛ'abəbtikəd} was the head chief. He and head chief, Waw-wit-kin, of the Sah-ku-meh-hu (Sauk) Tribe refused the Treaty because they were not assured a reservation of their own, though Dahtl-de-min, a subchief of the Sauk Tribe, did sign it. Ki-ya-hud, chief of the Mis-skai-whwa, also refused to sign. This later caused a great deal of confusion.

When the surveyors came to survey the land as a preliminary to giving title to white settlers, the Indians protested on the ground that the land still belonged to them because they had not signed the Treaty. While the talks were going on between the Indian leaders and the surveyors, two Indians, prodded by the fact that more white [23] settlers were moving in, procured some of the white man's bottled spirits and proceeded to take measures calculated to stop the survey.

They threw the surveyor's chains into the river, raided the cook shack, drove the cook away and tossed his cooking utensils into the stream, and then headed downriver for more firewater. This action of the Indians brought a company of soldiers upriver under the command of Lieutenant Culver Simons.

When Simons and his company reached Ball's Landing (Sterling) on a steamboat, Jimmy Jones, a young nephew of Chief Johnny Campbell, happened to be in the vicinity, (Johnny Campbell had succeeded his father as chief, since Sta-ba-but-kin had long since journeyed to the Happy Hunting Ground). Fearing trouble for his people, young Jimmy raced upriver ahead of the soldiers and warned the Indians.

Thus alerted, the Indians were ready and waiting for Simons. Chief Campbell had ordered all the guns and ammunition placed in a canoe and the craft moored just below the meeting place with two men standing by. When the meeting started the Indians were seated on the ground while the soldiers remained standing and armed.

Chief Campbell began his address by making the sign of the Cross. He said that the Chief Above, Saghalie Tyee (Chinook Jargon for God), had placed their ancestors on this land and that they wished to keep it; that the Saghalie Tyee had already surveyed the land by making rivers and mountains and placing them as the landmarks which divided their lands from their neighbors.

At this point he was asked by the Government agent if they believed in God, in Christianity. He replied that they were all Catholics and that God was the Creator of all mankind, and that the Indians and the white people were children of the one God, the Creator; that all they wanted was to have lands for themselves and their children to come. [b]

Simons ordered his men to stack arms and be seated. The Government agent assured the Indians that their wishes would be respected and lands reserved for them.

The meeting of Chief Campbell and his tribesmen, in the year 1881, near the mouth of the Baker River, with a representative of the Great White Father and a unit of the United States Army, temporarily brought a better understanding between the Indians and the pioneers. History was made. The survey went on uninterrupted and more settlers took up land as it was laid off.

However, the Indians waited many weary years for the Government agent to come back and give them lands. James Moore, Jake Harrison, Jimmy Jones, and other Indians, following the advice of white friends, did not wait for the Government agent, but took up homesteads along the river as did the white people.

When the agent did come, all of the land along the river was taken. Some of the Indians were given allotments along Illabot Creek on the mountain side. The upriver people, the Mis-skai-whwa, who once possessed and lived on the land from the vicinity of Illabot Creek to the headwaters of the Skagit and Cascade Rivers, were given allotments at the same time.

The Sah-ku-meh-hu (Sauk) Indians at the time of the Treaty owned and inhabited the entire drainage area of the Sauk and Suiattle Rivers. They had an important village at the confluence of the Sauk and Skagit Rivers. Chief Leo Brown remembered well the village on Sauk prairie, having lived there as a boy. The village consisted of eight large cedar board long houses, and was burned about 1884-5 by white people who had obtained title to the land.

Early in the 1890s the remaining members of the upper river tribes, the Mis-skai-whwa and the Sauk people, under the leadership of Captain Moses Ti-a-tmus and Chief Jim Brown, settled in the Suiattle Valley. For one reason or another, many of these people were [24] denied the right to take up land in the public domain. They received very little aid, if any, from the Superintendent of the Tulalip Indian Agency on the grounds that they were nontreated Indians. Later the opinion of the Superintendent was reversed, and these people were recognized as a party to the Point Elliott (Muckilteo) Treaty of 1855, but not until they had lost their last chance for allotments.

One must remember that the early white settlers did not find all of the Indian villages filled to capacity due to the smallpox epidemics which had ravaged the Indian population in the past. The older Indians tell sadly of seeing the planks from deserted cedar houses, made with so much toil with primitive tools, being split into fence rails by the white settlers.

Time and space wilt not permit us to go further into the history of these people. It will be enough to give the joint statement of Captain Moses Tiatmus and Chief Jim Brown, taken by this writer in 1912 at Sauk Crossing.

When the white people got title to the land on which our houses were, on the upper Skagit River, the Cascade River, the Sauk River, and Sauk Prairie, they burned our houses and drove us away. We then moved to the last land of our ancestors which was not occupied by white people, the Suiattle River area. We are asking the President of the United States to let us live here and to give us title to the land so we can have homes for our children.

The writer, a member of the Northwest Federation of Indians, at the request of Chief Campbell, helped these tribes organize for the purpose of suing the Federal Government for treaty rights. Although he is a descendant of Skagit River Indians he was, and is now, enrolled in the Swinomish Tribe.

Head men of the Suiattle group were the late William Moses, the late Chief Leo Brown, and Jimerson Price, with Edith Bedal of Darrington serving as secretary.

Suits against the United States Government must be based on tribal territories and tribal names as they [b] existed at the time of the Treaty of 1855. An organization, known as the Upper Skagit Sauk-Suiattle Tribes, has now been organized for the purpose of suing the Government for Indian rights. Officers of this organization are: Chairman, Charley Boome of Sedro Woolley; Secretary, Alice Cuthbert of Rockport; and the recently elected Chief, Pete Campbell of Concrete.

Tribes represented are: the Noo-wha-ah (often referred to as the Upper Samish); Noo-qua-cha-mish; Me-sek-wi-guilse; Sba-le-och; and Mis-skai-whwa. The last four named are often referred to as the Upper River Indians. Also included in the organization are the Cho-bah-ah-bish and Sah-ku-meh-hu for a total of seven tribes who, at the time of the Treaty, owned all the area of the Samish Valley and the Skagit Valley from Mount Vernon to the headwaters of the Skagit River.

Before and at the time of the Point Elliott Treaty these tribes and bands, for mutual security, were organized under one head. Chief Sta-ba-but-kin, a son-in-law of the Noo-wha-ah chief, Pat-teh-us, was Headman; second in command was Waw-wit-kin, chief of the Sah-ku-meh-hu. However, the authority of these men did not control the actions of the other chiefs, as is seen in the signing of the Point Elliott Treaty.

This organization was reactivated in 1915, without the Sauk-Suiattle bands participating, with Joe Campbell, son of Johnny Campbell and grandson of Chief Sta-ba-but-kin, as Chief and Chairman of the Allied Tribes of the Upper Skagit. Representing the various tribes were: Dick Williams, Noo-who-ah; George Washington, Noo-qua-cha-mish; Jimmy Charles, Cho-bah-ah-bish; Tommy Johnson, Me-sek-wi-guilse; Charley Moses, Mis-skai-whwa; Joe Campbell, Sba-le-och; with Martin J. Sampson, the writer, as secretary.

The suits for Indian rights brought by these organizations have recently been won by the Indians, but they are [25] still waiting for appropriations to pay claims upheld by the court.

8. *Noo-wha-ah*
dx^wa'ha

The Noo-wha-ah people are often erroneously referred to as the "Upper Samish." The tribe at one time possessed the land encircled by a line beginning at the Dwoch-chuch-um (Red Creek) south of Bayview and north of Telegraph Slough, thence north along the waterfront to the Nooksack River, through the west half of Whatcom Lake, around Warner Prairie, down the valley of the Samish River and the Olympic Marsh, and back down to the place of beginning.

Before the coming of the white man they were a large and powerful tribe and a bit warlike. Strong spirits of the Wolf and the Thunderbird hovered among the hills of the Noo-wha-ah land, giving these people a powerful advantage in war.

Under the leadership of Chadas-kadim I and Chadas-kadim II, father and son, they made war on tribes as far south as Puyallup and northwest to Vancouver Island. But at the time the land was settled by the pioneers the Noo-wha-ah were converts of the Catholic Church, a peace-loving people greeting their former enemies with the sign of the Cross and chanting the Ave Maria in place of their war songs.

But we are getting ahead of our story. Epidemics of some disease, probably smallpox, almost wiped out the whole tribe. There were still many Indians left after the first epidemic in the 1700s, since the people living on the upland lakes and prairies were not affected, but the last scourge in the 1830s reached every village, leaving only about 200 out of over 1000 people.

Only one out of a village on Jarman Prairie was saved, a baby girl. A visiting uncle found her in her dead mother's arms, moved her to the north side of the Prairie, and left her in a shelter. He then went back to the houses on the bank of the Samish River, and [b] after making sure that no others were alive, set the torch to all of the buildings. Checking the houses on Friday Creek and finding all of the inhabitants dead, he also burned this village. There, as a further sanitary measure, he took off all his clothing and tossed his garments on the flames.

Stripped naked and with the bare little orphan in his arms, he then set out over the long trail across Bow Hill to the village on the head of Edison Creek where his family lived. This was near what is now Bow, on what the Indians called "Du-wha-chub-ub," later called Edison Slough or the North Fork of the Samish River.

Arriving, he did not enter his house, but called from a distance for clothing and food which he took to the girl he had left some distance back on the trail. As a final precaution he made three different shelters, and fumigated each, together with their clothing, with cedar and fir boughs. Upon reaching the village they spent a few more days away from the houses until he was sure they were free of the dread smallpox.

The story of the smallpox among the Noo-wha-ah is that of all the other tribes of the Puget Sound area. It is believed that the first epidemic came about the time the Spaniards landed in California since it came from the south. The second scourge of smallpox also came from that quarter.

Some time in the early 1800s, after the first epidemic, the last war between the Indians of the Puget Sound country was made between the Noo-wha-ah and the Saanich Tribe of Vancouver Island. The Noo-wha-ah, headed by Chief Sat-hill, invaded the Saanich at Sydney to recover the head of their last War Chief, Chadas-kadim II, lost in a previous war when the Saanich invaded Noo-wha-ah territory in Skagit County. A very meager account of the battle has come down to us. A few were killed, the houses all burned, but no slaves were taken. Apparently the operation was not very successful since the head of Chadas-kadim, the prime [26] motive for the invasion, still remains somewhere about Sydney.

The descendants of Chadaskadim are Frank Bob of Alger, Alfred and Gene Sampson and their sisters of the Swinomish Reservation, the descendants of Julie Barkhousen of Summit Park, and the descendants of Ruth Shelton of Tulalip.

The descendants of Sat-hill are the children of the late Thomas F. Williams of the Swinomish Reservation, the McLeod family, and Susan Sampson Peter and her family of the Swinomish Reservation.

Thomas F. Williams once described his great-grandfather as a kind old man who would not harm a fly. This was before Susan Sampson Peter, his cousin, told him that their ancestor was the last War Chief of the Noo-wha-ah and that he howled the war chant of the Thunderbird among the Saanich. Catholicism did make a new being of the old warrior.

It was interesting to hear Mrs. Susan Sampson Peter, a tribal historian, speak of Noo-wha-ah history as if it were yesterday. Until her death in 1961 although she was 95 and quite blind, she could still give graphic descriptions of places as she last saw them.

Before Christianity changed their mode of life this tribe maintained a fort at the mouth of Edison Creek which was always guarded against surprise attack by northern or island enemies. This strategic spot was the gateway to an inland kingdom, since it was the point of entrance to the canoe route from the Sound to the Indian village near where Bow now stands, the head of canoe navigation on this stream. From this village a trail led over Bow Hill to a village at Belfast on Friday Creek.

Here the trail forked, one branch following up Friday Creek to the village on the lower end of Lake Samish. The other fork led to a village on Jarman Prairie, thence up the "Squil-col-lich" (Samish River) to Warner Prairie and another village, then [b] upriver to Wickersham and through the gap to Lake Whatcom.

Jarman Prairie, with Granny's Hill or Granny's Hump and the Indian fort in the background. The trees mark the course of the Samish River. The picture was taken from the site of the old Indian village. —Ray Jordan

Jarman Prairie, with Granny's Hill or Granny's Hump and the Indian fort in the background. The trees mark the course of the Samish River. The picture was taken from the site of the old Indian village. — Ray Jordan

A short distance southeasterly of Jarman

Prairie across the Samish River is a high, rocky hill known locally as "Granny's Hump" upon which the Noo-wha-ah had another fort to which the warriors could retire in the event that enemies appeared in overwhelming numbers.

Mrs. Peter remembered the Warner Prairie village as a good one, except that during the dry season the spring on which they depended became short of water and they were some distance from the Samish River. The spring had a peculiar action which she described clearly. After all the water was dipped out the spring would remain dry for a time; then after a certain interval there would issue a great gurgling sound and it would fill up again with a rush. The Indian name for this watering place was "Ha-cub-thluk," meaning "the doubling or stretching of one's legs," thus the action of the spring.

Upon checking with Charles Meins, who came to Warner Prairie about 1902, regarding springs on the prairie, the writer learned that his family had [27] used the only spring of any consequence in the locality for their water supply. Around this spring were clam shells, evidence of Indian occupation. And the spring did fail during dry weather, which fits Mrs. Peter's description.

Jarman, Warner, and Young Prairies, in and near the Samish valley, were highly regarded by the Indians as a source of the many roots and bulbs essential to the native diet. The Headman of the village on Warner Prairie was known as "Mowitch Man" or "Statileius," Chief of the Prairies.

Pat-teh-us, a famous chief whose home was near Bayview, signed the 1855 Treaty for the Noo-wha-ah.

Old Friday (Plidy to the Indians, who could not cope with the "F" sound) for whom Friday Creek was named was a member of this tribe. He was well known around Belfast, Bow, and Edison in the early days and was noted among the Indians as one of the Fire Dancers. He died in 1923 at the reputed age of 108.

9. *Squin-ah-mish*
sk^{w}idabix^w

The Squin-ah-mish people were a small band of the Swinomish, or very closely related to them by association and intermarriage, who lived in the territory between the Kik-i-allus and the Swinomish, namely on the North Fork of the Skagit River from its mouth at Bald Island upstream to Dry Slough, then south and west across Skagit Bay to the south half of Dugualla Bay on Whidbey Island, and then south on Whidbey to Brann's Camp.

The remaining members are very few. The family of Sats-kanam survived the smallpox epidemic, and Sats-kanam signed the Point Elliott Treaty for the band. The late Joseph B. Billy of the Swinomish Reservation was his great grandson, and is survived by his son, Archie Billy, Joseph Billy was also a grandson of Kwal-lat-sum (General Pierce) who signed the Treaty for the Skagits. In addition he was a grand-nephew of Chiefs Be-lole and [b] Sto-dum-kan, signers of the Treaty for the Swinomish; At-tak-be, his mother's father, was the brother of Be-lole and Sto-dum-kan. Joseph Billy was enrolled in the Skagit Tribe.

10. *Swinomish*
sx^wadabš

The domain of the Swinomish once included the east half of Fidalgo Island (known in the Treaty of 1855 as Perry's Island), up Deception Pass, the north end of Whidbey Island including the northern half of Dugualla Bay and west to the shoreline including the present Naval Base. Their territory extended to the mainland in an area encompassed by a line beginning at Dugualla Bay and running in an easterly direction to Bald Island, then northeasterly to a point about halfway to Mount Vernon, then north to Red Creek (north of Telegraph Slough), then through Padilla Bay between Bayview and Fidalgo Island to Hat Island, then south along the middle of Fidalgo Bay to the south end of the Bay, then in a southerly direction to the northwest end of Deception Pass, thus including the eastern half of Fidalgo Island, as already stated,

The remains of the Swinomish who had lived on the site of the present Naval Base before the first epidemic of smallpox were unearthed during the building of the base, placed in a large box, and buried in the base of the airfield tower. Joseph P. Willup was one of the people who helped gather the remains of his ancestors.

Sometime back in the dim past a band of the Kik-i-allus had emigrated from the Utsaladdy area to where the Model Village is located just across the Swinomish Channel from LaConner. Here they settled, multiplied in numbers, and prospered to such a degree that they extended their holdings to the large territory outlined above. In due time they became known as Swinomish.

A population of one thousand was quite evenly distributed over all the area owned by the tribe. One of the larger villages was at the headwaters of Sullivan Slough. The houses were well [28] fortified with deep ditches surrounding them, filled with sharp ironwood stakes. Its location was strategic because it could be reached by large canoe only at high tide, or by small canoe through the many small sloughs that led from Swinomish Channel.

But smallpox conquered this stronghold. Only one family, that of La-hail-by, the Prophet, survived the first epidemic. He gathered his people and told them that unless they prayed to their gods they would be overcome by some very powerful sickness, the like of which they had never seen before. It had been revealed to him in a dream that the Medicine Man would be powerless against the new sickness and that only group praying would save them. He was ridiculed by old and young, and referred to as "the crazy old man. How does he know?"

Only his family group came in and joined in prayer. They lined up in rows across the council house, facing south, with their hands in front of them making the motions of pushing something away. They sang and danced to a slow rhythm for many days and nights, stopping only to eat and sleep. Finally the east end of the line commenced to move forward and at the same time the west end started to move back, ever so slowly, but moving. After many more days and nights the lines of dancers found themselves facing west. It was then that La-hail-by ordered his people to stop, telling them that the sickness had passed and that their prayers had been answered. Many of the Swinomish today are the descendants of La-hail-by, the Prophet.

Two names still being used have come down to us from the very beginning of the Swinomish Tribe, that of an earlier La-hail-by and Too-whl-kadim, the sons of Huah-le-tsa (He of the Magic Robe), the father of the Swinomish Tribe.

The caste system was very much in evidence among the Swinomish until the coming of Christianity. The principal village of the chiefs was the original one across from LaConner while the [b] lower caste lived at Dugualla Bay. These two classes did not mix, but the middle class moved at will, free to associate with all others.

It is said that, when the Chiefs answered the call for help from the Dugualla Swinomish who were without fire, they brought the fire within arrow flight, placed the burning coals in a clamshell, tied it to an arrow, and shot it to the beach. After 1840 the adoption of Catholicism as the religion of the Swinomish gradually eliminated the caste system.

Worthy of note in this short history is the fact that these Indians used fish traps with hearts and leads much like our present ones on the west side of the Swinomish Reservation. The original traps led the fish from deep water to the tidelands where they were picked up off the ground when the tide went out. In the old days there were fish traps at Dugualla Bay, Turner Bay, the North Fork of the Skagit River, and along the Swinomish Channel. Stakes still mark the old locations.

Chiefs Be-lole, Sto-dum-kan, and Kel-kahl-tsoot signed the Point Elliott Treaty of 1855 for the Swinomish. After the death of the above three chiefs, the succession has been respectively: Frank Dicwalla, Charlie Belole, Peter Charles Stodumkan, and Martin J. Sampson, the writer.

Serving as chief with Sampson at the present time is Henry Cladoosby. In case of the termination of the Treaty of 1855 these chiefs will sign for the Swinomish Tribe. Until such time, it is the duty of these chiefs to see that the provisions of the Treaty are enforced.

11. *Samish*
sabš

At the time of the Point Elliott Treaty the Samish Tribe owned Guemes, Samish, Cypress, Lopez, and the western half of Fidalgo Islands, though they occupied only Guemes and Samish Islands permanently.

One of their houses on the southeast part of Samish Island measured 1250 feet in length; another on the northeast [29] part taped 1000 feet, while one on the west side of Guemes Island is recorded as being 999 feet long. These statistics were taken from pillars remaining in the ground in 1917.

There were fishing villages on Lopez Island in the late 1890s where the tribe fished with reef nets. They were still using twisted cedar saplings for leads and anchor rope. There were also fishing villages on Cypress Island, used while the Indians fished for halibut, and for hunting.

Some time in the remote past Samish Island was owned by the Noo-wha-ah Tribe (wrongly referred to as the Upper Samish). All of the Indian names on the Island are of the Noo-wha-ah tongue. "Bus-bus-sech," the name of the west end spit, means "then covering;" "Qua-qua-leuks," the southeast end, "grassy point," while "Stup-us," the name of the northeast end, means "deep point." The Samish and Noo-wha-ah were closely related through intertribal marriages and both languages were spoken on the Island; however, Samish was the dominant language there.

The Samish and the Lummi are of one language group. There is very little difference in the tongue spoken, and both had the same type of songs and dances. They at one time owned and occupied jointly all the San Juan Islands. Some time in the past they were of one tribe. As before stated in this work, the Samish Tribe spoke a language different from that of the other ten tribes of Skagit County who had a common tongue.

The Samish were master craftsmen. Besides building the large cedar plank houses they excelled in canoe building and carving. The totem pole on the Swinomish Reservation reflects the skilful art of the late members of the Samish Tribe, Charles Edwards and George Cagey. Charles and Dick Edwards built the famous racing canoe, the *Telegraph* of Swinomish, and George Cagey was the master builder of the *Lone Eagle*, another noted racing craft.

This tribe was especially noted for holding great Potlatches given as memorial services to the departed [b] chieftains. A great deal of responsibility rested on the host tribe in keeping order, housing and feeding the guests, and policing the different games, canoe races, foot races, bone games (*slahal*), mock battles between tribes, and intertribal marriages. Then there was the more serious business of the host tribe, the "coming out party" for their young men and women who, taking the names of their noted ancestors, were expected to carry out the best traditions of the tribe.

Each guest was paid for being present at the party for the young people. Orators received gifts for making comments on the ceremonies that took place during the Potlatch, especially those given by the older men whose opinions might be of great help to the future success of the younger generation.

These Potlatches were held for many reasons besides the good name of the tribe, good neighbor policy, and its commercial value. One potent reason was that the more one gives, the greater the prestige.

The Samish held the last big Potlatch on Guemes Island in the 1880s. Delegates came from all the tribes on Puget Sound, from the Makahs, Vancouver Island, and the Fraser River area. It is said that one old orator from the Snohomish Tribe had to hire two young men to carry the blankets presented him for making the best speech of the day.

The Potlatch was an observance similar in many respects to our modern Memorial Day; it was an occasion for the young men to come out in their feathers and paint, and likewise for the girls to display their finery of buckskins, shells, beads, feather adornments, and paint. It was also a time for freedom of expression in song and dance.

Interpreters were in great demand and were well paid for their services since there were many tribes of many different languages present. The Medicine Men were there to serve the sick. This was a gathering of free people, a [30] democratic society, and yet before the treaties these people held captives of war as slaves who were freely exchanged or bought and sold at the Potlatches.

The Samish Tribe is said to be the only one in Skagit County which had a secret society, the Wolf Clan, perhaps adopted from their more northerly neighbors along the British Columbia coast where such clans and others were numerous.

Chow-its-hoot of the Lummi Tribe signed the Point Elliott Treaty for the Samish in 1855.

Members of the Samish Tribe on the Swinomish Reservation are: Tommy Bobb, Lawrence Edwards, Alfred [b] Edwards and their families; and James Snohomish and his sister, Marian Cladoosby.

Present Day Numbers of Indians in Skagit County

Fish trap, Swinomish Reservation.   — Oscar C. Upchurch

Racing canoe, "Question Mark, No. 1," built by Charlie Anderson, which
won two races in Victoria in 1931.   — Darius Kinsey

Enrollment of the seven upriver tribes is close to 500, while the four coastal tribes number about 350, making an Indian population of approximately 850 for Skagit County. [31]

The... Swinomish Totem Pole

The Swinomish Totem Pole

Tribal Legends

As told by
MARTIN J. SAMPSON
to
ROSALIE M. WHITNEY

1938

Cover Design by E.M. ALEXANDER

*Dedic*ation
This history is dedicated to the memory of Chiefs or heads of the different tribes whose stories are told here. May their teachings outline the Totem on which this record is carved.

Press of Union Printing Company
Bellingham, Washington

Introduction

THE TOTEM POLE at Swinomish Reservation is a monument to the Swinomish, Skagit, Upper Skagit, Samish and other tribes whose remaining members are now living on the Swinomish Reservation. It was carved from a cedar log sixty-one and a half feet long, five feet thru at the large end, three feet thru at the small end, and is believed to be the largest and best in the State of Washington, or in the United States for that matter.

The carving was under the direction of Charlie Edwards, whose age is well past three score and ten. His ancestors were carvers and canoe builders from time immemorial. The Samish tribe from which he comes is famous for their skill in making fine war canoes, among them being the famous "*Telegraph*," and they were also noted for their building of the large tribal council halls of cedar.

The Totem Pole is an Alaskan idea and it is not our aim to copy the recording of a family history on the pole or to copy the style of carving, but rather to build a monument for the Northwest Indians, reproducing a collection of carvings hitherto seen only on the pillars of the large council halls of the various tribes. Some of these houses measured a thousand feet long and the carvings on the pillars supporting the roof depicted the history, tradition, legends and religion of the Northwest Indians.

Let it he known also that this Totem Pole is [6] but a demand of the general public as far as the sponsors of the W.P.A. project were concerned, was only incidental to the remodelling of American Hall and the building of a large playfield and other improvements. However, the writer, who is largely responsible for the W.P.A. project, is grateful to the men and women who saw the good of having on record the art and history of the Indian in his own way of keeping such a record.

No one knows exactly where the first Indian came from, but the mythology and legends which have been whispered from father to son thru the many generations claim that at one time the Indian and all living things, trees, animals, birds, etc., had a common language and helped each other in their struggle for a primitive existence.

The teaching of history, which is largely based on the family history of chiefs, legends and mythology, was generally carried out by the women, thus we find women historians still recognized to this day. Mrs. Joshua is an authority on the Lower Skagit history. She is nearing the century mark and we owe a great deal of our knowledge of Indian lore to her.

Mrs. William Peter, who is about eighty years old, is an authority on the Upper Skagit and Upper Samish histories. She is also well versed on Swinomish, Samish, Snohomish, Snoqualamie, Nooksack and Lower Skagit histories. Her grandmother was an authority on Upper Skagit history, her father was a doctor who descended from a long line of doctors. Mrs. William Peter is my mother and I would like to write more [7] about her people but this is a story of the Totem Pole. But enough to say that what made her forefathers the great doctors they were was their spirit guide, a grizzly bear, who had its home on the mountains across the Skagit River from the town of Hamilton.

Family tradition was never taught in public, but was whispered to the children in the family's own council. This was done to keep the knowledge which made them great doctors and leaders secret, as it was believed by them that when they told what the spirit was which guided them to greatness, then their power was lessened. Thus the knowledge gained by years of study is passing away without a written record except that which will be recorded on the Totem Pole.

Mrs. Susie (William) Peter
Tribal Doctor of the Upper Skagit

It was believed that when a man told what his guiding spirit was, whether it was a bear, a fish, a tree or a bird, as soon as it was told his power was weakened. Therefore, many of the stories cannot be told yet, but a few legends of spirit guides which are repeated in this book can be told because the principals involved have passed on to the great beyond.

Realizing that this valuable knowledge might die without any record being kept, I have secured permission from the few remaining Chiefs and Doctors to repeat a few of their secrets, which I shall do farther on in this book.

Spiritualism is or was the religion of the Indian. All activity of any importance centered around spiritualism. When the Indian doctored, danced, sang, or went to war, spiritualism played [8] a great part in his life. To the Indian in his native state everything had life or spirit, the earth, the rocks, trees, ferns, as well as birds and animals, even   the hail which fell from the sky had a spirit and a language and song of its own and might be an inspiration to a warrior.

My knowledge of spiritualism was gained by the whispered instructions from the family and from living among Indian Doctors who practiced it extensively. True there was an order from the Indian office many years ago prohibiting the practice of spiritualism, but my people, whose homes were at Trouble Point on the west shore of Swinomish Channel, practiced without interference from the authorities.

But to become a spiritualist one must be clean of body and mind; he must bathe in the waters of the lakes and rivers and fast for many days. No, I am not a spiritualist, much less a doctor. My mother's pies were too delicious and we never had a cupboard to lock.

The cedar tree came in for a great share in the life of the Indian. He made houses, canoes, buckets and other household articles with it. From the young cedar he made rope, from the bark he made a canoe baler and clothing. In the winter dances they used cedar poles and boards to manifest the presence of the spirit. This will become more clear to the reader as we discuss the carvings on the Totem Pole.

The foregoing is written to enable the reader to get a better understanding of these carvings.

MARTIN J. SAMPSON.

Mrs William Peters [9]

Stories of the Carvings on the Totem Pole

The Maiden of Deception Pass

On the Samish side of the Totem Pole, at the foot, appears a maiden, "Ko-kwal-alwoot," the Maiden of Deception Pass [10].

At one time a portion of the Samish Tribe lived on the land which is now known as Rosario Beach. They were known as fish eaters and lived mostly on the fish, mussels, clams and other sea food which abounded in the adjacent waters. They have told this story of "Ko-kwal-alwoot" who has been their inspiration thru-out the years.

"Ko-kwal-alwoot" and other maidens were gathering sea food on the beach one day when one of the shellfish slipped from her grasp and fell into deeper water. She reached for it and it slipped from her hand again and again and she kept following it until she was in deep water, well over her waist. Suddenly she realized [11] that what seemed to be a hand had grasped hers and was holding her there. Terrified she attempted to free herself but a voice told her not to struggle or be afraid, that she was very lovely and he was merely holding her there so that he could look upon her beauty. Soon her hand was released and she returned to her people.

After a number of such meetings during which the spirit held her hand longer and longer each time and spoke soothingly to her, telling her of the many beautiful things which were in the sea, there came a day when a young man emerged from the water and accompanied her to her father's house to ask for her hand in marriage.

The people of the village knew not from whence he came or who he might be, but they noticed that in his presence they were chilled as though icy winds were blowing.

At first when he asked for "Ko-kwal-alwoot's" hand her father was indignant and said:

"No," my daughter cannot go into the sea with you — she would die."

"On the contrary," said the young man, "she will not die; we will give her eternal life and we will be very good to her, for I love her dearly."

Then he warned the father that if he could not have "Ko-kwal-alwoot" for his bride all the sea food would be taken from them and they would be very hungry, but the father still would not agree.

As time went on there was a great scarcity of [12] food of all kinds and even the streams started to dry up so that they could have no water to drink.

When she could stand it no longer, "Ko-kwal-alwoot" went out into the water and called the young man, begging him to give her people food, but he replied:

"Tell your father that only when you are my bride will the waters teem with fish and your people may again live in plenty."

At last, her father realizing that his people were starving, reluctantly agreed to give up his daughter so that the many members of his tribe might live. He made one stipulation, however, and that was that she was to return to her people for a visit once each year, so that they could see if she was being well cared for and was happy. This was agreed upon, and "Ko-kwal-alwoot," wrapping her garments about her, walked into the water, farther and farther until she was out of sight and only her hair could be seen floating in the current.

True to the agreement there was food in plenty and the tribe prospered. And "Ko-kwal-alwoot" returned to her people once each year for four years, and before her coming there was always more food than ever before. Still each time she came her people noticed more and more of a change in her. Barnacles grew upon her hands, up her arms, and the last time she came they had started to grow upon the side of her face which had been so beautiful and her people felt the chill winds wherever she walked, and they noticed that she seemed to be unhappy out of the sea. [13] On her last visit they told her she did not need to return to them again unless it was her wish to do so.

Since that time she has been their guiding spirit, and through her efforts there has always been plenty of shell fish and food of all kinds in that vicinity and the spring water has always been pure and sweet.

The tribe believes that as the currents flow back and forth thru Deception Pass her hair may be seen drifting gently with the tide and that she is always there to look out for the welfare of her people.

————

The Samish Tribe was supposed to have originated on the north shore of Guemes Channel and with them came the custom of the Masked Dance or "Shwi-qui {*sweyxwey*}." In this dance a mask was used which was so constructed that there was very little breathing space, requiring great stamina on the part of the dancer.

In later years thru intermarrying with neighboring tribes the customs of this dance passed to the Northern Indians, but its origin was with the Samish tribe.

The original holdings of the Samish tribe was the west half of Fidalgo Bay from Smilik Bay west, Guemes Island, Cypress Island and Samish Island and they also had an interest in the common fishing grounds at the mouth of the Samish river. ______

Members of this tribe now remaining on Swinomish Reservation are Mrs. John Lyons, George Cagey, Tommy Bob and Charles Edwards, the carver of the Totem Pole. [14]

CHARLIE EDWARDS
BUILDER OF THE TOTEM

The Boy and the Magic Robe

On the opposite side of the Totem Pole at the foot appears the figure of the Boy of the Magic Robe and his little Spitz dog. This is the legend of the Swinomish Tribe.

The boy's name was "Twu-yalets-sa," meaning the Magic Robe. His son's name was "Twu-whil-Kadim," meaning that which is just visible; and his son's name was "La-Qual-by," meaning The Break of Day. These names of Kadim and Qual-by are still in evidence on Swinomish Reservation.

"Twu-Yalets-sa" or the Boy of the Magic Robe, liked to kill animals and he always saved their skins and kept them in a little box which he had made. His father warned him many times against killing the animals and birds, saying:

"The animals and birds are our friends and you must not kill them except when you are hungry — else evil will befall you."

But the boy kept on killing them and bringing [15] in their hides and putting them away in his little box.

After he had warned him many times, his father became angry one day and said:

"This has got to stop — we will teach that boy a lesson."

While "Twu-Yalets-sa" was out hunting, his father took all the tribe in their canoes and went away with all their possessions where he could not find them, as he had warned him so many times that he would.

"Twu-Yalets-sa's" grandmother, the crow, felt sorry for him and urged the father not to leave him, saying that after he had been punished he would be a good boy. His father was very angry and would not stop, so she flew back and buried his box of skins and some coals of fire far down under the sand. Then she tied his little dog near the place where she had buried these things, and after she had done this she flew back to where his people had gone.

When "Twu-Yalets-sa" returned he did not know what to do. All his people were gone, there was no fire and he was very lonesome and hungry. His little dog kept whining and he untied it and immediately the dog began to scratch and dig at a pile of sand and at last uncovered the box and the coals of fire.

Then a voice came to him, telling him to gather all the sticks and rubbish he could find on the beach and put it into a pile and put the coals of fire into this pile and he would have a fire to warm himself and on which to cook his food. He [16] did this, and went out into the waters of the channel and caught a fish which he roasted and ate, but he was still very unhappy as he had no one to talk to except the little dog which stayed faithfully at his side.

The voice came to him again, telling him to make a robe of his skins and when it was completed to wave it over his fire four times. This he did, and when he had waved it over the fire for the fourth time many people sprang out of the fire and he had a tribe of his own.

The crow flew over the camp and saw that he was happy and then she went back to where his father was and told him that his son was a great chieftain and had a tribe of his own already, and she laughed at the father for being so foolish as to go away and leave him. Foolishly in her glee she explained to the father how the boy had come by all these people, and he became very angry and ordered all his people to get in their canoes and follow him.

When he and his people landed they drove all the boy's new people out into the water and they floated away.

"Twu-Yalets-sa" cried out, "Why have you done this, my father?" and the father replied:

"They are nothing but rubbish and they cannot stay here with the fine Swinomish tribe who are of a pure strain. They can have no rubbish with them."

He allowed the little dog to stay as he had been with the boy all the time and the new people floated away and landed in various spots on [17] the Sound and that is supposed to be the origin of the many smaller tribes which dotted the shores of Puget Sound.

Those of the Swinomish Tribe still on the Reservation are Chief Peter Charles and his family, Jerry Willup and his family, Ignatious Willup and Laura Wilbur and their families.

The Sun, Moon and Stars

This is the symbol of the Nookactiamish, a member of the Upper Skagit Tribe, and the story going with it is as follows: [18]

The chieftain's two daughters had been gathering Camas roots one day on a small prairie near Clear Lake and becoming tired they lay down side by side to sleep. As night came on the stars shone very bright and the two maidens looking up into the sky were talking. One of them said:

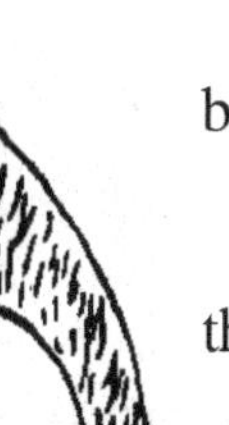

"I would like to have a husband like that beautiful big red star up there."

The other one said:

"I wish I had a husband as bright and beautiful as that white star up there."

So saying, they dropped to sleep and on awakening found that while they slept their wishes had been granted and they had been transported into the land of Stars and were married to the red and white stars, even as they had wished.

It so happened that the one who was married to the red star became very dissatisfied as her husband was not beautiful as she had thought he would be, but very ugly and disagreeable, but the other girl was delighted with her life and considered her husband very handsome.

They were sent out to dig Camas roots on a prairie which looked a great deal like the one on earth where they had been digging on the previous day. They were told that whenever a root went straight down very far they were not to dig that one but to go on to another one which did not go down into the ground so far.

The girl who was married to the red star wanted to see what she would find if she dug where the root went straight down and when she found one she dug very fast.

"Oh," gasped the other girl, "you must not do [19] that, they told us not to and surely we will get ourselves into trouble."

"Just the same," responded her sister, "I want to see what's down here," and she dug and dug as fast as she could, while her sister gathered roots faster than ever before so that the people would not know what the other girl was doing. At last there was an exclamation. "Look what I've found."

Her sister ran and looked down through a little hole that she had dug, and there beneath them was the earth. She had dug a hole thru the sky and could see where they had been on earth before they were brought to the land of the stars.

"Listen," said the girl who was married to the red star, "I'm going to get back there as fast as I can. I don't like my life up here, I don't like my husband and I am going to go back home."

"But how can you," replied her sister. "It's so far down there you'd hurt yourself if you jumped."

"I won't jump. We'll make a rope from cedar saplings and tie it to something up here and we'll go down to earth on that rope."

"Yes, but when can we make that rope? We are supposed to be gathering camas roots all the time. Besides I don't think I want to leave here," said the girl who was married to the white star. "I like my husband very much and the people are kind."

"Then," said her sister, "I'll tell you what we'll do. You gather roots twice as fast as you are doing now, and I'll make the rope. Then when it's done you can hold one end and I will climb down, [20] and then you can drop it down to me and fill up the hole again and no one will know where I have gone."

And so they worked hard for many days and when the rope was long enough they chose a dark night and the one sister slipped thru the hole and hanging to the rope she slid on down to earth. When she had landed she gave the rope a tug and her sister let it drop. This is thought to have been on the banks of a small stream running into Clear Lake, for to this day there is a large rock standing there looking for all the world like a coiled rope.

She could not find her people and she was all alone in the forest and she was very frightened, but a voice came and told her not to be afraid and to follow instructions and she would be taught to make little fish traps for gathering in fish and she would also be taught to gather other game for food. She followed the instructions very carefully and soon she had a nice little home built in the forest and had learned to gather in plenty of food and she was very happy.

When her little boy was born, however, she did not know what to do. She could not leave him alone while she went out for food and wood and she could not take him with her. The voice came to her again and directed her to turn an old fallen log into the shape of a woman and after she had done this she passed her hand over the figure three times and it came to life and she had a nurse for her child.

The spirit guide had warned her that if anyone found out that her baby was a boy it would [21] be stolen, and so she warned the nurse never to mention that it was a boy in her songs.

One day while the mother was away, two girls who were traveling from the Sauk River came near the hut in the forest and they heard the old nurse singing to the baby. She was singing about the beautiful boy he was, and then she said in a loud voice, "Oh, no that is a mistake, you are not a boy, you are a beautiful little girl." But the girls were not deceived and they watched their chance and stole the child. When the mother came back she turned the old woman back into a rotten old log and in her anguish she picked up the baby's clothes and wrung them in her hands and the spirit gave her another boy child to take the place of the one who was stolen.

About that time the Raven, who was chieftain of a small band of Indians living on the East bank of Skagit River, between where the towns of Lyman and Sedro Woolley now stand, saw her as he was paddling his canoe one day, and he took her to his home to be his wife. He was not very good to her and he was cruel to the little boy.

The mother told her son that somewhere he had a brother and that when he was out gather{ing} bark he should sing of this brother and try to find him. The Raven had taught him to fell a tree by burning it and as he sat waiting for the tree to burn enough to fall, he sang of his long lost brother.

In the meantime the two women who had stolen the older brother had raised him to be a fine man. He was different from anyone they had ever seen, as a sort of light shown from him all [22] the time. He was not content and roamed the forests all day, looking for something, he did not know what. He knew that the two women had stolen him when he was a baby, as he heard them talking of it when they were quarreling between themselves over which one the boy liked the most.

Then one day he heard this young boy singing in the woods, and when he heard the story of the song, he said:

"I must be that long lost brother," and he stepped out of the trees and spoke to the lad. But the boy could not see him at first as he shown so bright that the light hurt the younger boy's eyes. However, the older boy rubbed the little brother's eyes and then he could see him.

They started back to see their mother, and the older brother said he wanted to marry the finest girl in the tribe. She must be strong as well as beautiful and wise, in fact she must be strong enough to carry the body of an elk which he would shoot. The younger brother said he could recommend a girl for her character, but he feared she could not carry the body of an elk, and the elder brother said that if she had all the other characteristics she would be given the strength to carry the elk.

When they came to the place all the girls flocked around, the magpie came and the pigeon came, but none would do until finally the little green frog came and sat quietly on the river's bank, not saying a word but just looking sweet and wise, and the younger brother said:

"Look, that is the one I thought you should [23] choose," and the older brother was so pleased with her that she was given the strength to carry the elk and they were married.

The elder brother had heard how mean the Raven had been to his mother and younger brother and he said, "I will fix him." And at the wedding feast he threw a piece of tallow to him, throwing it so high into the air that when the Raven jumped to catch it he went on up through the roof and ever afterward he could fly and was a bird of the air and he did not bother the people in the camp any longer, except with his harsh, scolding voice.

At the wedding feast the older brother was asked why he out-shown everybody else, and he said he came from the land of the stars and that he was lighting the world. The two brothers put their heads together and decided that they would do a real job of lighting the world, so they went back up to the sky and took up their rightful places, but the older brother shown too brightly and made it too hot for the poor people of the earth, so he said:

"I will be the moon and shine at night and you, my brother, shall be the sun, for you do not shine too bright for the day."

And so they have been there ever since. The little green frog went with her husband and has been the lady in the moon.

Members of this tribe, the Upper Skagits, now remaining on Swinomish Reservation, are Jimmie Charles, Dewey Mitchell, Thomas W. McLeod, Mrs. William Peters, Martin Sampson, Alphonse Sampson, Eugene Sampson, and his sisters, and the Jack Day family. [24]

The Mink and the Fox

The Mink and his cousin, the Fox, were both very cunning and many interesting stories are told of their exploits.

One of the most interesting is the one told of the time that the Mink was boasting and bragging that he could do anything that any Spirit or Supernatural Person could do in the line of magic. The Supernatural Person could hear all that the Mink was saying and he chuckled to himself, vowing that he would play a trick on the Mink at the first opportunity.

One day the Mink had caught a salmon and was roasting it over a fire on the beach. He had worked hard all morning and he was very hungry, but he was also tired and sleepy and while the fish was roasting he fell asleep. This was the chance that the Supernatural One had been looking for. Quietly he stole up the sleeping Mink, rubbed fish oil all over his face, around his mouth, rubbed it on his hands, ate up all the fish himself, and then hid and waited to see what the Mink would do when he awakened.

The Mink looked around, saw that his fish was all eaten off the bones, felt the grease on his [25] hands and face and was completely puzzled. From all signs he had eaten his fish, but his stomach was still empty and he was very hungry.

Finally the Supernatural One showed himself and they exchanged tricks for a time. The Supernatural One admitted that the Mink had shown exceptional skill and told him that he would give him one last test to prove whether he was the best magician. He gave him a bell and told him to walk along the water's edge ringing the bell, and no matter how narrow the isthmus might be or how uneven the shore line, he must not take any short cuts but must follow the beach the entire distance. He warned him several times that if he attempted to make a short cut at any time he would die.

At first the Mink obeyed very well, but is was hard for him to do strictly as he was told and not play a little trick or two on the way, so that when he came to a very narrow isthmus which jutted a long way out into the water, he said to himself:

"That will take me a long time to go clear around, and just look, it's hardly more than a jump across to the other side of this isthmus. I could run across and no one would know the difference."

After carefully looking around to be sure nobody saw him, he took the short cut. But almost immediately his intestines started falling out of his body and lay along the path he had taken and soon he was so weak that he lay down and died.

His cousin, the Weasel, who was also gifted [26] in magic, came along. He gathered up the poor Mink's bones and put them together in their original shape, then stepped over them four times, pronouncing the magic word while he did so.

The Mink sat up and rubbed his eyes, then got up and shook himself, saying, "I must have been asleep a long time for I feel so very tired."

"Ho, ho," replied the Weazel, "you have not been asleep; you were dead. What is this bell for, anyway?"

As soon as the Mink saw the bell he remembered and then he told his story to the Weazel and they both agreed that they were not quite as cunning as they sometimes thought they were.

Another legend of the Mink is —

He decided that he was just as smart as the Sun and the Moon and he could do just as good a job of lighting the world as they did, so he went up to see them.

He arrived while the Sun was out and the Sun's wife did not know him, so he told her that he was her husband's son. Upon learning of this the husband decided to punish him for this falsehood, as he had had a great deal of trouble explaining to his wife that the Mink was given to playing jokes of this sort upon people.

The next day he dressed the Mink up in his shining suit, gave him his cane, and told him to go on his way and light the world, saying:

"It's perfectly easy, all you have to do is just walk around and let your light shine upon the world."

"I knew all the time," replied the Mink, "that [27] this was an easy job, but I don't want the cane, you don't use it for anything, do you?"

The Sun urged him to carry it, saying that it made him look so much more of a fine fellow; so the Mink started out swinging the cane along merrily.

When he came to the Milky Way he did not know how to get across. The current seemed to be very swift and it was quite wide. What he did not know and what the Sun failed to tell him, was that the Sun used the cane to lean upon to give him a start when he jumped across the Milky Way, and when the poor Mink just took a running jump, carrying the cane, he fell into the middle of the Milky Way, blotted out his light, and was quickly carried on the current right back to earth. (This is supposed to be the story of the eclipse.) [28]

Legend of the Hail

Susie "Kahl-la-los," whose name meant "small or tiny," lived with the Upper Skagits. She was a very quiet, industrious little woman, but many of her tribe believed that she had been given a guiding spirit when she was young, although she never told of it.

One day one of their tribe, Jimmie Jones, was traveling up river on one of the passenger boats and got into an argument with another Indian. The disagreement ended in a fight with one man being killed and Jimmie Jones badly cut in the abdomen. He was brought to his home and the best Tribal Doctors worked on him for days, but he steadily got worse. Finally, Susie Kahl-la-los came and stood by his bed singing a strange song.

She told in her song that when she was young she had fasted for many days and then while walking along a forest path a stranger came toward her from the East. He was toying with small objects, tossing them into the air and catching them again. They looked at first like tiny glass beads, but as she came closer she noticed that many of them were not being tossed by him but were falling all about him from the sky, and then she realized that it was hail.

He stopped and talked to her and while they spoke the hail fell all about them although the sun was shining brightly. He told her that she was to have a long and happy life and that whenever she needed strength for helping herself or [29] others she was to call upon the Hail and it would be given to her.

When she first stepped over to his side Jimmie Jones was very weak, in fact he was almost dead, and as she sang her song the people standing around them noticed that strength seemed to flow into his body and at the end of the song he sat up — he was better — and very soon he was entirely well.

Jimmie Jones is still living, a man about ninety years old, and some of those who witnessed this manifestation of spiritual strength coming from nature are still living. [30]

The Grizzly Bear and Rattlesnake

At one of the big potlatches on the Duwaumish Reservation the Chief's daughter became very ill and although her family hired all the noted doctors they could find, the girl grew steadily worse and finally became delirious — her people believed that the evil spirit had complete control of her.

In desperation her father called out: "Is there no one here who can help my daughter?"

And a young man from the Upper Skagit tribe stepped forward, saying that his name was "Yala-haut-so," that he was commonly called "Dr. Dick," and that he was willing to see what he could do.

At the same time another young man came [31] forward and stated he was of the Yakima tribe and immediately started to sing of his spirit guide which was the rattlesnake. Yala-haut-so did not tell what his guide was, but as soon as the Yakima Indian started his song he also began to sing a strange chant.

There was a huge fire and the Yakima Indian circled this several times and suddenly the smoke whirled around and took the shape of a rattlesnake which crawled slowly toward the bed where the girl lay. When it came within a few feet of the bed it stopped and coiled with its head raised as though it would strike.

All this time Yalla-haut-so had never ceased with his song and as the girl's delirium became weaker and faltered, he stepped up to the side of her bed and made a snatching motion and she became quiet — and in a few hours she was well.

When asked what he had done, Yalla-haut-so said he had done nothing — that his spirit guide, the Grizzly Bear, had snatched the evil spirit from the girl when it had become frightened at the sight of the rattlesnake. [32]

The Black Fish

The Black Fish is placed on the Totem Pole in honor of the late Sam Dan, the only Indian Doctor to ever defy a government doctor.

An interesting story is told of when he had a child who was very ill at the government hospital. Seeing that the child was getting no better, Dr. Dan came in one day while the government doctor was away and administered his own kind of doctoring, calling upon his guide, the Black Fish, to help him. When the government doctor returned the child had passed the crisis and was much better. He turned to Dr. Dan and asked him what he was doing there, whereupon Dr. Dan simply said, "I am curing my child as it seems that you are not able to do so."

Many years later, Sam Dan had another very sick child which he took to the office of a Mt. Vernon doctor. The late Dr. Howe of LaConner came in and upon seeing him sitting there he asked him what he was doing there and Sam Dan replied that he was waiting to have the doctor look at his child. [33]

Dr. Howe said, "Why don't you cure him yourself?"

An{d} Sam Dan replied, "This child has a white man's sickness and I cannot cure him."

Dr. Howe was so pleased at Sam Dan's honesty that he introduced him to the Mt. Vernon doctor as "Dr. Dan" and the Mt. Vernon doctor treated the child free of charge as he would have done for any other doctor.

The late Jim McLeod, brother of Mrs. Wm. Peter, also told of the guidance of the Black Fish. He was in a small canoe and wished to go to Lopez Island on important business at a certain time. There was a strong west wind blowing at the time and the tide was coming in thru Deception Pass, making traveling in a small boat very difficult.

Jim McLeod tried several times to go thru but he could not make it, his boat would swamp, forcing him to turn back. His business on the Island was so important that he had to go at that particular time and could not wait for the wind to stop blowing or for the tide to turn. Finally in desperation he called upon his guide, the Black Fish, to help him in his trouble.

Immediately two large Black Fish came toward him and lined themselves up, one on each side of his canoe, and took him safely thru the Pass and on over to the Island.

While no one saw this, there are several Indians still living who know that he arrived safely at the island during a severe storm and they firmly believe his story. [34]

The Mountain Goat

Thomas McLeod told one day of seeing the Mountain Goat as he floated down the Skagit River.

Thomas was very busy floating shingle bolts down the river when he heard a man's voice singing. He looked all around but could see no one and finally noticed this goat which was  standing on the water floating down stream, singing in a man's voice.

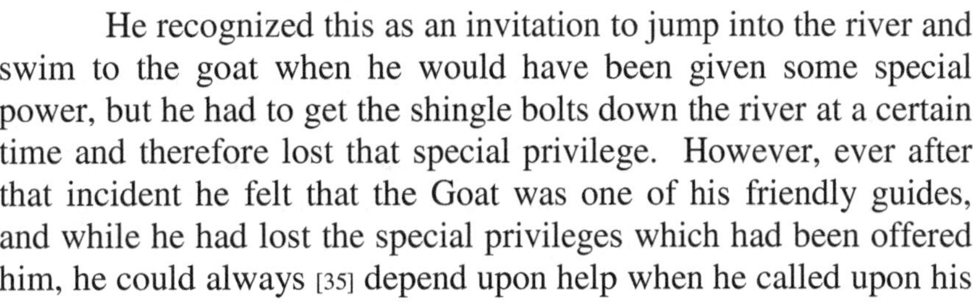 He recognized this as an invitation to jump into the river and swim to the goat when he would have been given some special power, but he had to get the shingle bolts down the river at a certain time and therefore lost that special privilege. However, ever after that incident he felt that the Goat was one of his friendly guides, and while he had lost the special privileges which had been offered him, he could always [35] depend upon help when he called upon his friend the Goat.

The BLACK BEAR — is universally respected and considered as a guide by all dancers, warriors and doctors in all tribes. He is shown on the Totem Pole in combat with the Alligator, which so far as is known by the Indians is just a large Lizard, which is used a great deal as a guide by the Indian Doctors of all tribes.

The TWO WILD CATS — are the guiding spirit of Pat Willup and his family, but as long as this family are still living, no actual stories of these cats can be told.

The TWO LIZARDS — represent the spirit bringing luck and are used in dancing. General Fornsby used them as guides in his doctoring, as the Lizard is always believed to bring good luck. General Fornsby and John Edge are the only real Indian Doctors left on the Reservation.

The COUGAR — was the guide of Elze {LZ} Andrews, who always sang his song to this animal no matter what he was doing, working, dancing, or preparing for war.

George Williams had as his guide Two Ladies who came from the East. They traveled thru the day, coming from the East with the dawn and leaving again with the night. In this circle they visited all the tribes. [36]

The Wilbur family also have the Hail as their talisman. They descend from Chief Sna-Atel-Em of the Lower Skagits, whose chief guiding spirit was the Hail. He was known as one of the most powerful chieftains, Mrs. Joseph Joe is a great great niece of Sna-Atel-Em. {Sneatlum?}

The TOAD — Most Indian Doctors, like the late Elze Andrews, used the toad for inspiration in their dances and doctoring. The toad stayed under water and made bubbles appear. In many of their songs, the bubbles are likened to whirlpools in Deception Pass.

The Man Swallowing the Shark is meant to show that man is superior to all living things.

The Canoe, which appears on the Totem Pole, is the family canoe. This type was originally made and used by the Makaw or Neah Bay Indians and the Indians on the west coast of Vancouver Island, but was later adopted by all tribes on the Sound as a family canoe. The high prow was designed to go thru the rough waters of the Straits, and it is much safer for families to travel in than the narrower, longer racing canoes.

The American Eagle, both male and female, appear at the top of the Pole, as the Eagle is greatly respected by all tribes and is supposed to be the friendly bird of the Indians.

Directly beneath the Eagle is the figure of [37] Franklin Roosevelt, who is known to the Indians as the Great White Father, or Chief of Chiefs, inasmuch as it was under his jurisdiction that the re-organization bill was signed giving the Indians self government. Therefore the Indians feel that carving his picture on this Totem Pole was the proper gesture to make as it is a monument to this particular age.

Of all these tokens and signs there are three things which are still being used today in songs, dances, etc., as talismen of the Indians. They are the two small figures made to look like ducks, called "Tchaz-u" and the round cedar discs, or "Qued-al-ich" {*sg^{w}ədilič*} and the cedar poles "Tusted" which are used in the dances and games at all the Indian celebrations. These are all used in the smoke houses today as manifestation of the spirit which comes to guide the Indians during the winter season. They are used generally as guides for hunters and fishermen.
[38 end]

Legend of the Nookachamis

An Indian of the Nookachamis Tribe, fasting and seeking power near Big Lake, was told by a voice to go and dive into Clear Lake after fasting for many days. He obeyed and the result was that while in a trance he was taken into a large house at the bottom of the lake where there were many people and after being honored and feasted he was sent back with two companions. These were the two cedar discs "Qued-el-ich" and when he came back to life he had them with him. They are supposed to be strong guides for the Indians and from that time on all thru the years every Indian has this token with him. They are now made from cedar bark, vine maple and buckskin.

Slo<u>x</u> ~ The Home of My Ancestors

A long time ago, this is how the homes of my ancestors looked.
ʔal tudi tuhaʔk^w g^wəl ʔəsista ʔə tiʔəʔ k^wədi tuʔalʔal ʔə ti tudyəl'yəl'ab.
This was the kind of a home the father of my father had.
ʔəsistə k^wədi tuʔalʔal ʔə ti bad ʔə ti tudbad.
It was located at slo<u>x</u> (between Hamilton and Lyman, Wn.) near the shore of the Skagit river.
ʔal slu<u>x</u> k^wədi tusʔaʔs, ilg^wił ʔə ti sqajət stulək^w .
Many people lived in that one house because it was very big.
qaʔhaʔ k^wədi t(u)əsłałlil ʔal tiʔił dču ʔalʔal yə<u>x</u>i həlab tuhik.
However big it was.
k'^widəs tał k^wi tushik^ws.
Maybe it was one hundred feet long and eighty feet wide.
x^wuʔələ ʔulub ʔi k^wi cəlac tał k^wi shaacs g^wəl ʔulub ʔi k^wi łix^w tał k^wi sbaʔs.
My mother and my father lived in that house at slo<u>x</u>.
t(u)əsłałtlil ci tudsk'^wuy, ʔi ti tudbad ʔal tiʔił ʔalʔal ʔal slu<u>x</u>.
My mother told me, she said that my grandfather used to wake them up early in the morning, sending them to the river.
tuyəcəbtubš ci tudsk'^wuy, tuʔuqəłtubk'^wəł həlgə ʔə tiʔił tudscapa ʔal k^wi łup dadatuʔ g^wəl tučəsatəb dx^wʔal ti stulək^w.
He would say to them, "Do not just be laying there in bed smelling your bodies, get up now."
cutəb, "x^wi k^w(i)ads<u>x</u>^wul ʔəstad^zil ʔəshaq^wʔabacəb, g^wədiləx^w.
They were told, "You will go and bathe in the river." She said that, that was his custom with them all of the time, summer or winter. [He was the head of the family and this was one of the rules to be obeyed by his training].
cutəb, "łut'it'əb čələb ʔal tiʔił stulək^w." ʔəsistə k^wəł k^wi tuʔalustubs, bək'^w pətab, pədhədəb, pədt'əs. [yə<u>x</u>i sd^zix^wqs ʔə tiʔił ʔiisəds g^wəl dił <u>x</u>əčusədads]

Three fires large in size was this house, but only the near first fire was used for cooking the food. See the salmon being cooked, skewered on cooking sticks.
łix^wʔaličup k^wi shik^w ʔə tiʔəʔ ʔalʔal g^wəl <u>x</u>^wul tiʔəʔ čit, iłd^zix^w hud k^wi ƛujəctub dx^wal sq'^wəldaliłəd. šuuc tiʔił sʔuladx^w sq'^wəlb ʔəsšic' ʔal <u>x</u>ək'^wəd.

Let us talk about what you see in this house.
g^wəg^waʔg^wəbid čəł tiʔił ʔəsšuuc čələb ʔal tiʔə ʔalʔal.

1. *There are two Mallard ducks. They are laying on top of the small place for putting things. This was the game of the man laying down at the other end of the house. He is resting because it was early in the morning that he went hunting.*
  The woman will pluck the ducks and she will make soup of it. Excellent tasting soup, is the soup of the duck.
1. ʔa ti saliʔ <u>x</u>ət<u>x</u>ət. ʔəsłaq' šəqabac ʔə ti miman səx^wt'ag^wtalik^w. sx^wiʔx^wiʔ ʔə ti stubš ʔəstəd^zil diʔadi. ʔuqag^wəx^w yə<u>x</u>i tułup dadatuʔ k^wi tusʔyu<u>x</u>^ws, x^wiʔx^wiʔs.
  łu<u>x</u>əciustub ʔə ci sładəyʔ ti buq^w g^wəl łučəł; słub. ad^zaləqəp słub, tiʔił słub ʔə buq^w.

2. *There are clam baskets. Clams are put in there when they go clam digging.*
2. ʔa ti xʷʔax̱ʷaʔəd. x̌ʼudəgˇaʔtub tiʔił sax̱ʷuʔ x̌ʼuʔax̱ʷuʔilułəs həlgʷə.

3. *There are cedar root baskets everywhere. That is where many varieties of dried berries are put. Possessions of other kinds are also put into cedar root baskets, wooden containers, and cedar bark containers.*
3. qaha kʷi yiqʼyiqʼus bəkʼᵂ čad. ʔal tiʔił kʷi bəkʼᵂidup sqʼᵂəlaləd ʔəsšabtub gʷəl ʔəsdəkʷ ʔal tiʔił. gʷəl x̌ʼ(u)əsdəkʷtub kʷi bəkʼᵂ stab, stabigʷs ʔal yiqʼᵂus, ʔal wəqʼəb, słuəyʔulč.

4. *They have a dip net leaning at the pole. They use this dip net at the river. They put it into the water and the knowledgeable fisherman is rewarded with salmon.*
4. ʔa ti qʷuləč ʔəsʔiltub ʔal tiʔił; cəqʷuł. x̌ʼujəctub tiʔił qʷuləč ʔal ti stuləkʷ. x̌ʼujiqʼaladᶻəd gʷəl x̌ʼudaha ʔə kʷi sʔuladxʷ kʷi sčəwat dxsxiʔxiʔ.

5. *There is an old man telling stories to the children. They are sitting nicely and listening intently. They are not playing around, disrespectfully.*
5. ʔa tiʔił lux̌ ʔuʔəyəhubtxʷ tiʔił stawixʷał. ʔəsgʷədil ʔə kʷi haʔł həlgʷə gʷəl ʔuləqəladi. xʷiʔ gʷəsukəlpcuts həlgʷə.

6. *There is a woman twirling the leg spindle, she prepares the wool of the sheep for Knitting and weaving all kinds of clothing to keep them warm.*
6. ʔa ci sładəyʔ ʔucəlpad ti dᶻulaqʼ, x̌ʼuqʷibid tiʔił labatulqiʔ dxʷʔal kʷi gʷəsqəlkʼalikʷs ʔə kʷi bəkʼᵂ stab sx̌ʼalabac gʷəsəsqəbłs həlgʷə.

7. *There is a woman weaving a clam basket. She has her cedar boughs in the water, soaking.*
7. ʔa ci sładəy ʔučəł xʷaxʷaʔəd. ʔəsjiqʼtxʔ ti stidgʔə ʔal ti qʔu, ʔəsbasild.

8. *The woman, who is sitting at the other end of the house, is taking care of her two grandchildren. Their mother is berry picking.*
8. ciʔił sładəyʔ ʔəsgʷədil diʔadi gʷəl ʔəstixədxʷ ti ʔibʔibacs, səsali. ʔucʼəbəbiluł ci skʼᵂuys həlgʷə.

9. *And the woman, who is moving toward the center of the house, has a cedar root basket. She dipped water from the river.*
9. gʷəl ciʔił sładəyʔ ləsulacut gʷəl ʔəskʷədad tiʔił yiqʼᵂus, tuyax̌ʼəd kʷi quʔ tulʔal ti stuləkʷ.

10. *Look at the rocks near the first fire. They keep those brushed to put into the fire until they are hot. They then put them into the cedar root basket for boiling their food.*

10. šuuc tiʔił čəčəƛa čitbid ʔə tiʔił; dᶻixʷ hud, dił ƛ(u)əst'ixʷtub gʷəl ƛuhudutəb dxʷal sədils gʷəl ƛudəgʷatubəxʷ dxʷʔal kʷi yiq'ʷus gʷəl dəx ʷʔuqʷalcalikʷəxʷ ʔə kʷi sʔəłəd.

11. There *is a lot of food up above, hanging. Dried salmon, dried meat, meat of the deer. Dried horse clams. They dry the heads of salmon.*
11. ʔa tiʔił qaha sʔəłəd šəqaltxʷ, ʔəsk'ił. ʔəsšab sʔuladxʷ, ʔəsšab biac, sqigʷəcałc'iʔ. ʔəsšab haac, ʔəsšabqitəb ti sʔuladxʷ.

12. *You see the pole in the middle of the house. They have power poles tied there, two long ones. They have power boards tied there, two of them. They belong to the owner of the house. In the winter time he sings for them and they go. They work. They help those who are sick. They find something that is lost. They point out a thief. They help in many ways.*
12. šuucəxʷ tiʔił cəqʷul ʔudəgʷabac ʔə'ʔa ti ʔalʔal. ʔəsłidtəb tiʔił təstəd, sali haac. ʔəsłidtəb tiʔił sgʷədilič sali. gʷəł tiʔə absʔalʔal tiʔə diʔəʔ. ʔal pədt'es gʷəl ƛuʔilucitub tiʔiʔaʔ gʷəl ƛuxʷ. ƛuyayus. ƛukʷaxʷad kʷi ʔəsxeł. ƛuʔəydxʷ kʷi stab ʔəsxʷil. gʷəlaʔəd kʷi dxʷsqada. bəkʷ stab gʷəskʷaxʷaxʷs.

13. *There are three wooden ladles which they use for dipping soup, for food, for water.*
13. ʔəsk'ił kʷi łixʷ łabqs, dəxʷ ʔuyaƛalikʷs həlgʷə ʔə kʷi słub, ʔə kʷi sʔəłəd, ʔə kʷi qʷuʔ.

14. *There are deer hoof rattles hanging near the ladles.*
14. ʔəsk'ił kʷi k'ʷətilšəd, čitbid ʔə ti łabqs.

15. *There are dried horse clams hanging near the dip net.*
15. ʔəsk'ił kʷi ʔəsšab hac, čitbid ʔə ti q'ʷuləč.

16. *There are drums at the other end of the house. One is behind the old man telling stories and one is near the man who is sleeping.*
16. ʔa ti təsadi diʔadi. ʔa ti dču qadbid ʔə ti luƛ ʔuʔəyəhub, gʷəl ʔa ti dčuʔ citbid ʔə ti stubš ʔəsʔitut.

17. *Look at the cattail that have been made for beds, are made for the [mat] walls. And there are animal skins used for blankets.*
17. šuuc cəxʷ tiʔił ʔulʔal ʔəsčəłtub słagʷid ʔəsčəłtub k'ʷat'aq' gʷəl ʔa tiʔił (čaʔəd) (k'ʷəlu) – sčəł sqəlikʷ

   Where our ancestors lived was very good. They helped each other, they knew each other. Their customs were good long ago.
Haʔł tiʔił tusəsłałil ʔə tiʔił tuyəlyələb čəł, tuʔukʷaxʷatəgʷəl, t(u)əshaydəgʷəl. haʔł tiʔił tuʔalʔaluss həlg'ʷə ʔal k'ʷədi tuhaʔkʷ.

This is taqʷšəblu talking 8-10-76
taqʷšəblu ciʔəʔ ləcu gʷagʷəd 8-9-76

As Vi Hilbert further explained (Miller 1999: 87, 155):

Along the Skagit River, six houses at *slox* are well reported.[14] Located between modern Lyman and Hamilton, the best known of these houses (that of Vi Hilbert's father's father) was eighty feet long and fifty feet wide, with six to eight fires. The site included an important fishery, for both salmon and trout, where people used dip nets, spears, and hooks but no weir. Every day, those who fished shared their catch with everyone in the house.

Owners of this house were four brothers and a sister, with their families, at five fires. One of the brothers was the father of Charlie Anderson, whose own sister and her husband had a sixth fire. The other two fires were occupied by the families of other grown children of the brothers. These first cousins were regarded as siblings in the native terminology, so the household consisted of parents and their children, who regarded each other as brothers and sisters.

Indeed, this house provides the dearest illustration of the link between [88] siblings (family core), house, and place. Each year to this day, the salmon fishing season begins with a blessing of the Upper Skagit fleet at *slox* as a reminder that the man appointed by the Skagit Prophet to be head fisherman for the river always belonged to that community.

#14 [155]   Both Sally Snydcr and June Collins erred in limiting *slox* to a single house, probably because they did not talk to anyone belonging to this family, such as Vi Hilbert.   Collins regarded it as the village of the *basla'{s}alox* band, but this term merely describes those living at *slox*.   Of the six houses there at one time, owners are known for four.   In addition to that [156] of Charlie Anderson's father *(su'yius),* homes were owned by Dora Solomon's father, Smokey Lyle's grandfather *(hyus slosh),* and a man named Shoemaker·{see p26 herein}.   Charlie's sister was the mother of Dewey Mitchell, a famous Swinomish elder, and of two daughters.

After the plank houses were abandoned, a European-style house was built at *slox,* where Vi Hilbert lived as a girl.   When John Fornsby's daughter-in-law died there of pneumonia, Louisa prepared the body, and she was buried in a grave behind the house, suggesting a parallel to the final burial of Fornsby's grandfather *k^{w}əskadəb* at his potlatch house near Skagit City.

Susie's Training to Become an Indian Doctor

1 training 14 memories 26 revenge 31 windstorm

Prominent families were noted for certain distinctive abilities, passed down through generations. Both men and women of a family shared these talents, blessed by spiritual help. The ordeal of becoming a native Indian doctor, one of the most important careers, began early for Susie Sampson Peters. Her father urged her to fast and plunge into an icy creek (where gravel froze to her feet). Though an orphan, her father had disciplined himself to gain spiritual help from a Butterfly, who also provided him with the names of his future daughters. Susie's own powers, never used in public, were contacted near Day Creek, Jarman Prairie, and Hamilton. As an adult, she joined the Indian Shaker Church, and her property, powers, and spirits converted with her. While questing of old taught respect and reserve, schools which replaced such training did not benefit children in the same way. Successful doctoring gave wealth and generosity that classrooms can not match. Revenge killings of her Indian doctor kin are sadly told, followed by her account of a terrific wind story, with a humorous aside abot an old woman named tidišəʔ who builds a fire on the threatened beach, unaware of the growing hazards.

Susie's son Al [AS] aided her taping by Leon Metcalf and later her son Martin [MS] offered translations to Vi Hilbert when she undertook the transcription and translation of the Metcalf tapes.

1. AS: yəhəẇ, ʔux̌ʷalikʷəxʷ k̓ʷuyəʔ.

   AS: Now, begin telling your information, Mother.

2. SSP: ʔu tuʔəshuytub čəd sʔušəbabtxʷ ʔə tiʔił tudbad yəx̌i tudxʷdaʔəb.

   My father made life very arduous for me because he was an Indian doctor (a shaman). [MS, her other son, translated this: He gave me strict discipline.] [Father said]

3. tuʔəscuucəbš, "p̓aƛaƛ gʷəsładəyʔəxʷ tux̌ʷ čəxʷ łudxʷdaʔəb.

   He said to me, "It doesn't matter that you are merely a woman, you shall become an Indian doctor (in keeping with the prominence of your family ancestors).

4. xʷiʔ kʷi ładsʔubəq̓əd tiʔəʔ sʔəłəd. xʷiʔ kʷi ładsʔuhuydxʷ ʔə kʷi qa."

   You will abstain from putting food in your mouth. You will not eat much." [MS: "You will fast."] [Susie agrees]

5. hay čəd tuʔəsčalad.

   So, that was what I did. [MS: I followed instructions obediently.]

6. ƛukʷədyidtəb čəd ʔə tiʔił səpləl, mimaʔən.

   A little bit of bread was given to me, a small portion.

7. gʷəl ƛutugʷutəb dxʷʔal tiʔəʔ dq̓əyuq̓ʷ.

   It would be measured according to how long [the length of] my throat was.

8. siʔiƛub dxʷʔal tiʔił dk̓ətuʔ łudscəxʷəsbəł.

It would have to be enough to satisfy my stomach. [MS: to sustain me.]

9. liłaʔuʔxʷ čəd tiʔił tuʔəsistətub.

By this regime was I trained.

10. łułičitəb tiʔił k̓əyayəʔ gʷəl łuʔugʷutub.

Also, dried salmon would be cut off and measured (along my throat). [Father specified:]

11. "si, dił łuʔadəxʷəsbəł ck̓ʷaqid."

"Just so much, just enough, will serve to keep you appeased (while training)" [Susie confirms]

12. xʷiʔ gʷədsq̓əyil čəd tuluƛəxʷ.

I did not balk. I was maturing enough to understand (its purpose).

13. tuk̓ʷidaladxʷəxʷəd.

I am not sure of my age, however old I was.

14. ʔabiləxʷ čəd tuʔulubaladxʷəxʷ.

Maybe I was ten years old at that time.

15. xʷiʔ gʷəƛudswiliq̓ʷid tsi tudsk̓ʷuy.

Never once did I come crying to my mother (to intervene). [I submitted to all the hardships].

16. x̌ʷul̓ ləbəč tiʔił stul̓čaʔkʷ, cutəb, "łagʷic̓aʔəb čəxʷa saxʷəb.

When the West Wind blew, I was told, "Take off your clothes and run (as fast as you can).

17. dayəxʷ tiʔił ʔadsgʷig̓ʷədalqs kʷi ʔəsx̌altxʷ čəxʷ.

You need only to keep on your small undergarment (for modesty).

18. hiwil təlawil dxʷq̓ixʷ."

Alright, you go, run upriver."

19. ʔal tiʔił ʔal sx̌ad̓x̌ad̓adis.

Toward there at sx̌ad̓x̌ad̓adis [above and across from Lyman on the Skagit River, where Day Creek flows out.] [Susie reluctantly agrees]

20. xʷiʔ gʷədsəsx̌abid kʷi stab x̌ʷul̓ čəd ʔu xʷəc tiʔił dsx̌alalic̓aʔ čəda baləsaxʷəb.

I did not pout or fuss (though I hesitated). Nonetheless, I took off my outer dress and I ran.

21. baləxʷəcəd čəd tiʔəʔ dsčayəp, tiʔəʔ ʔəsx̌altxʷ čəd čəda łaqaš ʔilgʷił ʔə ti stuləkʷ čəda ləx̌ʷijəd ʔə tiʔił čəƛa balətičib čəd dxʷčaʔkʷ.

I removed my skirt, placed it beside the river, weighted it down with a rock, and I swam out into the current, away from shore.

22. čaʔkʷ ti dsʔup̓əq̓ʷagʷil ʔə di łax̌.

Out in the stream I floated in the pitch black night.

23. xʷiʔ gʷədsəsx̌əc.

[an aside] I was not afraid.

24. xʷiʔ kʷi stab gʷəʔəsx̌əcbid čəd.

Nothing was allowed to scare me.

25. hay, diɬ cəxʷhaydxʷ tiʔəʔ sxʷədaʔəb dču̓ʔ, ʔəskʷaxʷacəxʷ ʔə tiʔiɬ dsəluX̌il.

So, that is how I found this particular power which always helps me even as I grow older.

26. ʔəskʷaxʷacəxʷ tiʔəʔ sxʷdaʔəb.

Even now sustaining me is this doctoring power. [Doctor spirit speaks:]

27. cuucəbš, "ʔabiləxʷ čəxʷ ɬuluX̌il gʷəl ɬ(u)adsqʷid̓ʷəxʷ čəd.

It says to me, "If you happen to get old, I will be your strength![1]

28. ɬuʔəskʷaxʷacidəxʷ čəd."

I shall help you." [Susie explains]

29. ʔabsdaʔ tiʔəʔ sxʷdaʔəb, ʔabsdaʔ ʔə tiʔəʔ ʔalʔuyəli, tiʔəʔ xʷdaʔəb.

This power has a name, it is called ʔalʔuyəli, this power, indeed! [Spirit speaks:]

30. "x̌ʷuɬ čəxʷ ɬuʔuxaX̌aX̌il čəxʷa ɬuʔəyilc."

"When you have trouble, call on me!" [Susie affirms]

31. gʷəl ʔəsistə čəd ʔal tiʔəʔ sləx̌il.

That is just what I always do.

32. bək̓ʷ ti dxʷdadaʔəb ʔəxʷsgʷəlaldubšəb.

All the Indian doctors wanted to wipe me out (kill me).

33. xaX̌txʷ gʷədsʔatəbəd ʔal tiʔəʔ diʔəʔ, dəxʷ ʔa ʔə tiʔiɬ dsqʷid̓ʷ.

They wanted me to die, here, where my strength lies (my power).

34. ʔa tsiʔiɬ dsxʷdidaʔəb ʔa.

Still (through skill), there continues to exist within me a bit of doctoring power, here, inside.

35. x̌ʷuɬ čəd ʔuxaX̌il čəda baʔləcuʔilidupəd tiʔiɬ dsxʷdaʔəb.

When I have trouble of any kind, I have only to sing my doctoring power song to get relief. Here is the song.

36. s̓tilib:

Song:

ʔad̓ᶻəq̓əcutəxʷ tiʔəʔ

It turns itself around,

37. tə yalʔuyəli

this very ʔalʔuyəli

38. ʔal tuyəlikʷ

[vocables, sung sounds]

39. xʷuyə, xʷuʔi

[doctoring breaths]

40. ʔad̓ᶻəq̓əqutəxʷ tiʔəʔ

It turns itself around,

41. tiyəluʔwəyi ʔi

Around it turns itself

42. ʔad̓ᶻəq̓əcutəxʷ tiʔəʔ

It turns itself around

43. tiyuləwi ʔi ʔuya, xʷuʔi.

[end of song].

44. balətəq̓ʷ. huy diɬ dsgʷa dsqʷid̓ʷ tiʔiɬ tuɬʔal ti tudsəshuytəb sʔušəbabtxʷ.

The song breaks off there. That is my strength gained from what I endured.

45.	ʔutitəb čəd bək̓ʷ sətax̌il, bək̓ʷ dadatu.	I earned it (by hardship). I bathed every evening, every morning.
46.	putəxʷ x̌ux̌əb tiʔəʔ djəsjəsəd čəda x̌ušig̓ʷag̓ʷildubut tuʔali,ədi ti g̓ʷədap.	My feet would be weighted down by the time I struggled to shore.
47.	łuʔibəš čəd.	I staggered on cold, numb feet.
48.	tux̌ix̌iqəxʷ tiʔił čəx̌a ʔal tiʔił djəsjəsəd čəda x̌uʔəxʷcutəbəxʷ,	Pebbles would freeze to the soles of my feet and I would think,
49.	"x̌aləxʷ tiditəbtəbušəd lił̓al tiʔił čəx̌a."	"The bottoms of my feet are made of rock."
50.	k̓ʷawa tux̌ʷ x̌uʔəsqaxʷ tiʔił čəx̌a g̓ʷəl x̌ux̌iq dxʷʔal tiʔił djəsəd g̓ʷəl x̌uxʷitiləxʷ x̌uʔabšədəbəd.	However, the frozen rocky layers stuck to my feet would fall off as I stepped forward on shore.
51.	ʔu, dił tudəshuytub ʔəcaʔ ʔal tiʔił tudsčačas	Oh, that was just what I was subjected to as a child.
52.	g̓ʷəl liłaləxʷ tiʔəʔ pastəd. lił̓aləxʷ tiʔəʔ skul tiʔəʔ dbədbədaʔ.	Now (however), everything is according to the ways of the Bostons.[2] My children go to school now.
53.	tiʔəʔ dəxʷqələlaluss.	Which is why they remain uneducated.
54.	dəxʷxʷiʔs g̓ʷəʔəshaydxʷ g̓ʷəsqəlalitut.	That is why they know nothing about spirit power.
55.	xʷiʔs g̓ʷəʔəshaydxʷ g̓ʷəstab.	Why they do not know anything useful.
56.	cug̓ʷəxʷ tiʔəʔ g̓ʷəł pastəd čəłx̌əčəb tiʔəʔ ləskʷədad həlg̓ʷə.	The only thing they learn about is the mindset of the Bostons.
57.	g̓ʷəl tiʔił tudbad g̓ʷəl tuʔəsistətub k̓ʷəł, yəx̌i tučačas g̓ʷəl tuʔiʔixʷədil.	Now, I suppose my father was treated similarly because he was still but a child
58.	tug̓ʷəlaltəb k̓ʷi tubads.	when he was orphaned, his father was killed (murdered). [He had no one to rely on.]
59.	g̓ʷəl tuʔutitəbtub, tuʔutitəbtub.	He was sent out to seek power, to ritually bathe and purify himself.
60.	k̓ʷidəłdat k̓ʷi x̌usʔals tiʔił sbadil x̌usəstədʷils.	Many days he was in the mountains, where he slept.
61.	xʷiʔ g̓ʷəsʔuʔələds. x̌ʷul ləcug̓ʷəčəd k̓ʷi xʷdaʔəb.	He fasted. He deliberately sought doctoring power.
62.	x̌ʷul ləcug̓ʷəčəd tiʔəʔ bək̓ʷ stab sqəlalitut.	He steadfastly searched for any kind of spirit power.

63. hay, gʷəl tuləʔuluɬ gʷəl cickʷ sʎ̓əp tiʔiɬ ʔilucid ʔə duqʷəč, gʷəɬ duqʷəčabš.

Then when he was canoeing, there along the deep edge of duqʷəč, belonging to the duqʷəčabš.

64. tiʔiɬ ʔuʔaʔil kʷədi qʷəłay gʷəl tudxʷdzaldzaləgʷab.

There, he came to a log which spun around in a whirlpool.

65. ʔu gʷəl stabəxʷ kʷi ləgʷəčəd čəd, bsʔatəbəd.

[aside, he thought] Oh, am I expected to risk my life here?

66. ʔu ƛ̓ub čəd ʔuʔusil. baləʔusil kʷəɬ. ɬulaʔiččut čəxʷ ɬubaɬəxʷ.

Oh, I had better dive. He then dove, it is said.

67. ɬulaʔiččut čəxʷ. "ʔusil kʷəɬ. tab, yuʔyuʔbəč tiʔiɬ dəxʷʎ̓əp ʔə tiʔiɬ ʔilucid ʔa duqʷəč ʔəsšigʷ."

"Call upon me whenever you doctor from now on. Return to me for help." [A voice said]

68. cutəb ʔə tiʔəʔ diʔəʔ, ʔə tiʔəʔ yuʔyubəč, sɬadəyʔ.

One Butterfly, a woman, said to him. [Butterfly speaks]

69. "ʔu ɬ(u)adsdaʔiɬ čəd, ɬusɬadəyʔ kʷi ɬadbədaʔ, sgʷəqʷulčəʔ kʷi ɬusdaʔ ʔə kʷəsi ɬadbədaʔ."

"Oh, you have a name for your offspring. Your child will be a daughter. Her name will be gʷəqʷulčəʔ. That will be the name of your daughter."

70. xʷiʔuʔxʷ gʷəčəgʷass, gʷəl ləcutəb.

He still lacked a wife when he was told this.

71. "tsiʔəʔ dbədaʔ gʷəl dsləx̌ʷulčəʔ, čičəbtəlax̌əd ʔə tiʔiɬ yuʔyubəč tiʔiɬ ʔucuuc bədaʔs."

"My daughter is sləx̌ʷuɫčəʔ, who is the wings of a butterfly." [He identifies his daughter.]

72. ʔu, sali tiʔiɬ sdaʔiɬtəgʷi tiʔiɬ tudbad.

Two female names (for two daughters) are given to my father to use.

73. diɬ ƛ̓usʔilids.

This is the song he was given.

74. stilib:

    q̓iltubəxʷ tsi sɬadəyʔ

Song:

    The woman puts him on board (to duqʷəč).

75.   čaxʷyid ɬi ti sɬuʔiʔəyə

    So pound sticks to assist this power.

76.   ʔuq̓iltubəxʷ ʔə tsi sɬadəyʔ

    The woman has him aboard.

77.   čaxʷyid ɬi ti sɬuʔiʔəyə ʔə

    So pound sticks for this power.

78.   wilxʷa tə sɬuʔiʔəyə.

79. ʔuq̓il tiʔiɬ yuʔyubəč. kʷa tux̌ʷ ƛ̓uʔadzəq̓əcut kʷəɬ, gʷəl ʔucut ʔuq̓il.

The butterfly landed on the canoe and took her (my) father into her own spiritual canoe.[3] [Susie explains]

80. kʷa tux̌ʷ ʔuʔadᶻəq̓əcut dxʷq̓ixʷusəb.

However (in ordinary time), the butterfly just turned around to say "I am here," even as he headed upstream.

81. huy tusxʷdaʔb ʔə tiʔił tudbad. diłəxʷ tudəxʷəshilics łutitəbəd.

This became the spirit power of my father. He sent me to quest (because I had to earn the name given by the spirit).

82. ʔutitəb. ʔəywasəd p̓aƛ̓aƛ̓ gʷəsładəyʔəxʷ tuxʷ čəxʷ łdxʷdaʔb.

She (I) quested: Changed herself. It did not matter that she is (I am) a woman because you (I) became an Indian doctor.

83. xʷiʔ gʷədsxʷdaʔb. xʷiʔ gʷədsxʷdaʔb, xʷiʔ.

But I am not really a doctor, no.

84. xʷiʔ ləʔasax̌id čəda gʷəʔuliltəb ʔə tiʔił ʔuʔax̌id.

I do not really have doctoring power, no. Anyone who wanted to do so could easily remove (kill) me. Yet I have other powerful abilities.

85. ʔa čəd tuʔuxʷiʔxʷiʔəxʷ. tuʔuxʷiʔxʷiʔəxʷ čəd ʔə tiʔəʔ sʔuladxʷ.

There I was out harvesting food. I was getting salmon.

86. ƛ̓uʔsgʷaʔəxʷ čəd ʔə tiʔił ƛ̓uʔuxʷuuc ƛ̓ucutəb.

I went along with those who fished with a bag net.

87. čətuləluƛ̓il. čəda wawaʔəxʷ ƛ̓uʔuxʷiʔxʷiʔ.

As I grew older, I fished alone, by myself.

88. ʔuʔəydxʷəxʷ čəd tiʔił dəxʷʔa ʔə tiʔiłəʔ sʔuladxʷ.

I found where the salmon were.

89. q̓ič sʔuladxʷ, ʔuxʷiʔxʷiʔbidəxʷ čəd.

Important salmon, I sought.

90. tuxʷiʔxʷiʔəxʷ, xʷiʔxʷiʔəxʷ čəd ck̓ʷaqid dxʷʔal tudsluƛ̓il.

I fished. I fished constantly until I grew up.

91. tucutəbəxʷ čəd ʔə tiʔəʔ cədił sqələlitut.

Then another spirit power came to me.

92. kʷədatəb čəd ʔə tsiʔił dsk̓ʷuy gʷəl čax̌ʷabacs čəda saxʷəb.

Once I was disobedient and my mother hit me. I ran away.

93. x̌ʷul̓ čəd l̓əsk̓ʷikut ʔə tsiʔił diičuʔ tudsc̓aʔči̓ʔəp čəda saxʷəb ʔal tiʔił baqʷəb.

I was dressed in only a little skirt and I ran onto the prairie.

94. sgʷaʔs swatixʷtəds ʔa.

That was where the spirit lived.[4]

95. čəda čadᶻil, ƛ̓uq̓ʷagʷil čəd dxʷʔal tiʔił č̓alasac qaʔ, čəda hiq̓ʷusəb.

There I hid, placing myself within many ferns. Lots. I pulled my skirt over my face (in shame).

96. ʔəstaʔtxʷ   čəd   tsiʔił   dkʷiʔkuʔt   čəda ʔəsq̓əpuʔcut.

Thus I had at least some clothing and I was hugging myself for warmth.

97. wiʔadəxʷ, wiʔadəxʷ, wiʔadəxʷ.

(Someone) hollered, hollered, hollered.

98. łalustəgʷi ti tustawixʷał.

This is what happened when children misbehaved.

99. wiʔadəxʷ tiʔił ləcu gʷəčəd, x̌ʷul čəd ʔəslililbid.

Those who searched hollered but I ignored them. [Susie felt very badly and said]

100. "ƛub čəd łuyubil. ƛub čəd łuʔatəbəd.

"I wish I were dead. It would be better if I died.

101. diʔaʔ kʷi łudsʔatəbəd ʔal ti."

Let me die right here."

102. ʔa, ʔa čəd ʔəsq̓əpuʔcut. dił tiʔił dsłčisəb ʔə tsiʔił luƛ̌.

There, there, I was hugging myself all together. Then a very old lady came to me.

103. luƛ̌ sładəyʔ, luƛ̌ sładəyʔ tsiʔəʔ, gʷəl ʔuwiliq̓ʷic

An old woman, she was an old woman, she asked me:

104. "ʔəsƛ̌ax̌ čəxʷ ʔu."

"Are you cold?"

105. "ʔu, cickʷəxʷ čəd ʔəsƛ̌ax̌."

"Oh, I am very cold indeed."

106. cuuc čəd tsiʔəʔ luƛ̌.

I said this to the old one.

107. xʷiʔ gʷəƛ̌udsəxʷəsšuuc.

I had never even seen her before.

108. "tiʔəʔ tə dsqəlikʷ. łux̌ačijid̓əb čəxʷ."

"Here is my blanket. Use it to cover yourself."

109. x̌ačijtəb čəd ʔə tsiʔəʔ luƛ̌ ʔə tiʔəʔ sqəlikʷ.

[aside] This old woman covered me with this blanket.

110. x̌ačičs gʷəl ləgʷəgʷatubš.

She covered me, then she spoke to me.

111. "xʷiʔ kʷi ładsƛ̌ax̌.

"You will not be cold.

112. łuʔabyicid čəd ʔə tədsgʷədgʷatəd.

I will give you my vocabulary (language).

113. łuʔabyicid čəd.

I shall give it to you.

114. łuʔabyicid čəd ʔə tiʔəʔ dsgʷədgʷatəd ładəxʷəshəd."

I shall give you my vocabulary by which you will keep warm!"

115. tiləb ʔuʔilid tiʔəʔ cədił xʷgʷədgʷatəds čəda ləcuʔilidəxʷ čəd.

Now, see, I have two spirit powers and songs.

116. šuhu, səliʔiləxʷ ti dsqəlalitut.

Then she sang her words, so I can now sing them. I now have two spirit power songs.

117. s̓tilib:

　　ləqədəxʷ łi

Song:

　　Listen you folks

118. tə łalali

to the Lady of the Prairie.

119. ləqədəxʷ łi

Listen you folks

120. tə łalali

to the Lady of the Prairie.

121. ləqədəxʷ łi

Listen you folks

122. tə łalali

to the Lady of the Prairie.

123. ləqədəxʷ

Listen.

124. xʷi xʷi xʷi xʷi xʷi

[vocables]

125. dił ʔəskʷaxʷac cəxʷluλ̓əb.

This (power) has enabled me to reach old age. As the lady said,

126. "ładəxʷ luλ̓əb tiʔił xʷgʷədgʷatəd."

"These words will give you a long life."

127. s̓tilib:

　　ʔabsʔukʷ ʷʔukʷucid

Song:

　　It has words of fun (of youth and gaiety).

128. tsə łalali

the lady

129. ʔabs̓tilibucid

It has words to sing.

130. tsə łalali

the lady

131. xʷi xʷi xʷi xʷi xʷi.

[vocables]

132. ʔudᶻəsəsəyaqi

It ripples its heads all over

133. tə swatixʷtəd

the world.

134. ʔudᶻəsəsəyaqi

It ripples its heads all over

135. tə swatixʷtəd

the world.

136. ʔi ʔi ʔi

[song ends]

137. sax̌ʷil həwə, sax̌ʷil tiʔəʔ swatixʷtəds.

So (you see), it is prairie grass, that is its world.[5]

138. put baləʔux̌ʷ, baləʔux̌ʷ, gʷəl ucuuc sq̓ədᶻuʔs.

It (the song) repeats, it goes again, and says that this (the grass) is its hair.

139. saliʔəx̌ʷ ti dshuyutəb ʔə tiʔił luλ̓luλ̓.

The old ones have now given me two powers.[6]

140. ʔəsx̌əł čəd, hagʷəxʷ tux̌ələd.

I was sick, I was sick for a long time [spiritually, supernaturally ill].

141. tuiʔal kʷi tuq̓il ʔə tiʔił sʔuladxʷ.

For the entire salmon season, during all of the runs.

142. tukʷədad čəł tiʔił həduʔ.

We caught humpback salmon first.

143. tiʔəʔ x̌̌uhikʷ hikʷ x̌̌uhəduʔ.

These humpies were very large.

144. ʔux̌ʷadᶻəd čəɫ, ʔux̌ʷadᶻəd čəɫ, ʔux̌ʷadᶻəd čəɫ.

We killed them. Indeed, we killed them.

145. kʷa(h)wəʔ ʔu kʷədac tiʔəʔ cədiɫ həduʔ gʷəl ʔux̌ʷtubš, ɫiq̌ʷtubš.

As a consequence, it seems, the humpies took me, they ran off with me (my soul).

146. huy čəd ɫaq̌əxʷ.

Then I was put down.

147. ʔaʔəxʷ čəd ʔəsx̌əɫ.

There I was sick.

148. ɫljixʷitəb čəd, x̌ʷul čəd lədxʷdidi.

I was medicated (treated), yet I became progressively worse.

149. ʔal tiʔiɫ ʔal hamton.

It took place there at Hamilton (Skagit River).

150. ʔa čəd ʔəsɫaq̌, dxʷʔaləs ʔax̌id gʷəl huy tiʔəʔ sɫuʔəb.

There I lay (for an indefinite time) until the dog salmon run finished.

151. tuɫʔal tiʔiɫ tupədhədəb čadəbidəs ʔə July kʷi dsɫaq̌.

For the whole summer time, from sometime in July, I was down.

152. putəxʷ čəd ʔəsx̌uʔx̌uʔil.

I became very thin.

153. putəxʷ ʔəstaʔbid ti tudk̓ətuʔ.

My stomach was compressed.

154. x̌ʷiʔəxʷ gʷəsʔəɫəd gʷəʔa

No food was inside.

155. putəxʷ čəd ʔəsx̌uʔil.

I was skinny.

156. x̌̌uʔil ti dsʔacus.

My face was thin.

157. x̌̌upəx̌̌əd čəd, x̌ʷuləxʷ šaʔw̓ kʷədi tudsʔacus.

[aside in pathos] When I would feel it, my face was only bone.

158. diʔɫ tiʔiɫ dsqəlqəlalitut, qəlalitut čəd.

Then I dreamed, I dreamed!

159. cutəb čəd, "ʔu, x̌̌ubəxʷ čələb ɫuʔabaqəd tsə ʔaciɫtalbixʷ.

I overheard talking, "Oh, you folks had better return that human woman.

160. ɫuʔabaqədəxʷ čələb tsə ʔaciɫtalbixʷ dxʷʔal tiʔiɫ swatixʷtəds.

You folks should return her to her own world.

161. ɫuʔabaqədəxʷ čəxʷ skʷayasəliwəʔ."

You, the one called skʷayasəliwəʔ, will return her."

162. daʔətəb tiʔiɫ siʔab, absq̓ilbid ʔə tiʔiɫ hikʷ.

The leader with a great big canoe was (thus) identified.

163. tiləb čəd ʔucutəb.

Then I was told (in song).

164. sɫilib:

Song:

    q̓ilidəxʷ ɫi

Put her on board,

165.   tsə ʔaciɫtalbixʷ

The human female.

166.   q̓ilidəxʷ ɫi

Put her aboard,

167.	tsə ʔaciɬtalbixʷ	the human female.
168.	ʔabaqədəxʷ	Return her,
169.	skʷayaɬəway [skʷaysəliwəʔ]	skʷaysəliwəʔ
170.	tsə ʔaciɬtalbixʷ	the human woman.
171.	ʔabaqədəxʷ	Return her,
172.	kʷayaɬəwayə [kʷaysəliwəʔ]	skʷaysəliwəʔ
173.	tsə ʔaciɬtalbixʷ	the human female
174.	ʔi ʔi ʔi ʔi ʔi ʔi.	[vocables, song ends].
175.	q̓ʷuʔq̓ʷuʔ ʔaciɬtalbixʷ tiʔəʔ ləsq̓il.	Many other people are also on board.
176.	ʔəshuyhuyʔaliqʷ.	With their red paint cedarbark headdress on!
177.	ʔušuuc čəd, yəx̌i čəd x̌ʷuɫ ʔəsɬaq̓tub.	[aside] I could see them because they had me lying on my back looking up.
178.	kʷawəʔ diɫ kəkəwič ʔə tiʔəʔ həduʔ tiʔəʔ cəxʷəsq̓iltub dəxʷʔuluɫs dəxʷʔuʔuluɫs ʔal ta.	I was traveling on the back of the hump of a salmon. That is how I was canoed.
179.	ʔəsx̌əc čəd gʷəxʷəɫabəd.	I was very afraid that I would fall off (and drown).
180.	ʔux̌ʷ.	It went on.
181.	tiləb tiʔiɫ bədscutəb,	Then again I overheard (the song).
182.	sɫilib:	Song:
	q̓ʷibidəxʷ,	Unload it now,
183.	kʷaysəliwəʔ [kʷaysəliwəʔ].	skʷaysəliwəʔ.
184.	ɬčiləxʷ čəxʷ dxʷʔal ti ʔadswatixʷtəd.	You have arrived back in your land.
185.	ɬuq̓ʷibəxʷ čəxʷ.	You will disembark.
186.	ɬucuuc čəxʷ kʷəsi adkia,	You will say to your own grandmother,
187.	dxʷəq̓yic kia,	Open the door for me, grandmother,
188.	ʔuɬčiləxʷ čəd.	I came back. [song ends]
189.	q̓ʷib čəd, čəda ləʔibəš.	I got off and I walked away.
190.	[ɬasəx̌iq̓id] tiʔəʔ ʔəsq̓iltubš	What can it be that had me aboard?
191.	hikʷ x̌ʷulab ʔə tiʔəʔ ship.	It was as big as a ship.

192.	Song:	Song:
	ʔuadzəq̓acutəxʷ	It turned itself around,
193.	ti skʷaysaliwəʔ.	skʷaysaliwəʔ did.
194.	ʔuadzəq̓əcutəxʷ.	Turned himself around.
195.	ti skʷaysaliwəʔ	That skʷaysaliwəʔ. [song ends]
196.	ʔadzəq̓əcutəxʷ, tu, hikʷ ləʔał.	They went away, turning around, going very fast, on the return. [Susie realizes]
197.	"ʔu, sdukʷ həwə, həduʔ həwə tiʔiʔił, hədhəduʔ."	"Oh, so it is not what it seems, those are truly humpback salmon, humpies!"
198.	xʷiʔ həwə baləsq̓ilbid.	Not canoes (at all).
199.	sdukʷ həwə.	They are very different indeed.
200.	ʔux̌ʷ čəd čuba, čələsdxʷtəsyax̌əd.	I went upland, I knocked on the door.
201.	"dxʷəq̓yic kia, ʔułčiləxʷ čəd."	"Open the door, Grandmother, I have arrived."
202.	tiləb čəd ʔucutəb.	[aside] They said of me (however),
203.	ʔuqəp čəd kʷəł.	I was crazy (confused, they said).
204.	qəp tsi ʔadʔibac, kʷədad.	"Your granddaughter is crazy, take her in,"
205.	cutəb tsiʔił dkia.	They said to my grandmother. [But Grandmother said:]
206.	"kʷədad, xʷiʔ gʷadsłčil tsi dskʷuy, didił ʔadsdiʔa, adsəsʔitut, didił."	"Get a grip on yourself, for you did not just arrive, my dear little one, you have instead always been here, asleep continuously."
207.	"xʷiʔ, daʔxʷ čəd ʔuq̓ʷibitəb.	"No, I've just disembarked." [Susie responds]
208.	daʔxʷ čəd ʔuq̓ʷibitəb ʔə skʷaysaliwaʔ."	"skʷaysaliwaʔ just let me off." [Her mother says to her grandmother,]
209.	"kʷaʔəd kʷuyə, xʷiʔ ləx̌ix̌q̓txʷ. kʷaʔəd."	"Let her alone, dear, do not disagree with her, leave her alone." [Just take care of her]
210.	hudičup tiʔiʔəʔ.	Build a fire, they said.
211.	"tuqəlqəlalitut čəxʷ xʷuʔələʔ."	"Maybe you were just dreaming."
212.	tuʔalustəgʷi ti tustawixʷał, tiʔił dzixʷ ʔaciłtalbixʷ.	That was their way with children, those humane Indians.

213.	x̌ʷuɫ čəd liɫʔaluʔxʷ tiʔiɫ ʔaciɫtalbixʷ.	[aside] I am still referring to the old Indian traditions.
214.	liɫʔaluʔxʷ čəd tiʔiɫ lux̌lux̌.	[I mean the real elders of old.]
215.	xʷiʔ gʷəsuʔəɫtxʷ kʷi bədaʔs.	No food was given to their children (so they would fast).
216.	xʷiʔ gʷəsuʔəɫtxʷs.	No food was given.
217.	x̌ʷul sqəlalitut dx̌əčtxʷs.	They were to think only of getting spirit power.
218.	x̌ʷuɫ čəxʷ ɫučačas čəxʷa ɫuʔatəbəd ɫuxʷiʔəs kʷi ɫuʔadsqəlalitut.	You would die young (defenseless) if you did not have spirit power.
219.	yuhu, diɫ dəxʷutitəbtəgʷi. tiʔiɫ čačas.	So, that was why they made children quest in earnest for help.
220.	ckʷaqid ʔucəsyayus, ʔəsyayusbitəb.	We still insist on such training.
221.	šuhu, tiʔəʔ cəxʷʔulux̌əb.	You see, this is the work that I have embraced. [That I managed to have an extended life, I have had lots of help.]
222.	ʔaliləxʷ čəd tiʔəʔ sčədəb čəda ləcutəb.	When I came into the Shaker Religion, I was told (by a spirit),
223.	"ʔabiləxʷ čəxʷ ɫuʔəsčalad tiʔəʔ diʔəʔ ɫuadscuucbicid čəxʷa ɫuhəliʔ.	"If you follow this that I tell you, you will have a long life.
224.	gʷəl ɫuhaʔkʷ kʷi ɫadshəli."	And you will live a long time."
225.	x̌aləxʷ čəd baləsʔistə.	[aside] Indeed, this is just the way I am.
226.	ləsčaladəxʷ čəd tiʔiɫ dsəcutəb ʔə kʷi x̌ax̌a šəq siʔab.	I follow the teachings of the Lord Above.
227.	tiʔəʔ cəxʷʔəʔux̌ʷalikʷ.	This is what I espouse.
228.	tiʔəʔ cəxʷʔəʔux̌ʷalikʷ. ʔu masi, ʔu.	This is what I voice continuously [in song and prayer]. *masi*, Mercy, Thanks be to God.
229.	ʔu tiʔiɫ adsəxʷshaydxʷəb kʷi səshuy ʔə kʷi dᶻixʷ tuʔaciɫtalbixʷ.	[aside to Leon Metcalf [LM] about Martin Sampson [MS]] Oh, that you sincerely wish to learn about the ways of our ancestors!
230.	šuhu tiʔiɫ bədbədaʔ ʔə Matin, tiʔəʔəxʷ tiʔiɫ səshilids.	Just look at my son Martin, this is what he tells kids today.
231.	tiʔəʔəxʷ tiʔiɫ səscuucs.	This is what he says (to youngsters).
232.	šaċəd ti ʔadsx̌al.	Finish school!

233.	kʷədad tiʔəʔ sx̌al.	Learn to write. [Get an education.]
234.	yəẃ čəxʷ łušaċədxʷ čəxʷa łuhaʔɬ, łuqaʔəł stabigʷs.	Only if you finish your education will you be successful, will you gain possessions.
235.	łuqa kʷi ładstabigʷs łušaċədəxʷ tiʔəʔ sx̌al."	You will have lots of valuable things, if you finish your schooling."
236.	yəẃ čəxʷ łuhaydxʷ tiʔəʔ xʷdaʔəb gʷəl łuqa kʷi ładstabigʷs.	But I know better, that only if you know doctoring power will you gain lots of things.
237.	łuqa kʷi łuadsqʷatigʷs.	You will have many, many things.
238.	tuʔəscut ti tugʷəł ti tudᶻixʷ tuʔaciłtalbixʷ.	That is what the ancient people preached.
239.	dəxʷʔubałəxʷ ʔə ti tudbad.	That is why my father doctored.
240.	gʷəl sq̇ʷuʔq̇ʷuʔ spəču?, xʷəltəbalc, tiʔəʔ sʔiċəb, tiʔəʔ tala.	[He gained fame and earned] many of those cedar root baskets, those guns, those blankets, that money.
241.	xʷiʔ gʷəsasx̌alas.	He was never needy.
242.	tiʔəʔ q̇ilbid, tiʔəʔ q̇ič q̇ilbid q̇əlusaa.	These canoes, expensive large canoes came as gifts compensating for the spirit help.
243.	tiʔəʔ sdəxʷił, tiʔəʔ ʔaʔutx̌s, tiʔəʔ stiwatł ƛ̕udaʔətəb.	This hunting canoe, family canoe, this other canoe.
244.	xʷiʔ gʷəsəsx̌alaʔs, huy dxʷdaʔəb.	Never in need, because he was a doctor.
245.	huy tuʔugʷəčəd kʷi gʷədəxʷhaʔłs, gʷədəxʷsiʔabs.	He quested for ability that would be good for him, bring him wealth.
246.	gʷəl ləliʔəxʷ tiʔəʔ.	Now everything is so different.
247.	yuhu, tiʔił bədbədaʔ ʔə tiʔəʔ. ʔaləxʷ kʷədi diʔi, ləcuƛaʔəxʷ skul.	See, the children of this one [MS]. They are over there, attending school.
248.	ʔu, lədxʷʔaləxʷ sx̌ilixʷ tiʔił dəxʷscuuci tiʔiłəʔ ʔiłluƛ.	Oh, except they say the oldest one (Ben) is going off to fight (in Korea).
249.	huy dił cugʷəxʷ səshuy ʔə tiʔəʔ liłlaqəxʷ.	This is now the only way known to these later generations.
250.	x̌ʷuləxʷ ʔəsx̌ədᶻəd tiʔəʔ bədaʔs.	They urge their children [to be like Bostons, as, for example,]
251.	gʷədil čəxʷa ʔəłəd, gʷədil čəxʷa ʔəłəd, gʷədil čəxʷa ʔəłəd.	"Sit down and eat up, sit down and eat, sit and eat." [Don't fast.]

252. x̌ʷuləxʷ ʔəscut.

That is what is said (to them).

253. x̌ʷiʔəxʷ gʷəscuuci, "hiwil ʔux̌ʷ t̕it̕itəb, t̕it̕itəb, bək̓ʷ sətax̌il.

No one ever says to them, "Go fast to quest, quest, every day.

254. t̕it̕itəb."

Quest with determination."

255. čəsaʔtəb, tuʔsəcaʔəs tučačas.

All were sent out, when I was a child.

256. x̌ʷiʔəxʷ gʷəʔəsistəʔ ʔə tiʔəʔ stawixʷał, x̌ʷiʔəxʷ.

Not anymore, not with these children, no longer.

257. lab x̌ʷiʔəxʷ.

Truly, no more.

258. haʔł tiʔił tusəshuy ʔə ti tudᶻixʷ tuʔaciłtalbixʷ.

The ways of our first people were indeed very good. [They shared.]

259. tuʔəłtagʷəl.

They fed each other.

260. ʔuʔəłtxʷ ti ʔiišəds.

They fed their friends.

261. ləʔuluł təʔiišəds gʷəl ləłaliltxʷ, ʔučəłtxʷ t̕atəgʷt həwə.

When their friends were canoeing, they had them land and they served lunch to them. He (SSP's uncle) said:

262. "łalil łi čələbə q̓ʷib čələbə łuʔəsx̌ic čələbə łubahiwil."

"You folks come ashore and get out. Have a bite to eat before you go on."

263. gʷəl tiʔił tudqəsiʔ, diičuʔ tudxʷdaʔəb tuʔiłluƛ̓.

That is the way of my oldest uncle, who was an Indian doctor.

264. x̌ʷiʔ gʷəsʔubəlx̌ʷ ʔə kʷi dčagʷił q̓ilbid.

Not a single canoe ever went by (his home without being invited in).

265. łaliltxʷ gʷəl ʔuʔəłtxʷ, gʷəl ʔuʔəłtxʷ. tiʔəʔ tudxʷq̓ixʷ.

He invited them all to land and he fed them, he fed those coming from upriver.

266. cugʷukʷ ʔəsistə tiʔił tusəshuys.

That is what he always did.

267. ləliʔəxʷ tiʔəʔ səshuyəxʷ ʔə tiʔəʔ stawixʷał, ləliəxʷ.

The ways of the young people are different now, very different indeed.

268. tux̌ʷəxʷ tiʔəʔ x̌əltəb ƛ̓ułčisəbuł, dukʷibəł, ʔəxʷshaydxʷəb kʷi bək̓ʷ ʔəsčal.

Yet I remember the old ways and I will ever recall them, because now this Boston has come here to us, this changer [LM] who wishes to know all about these other things.

269. ʔəxʷshaydxʷəb kʷi sqəlalitut.

Especially, he wished to know about this power from the spirits.

1. This indefinite construction was used so as not to jinx things. (L 27)

2. Bostons = Americans. (L 52)

3. SSP here distances herself from her own questing by using "she" and "you," again not to expose herself to danger. (L 79-82)

4. Jarman Prairie was her mother's homeland, observe the symmetry of her mother's land compensating for her own human mother. (L 94)

5. The entire prairie is here speaking to her. (L 137)

6. Alternatively translated, My ancestors have now provided me with two powers. (L 139)

Memories

As part of a taped exchange with Ruth Shelton at Tulalip, Susie reflects on her Shaker beliefs, help from her grandchildren, death of older relatives, and her first marriage to "the father of my children." They lived in a board cabin, planted russet potatoes, and dried salmon to exchange for flour, bread, and sugar at a store. As a young bride, she was unsure how to treat her inlaws, who therefore taught her. Susie added apple trees and berries to the homestead. Her husband sold firewood. The family picked hops and camped. While away, illness struck the Skagit and their cabin was contaminated, so it was burned and abandoned.

Other family tragedies were the revenge killings of her grandfather, father, and brother. Drunks beat on her father "like a drum," then stab him.

Warned of a huge windstorm, people's plans and reactions are dramatically described.

Natives sold duck feathers in Victoria, killing island sheep with a hard biscuit for lunch along the way. Dangers of intertribal mixing with enemies in Victoria are also mentioned.

1.	ʔu masi ʔal kʷi dsluucidəxʷ, dəgʷi tsi dsqaʔhaʔɫ, ʔal kʷi dsləqcbicid, ʔal kʷi adscugʷugʷəxʷ ʔal tiʔiɫ tuswatixʷtəd ʔə tiʔiɫ t(u)adsixʷsyayayaʔ.	Oh, mercy, (I give thanks) that I have heard you now, you my (beloved) older cousin, when I heard you, when you are alone now there on the land of your relatives (by marriage).
2.	gʷəl huyatxʷ kʷi shaʔɫs kʷi dsəsləqcbicid, adsəstəɫildxʷ tiʔəʔ stiwiɫ.	And I'm grateful to have heard you, that you believe in this prayer stiwiɫ.
3.	ʔəsʔistəʔ čəd, adsuq̓ʷa, adsqəlajut, gʷəbabək̓ʷəs c̓ək̓ʷadəd gʷələʔux̌ʷtx čə(d).	That is the way I am, your younger cousin, your niece, if I were to include all of the ways we are related to each other.
4.	ʔəsʔistəʔ čəd.	That is the way I am.
5.	ʔa tiʔəsdukʷ x̌əɫ ti ʔuluudxʷ čəd gʷəl ƛudəxʷ d̓aƛ̓əb ʔə tiʔiɫ dx̌əč.	There are some things that I hear that cause me to have confused thoughts.
6.	x̌ʷiʔ ləhaʔkʷ čəda ƛudxʷscutəb, "ʔu p̓aƛ̓aƛ̓ dxʷʔal ʔəca," ʔu ʔəscut ti ƛudx̌əč.	After a short time I would think, "Oh, that is unimportant to me," those are my (end) thoughts about that.
7.	gʷəl tiʔəʔ haʔɫ ƛuluudxʷ čəd, diɫ cəx̌ʷwiliq̓ʷid tiʔiɫ dbədaʔ.	And these good things that I hear, this causes me to ask my son [Al].
8.	gʷat kʷi ʔuɫčil ʔə kʷi ʔutiwiɫ, dəxʷhaʔɫ ʔə ti dx̌əč, ƛudəxʷʔəsju̓ʔils.	Which of the praying people arrived, that my mind is good, causing me happiness.
9.	tiʔiɫ gʷəl ʔaliləxʷ tiʔiɫ bədbədaʔs, kʷi ʔuc̓ədəb.	That has now come to his children, who have become Shakers [members of the Shaker religion].
10.	tiʔiɫ saliʔ bədbədaʔs gʷəl ʔaliləxʷ tiʔəʔ sc̓ədəb dəxʷliɫʔa čəɫ	His two children are with this Shaker religion that we follow.

11. cəxʷ liłʔa dxʷʔal dsbadil.

That I have followed until I became blind.

12. gʷəl ʔaʔuxʷ čəd lʔəskʷədad.

And I still have it yet (as an active part of my life).

13. ƛuləd̓aƛəb ti dx̌əč ʔə tiʔiłəʔ x̌əł ti ʔəsc̓əq sgʷaʔgʷəd ƛuluudxʷ čəd.

My mind becomes disturbed by unclean gossip that I hear.

14. xʷiʔ ləhaʔł čəda ƛupaƛaƛ.

It is not good and I (become depressed).

15. ʔu p̓aƛaƛ kʷi lədiłcut ʔə kʷi ʔuʔəẏdubutəd.

Oh, it doesn't matter (after all).

16. tiʔił d̓ibʔibac gʷəl cəxʷəshəliʔdubutəb.

My grandchildren are what I live for.

17. x̌aƛtxʷ čəd kʷi sluƛuƛils gʷəl ʔəẏwaʔs tiʔił słaladəy.

I want for them to grow older and for the girls to change their ways.

18. gʷəl ləhikʷ čəd ʔəshiił ʔə kʷi adsəstix̌dub ʔə kʷi ʔal tiʔił ad̓ibʔibac, yəxi luƛluƛəxʷ, baslaʔlaʔxʷ.

And I am so very happy that your grandchildren take care of you, because they are older now, they have some sense now.

19. gʷəl tiʔəʔ dsgʷaʔ d̓ibʔibac gʷəl ʔəsx̌ʷaÌx̌ʷaÌʔuxʷ labʔuxʷ ʔəsx̌ʷaÌx̌ʷal, ʔəsd̓aƛəb ʔə kʷi x̌əč.

But my grandchildren are still not strong enough, they are very unprepared, with minds that are undeveloped.

20. ləyayusʔas əlgʷəʔ ʔal tiʔəʔ ƛussəd̓aldubuts gʷəl cukʷ tiʔił sx̌alalićaʔs əlgʷəʔ kʷi ƛukʷədxʷ.

When they are able to get out to work, then it is only their clothes that they (get for themselves).

21. ʔu, gʷəl tiʔił ad̓ibʔibac gʷəl haʔł kʷi səshuytubicids, gʷəl ʔiłd̓ixʷ sẏuʔilabtxʷ kʷi səstix̌dubicids əlgʷəʔ.

Oh, but your grandchildren are good to you, and it is indeed a great joy the way they take care of you.

22. huy ʔiłd̓ixʷəxʷ bədbədaʔčəł tiʔəʔ ƛuʔibʔibac čəł, tsi siʔab tsi dsqaʔhaʔł.

As it is that our grandchildren are first our children, my dearest, my beloved older cousin.

23. ləʔəx̌iʔtub tiʔəʔ dsbadil.

What was the reason for my blindness?

24. haʔłʔuxʷ ti dx̌əč čədaʔ badil.

My mind was still good and I became blind.

25. ʔa tiʔił sšəxʷ ʔə ti dsacus čəda badil.

When my face swelled, then I became blind.

26. gʷəl cickʷ čəd ʔəshiiɬ ʔal tiʔəʔ dsəsləqcbicid, gʷəl ləhuy čəxʷ, huy čəxʷ, huy čəxʷ ʔə tiʔiɬ ƛ(u)adsləqdxʷ tiʔəʔ dsgʷa ƛudsəstigʷicid.

And it makes me so happy to hear you, and [and I know that you are there for me to be able to hear]. You are there, and how [comforting] to know that you can listen to me as I give thanks to you, voicing my appreciation for your presence.

27. tux̌ʷʔuxʷ čad kʷi dəxʷlil čəɬ, tux̌ʷ babəkʷiləxʷ tiʔəʔ dyəɫyəlab.

But why is it that we are far away [apart, caused yet by the deaths of all of my ancestors].

28. tux̌ʷəxʷ swatixʷtəd kʷi bədəxʷ ʔa ʔi tiʔiɬ tuswatixʷtəd ʔə tiʔiɬ t(u)adsixʷsyayayaʔ, adəxʷluƛil, adəxʷəsƛalab tsi siʔab tsi dsqaʔhaʔɬ.

It is now only the land [Tulalip] where you are and the land of those who were your relatives [Sehome], where you grew to maturity, where you have established yourself, my dearest older cousin.

29. ʔu, huyatxʷ tiʔiɬ adx̌əč, haʔɬ.

Oh, appreciation for your mind, good.

30. adsuɬəgʷəldubəxʷ ʔə tiʔəʔ adʔiišəd.

As your people are leaving you (in death).

31. ʔal tiʔiɬ sʔux̌ʷ ʔə tsiʔiɬ tudsqaʔ, xʷiʔ čəd ləɬaʔtild.

When my older cousin left (died), I did not get there to her (funeral).

32. x̌ʷuɫ cugʷəxʷ dəxʷʔəslaʔtəds kʷi sdaʔs dᶻəluličəʔ.

The only thing that will be left to identify her will be her name dᶻəluličəʔ [Mrs. Sheldon].

33. čəd dxʷx̌ʷaligʷədəxʷ.

And I give up now.

34. gʷatəxʷ kʷi ɬubačəkʷaʔ čəd ɬudsyayaʔ.

Who will I be able to claim as my relative?

35. gʷatəxʷ kʷi ɬubačəkʷaʔ čəd.

Who will I (now) be able to call my relative?

36. huy čəxʷ, diɬ sšaċs kʷi dshuyucid, dstigʷicid.

Goodbye to you, this ends my greetings to you, my thanks to you.

37. ʔu masiʔ čəxʷ ʔə kʷi adsəstəɬild gʷəɬ šəq siʔab čəɬx̌əčəb.

Oh, praises to you, as you believe in the teachings of our supreme one.

38. dxʷʔal ksna kʷmans, titəmənaʔs, ti tə santus pli, ƛum ʔəsʔistəʔ.

In the name of the father, and his son, and the holy spirit, Amen.

39. AS: x̌aƛtub ʔə tiʔəʔ diʔəʔ kʷi gʷ(ə)adsləlaiɬxbid tiʔiɬəʔ tudᶻixʷ t(u)adsbəlyitxʷ kʷi dbad.

[AS speaks to his mother, translating LM's wishes] This one wants for you to talk about when you first married my dad.

40. ʔu,

Oh. [SSP acknowledges the question]

41. AS: ʔ tudəxʷʔupədalikʷləb ʔə tiʔiłəʔ, dxʷʔal kʷi tubasdᶻəx̌ʷtxʷləb dxʷʔal kʷi tubasʔux̌ʷləb dxʷʔal puyaləp, dxʷʔal tiʔəʔ diʔəʔ tubadəxʷʔuyayusləb ʔal tiʔəʔ diʔəʔ stuləgʷabš.

[Al continues to explain what LM wishes from her.] When you folks planted those things, until you folks moved to Puyallup, until you folks worked at Stillaguamish.

42. tiʔiłəʔ tudᶻixʷ t(u)adshuygʷas dxʷʔaləxʷ tiʔəʔ sləx̌il.

From when you first married until the present day.

43. AS: ʔəshuyəxʷ, yəhaẃtxʷ.

AS: It [recorder] is ready now, go ahead (with your information).

44. SSP: ʔu, masi čəxʷ, tuʔalil čad tiʔił tudsq̓ʷuʔ, baʔad ʔu tiʔił tudbədbədaʔ.

SSP: Oh, praises to you, I was with my companion, many were my children.

45. xʷiʔ gʷətudx̌əč, xʷiʔ gʷətuʔascal gʷətudx̌əč.

I had no sense. [I was completely immature mentally and emotionally.]

46. ʔa čəł ƛuʔuyayus tuʔupədalikʷ čad ʔəsq̓ʷuʔ ʔə tsi dskʷuy.

We were working, planting along with my mother.

47. huy čad cuucəxʷ, cutəxʷ, ƛubkʷəł łučəł ʔalʔal ʔal tiʔił q̓əxʷax̌ad, papstədʔaltxʷ.

Then I said (to someone) I said, it would be good that (he) build a little white man style house on the upriver side.

48. sʔubəkʷʔalətxʷs tiʔiłəʔ stə sx̌əlaʔs, stab.

The wall boards and things he had salvaged from different places.

49. huy dᶻəx̌ʷtxʷəxʷ tsiʔəʔ ʔaʔəlʔal, tubasčəls ʔalʔal ʔal tiʔił tusxʷuĺs tustubš.

Then he moved this little house, a house that he had built when he was just a man yet (before he was a husband).

50. gʷəl ʔa huyud gʷəl huy.

He then made it, and finished with it.

51. huy təqalikʷəxʷ tiʔił bads.

Now his father trapped.

52. pədəxʷ dᶻəlabac.

It was the change over time of the year.

53. tupəd kʷaʔ słuʔəb tiʔiłəʔ tudsʔalil tiʔił kʷi bad ʔə tiʔił dbədbədaʔ.

It was, however, in the season of the dog salmon that I came to be with the father of my children.

54. ʔa čəł, čəła ʔacac ʔəsłałlil čəłaʔ ʔuʔuləx̌əd tiʔił qiwx̌.

We were there, and we lived there and we helped ourselves to steelhead salmon.

55. ƛuċəbidupəxʷ čəł dxʷʔal kʷi łuspədalikʷ čəł.

We cleared land in preparation for our time of planting.

56. ċəbidup čəł ʔə tiʔił ba.

We cleared a great area of ground.

57. ʔu, qa ti sqaẁc ʔə tsi k̓ʷuyəʔ, ɬukʷədalikʷ čəd, qa ti tudsgʷaʔ tudsəskʷədalikʷ.

Oh, mother had lots of potatoes, I will help myself, lots of them are mine that I have taken.

58. yəx̌i čəd tubasʔi ʔə tiʔiɬ sqaẁc, haʔɬ sqaẁc.

Because I had found those potatoes, good potatoes.

59. šəqaydi ʔə tiʔiɬ hikʷ qəladi q̓ʷədiq̓ʷac, gʷəɬ kaykay.

On top of a big cottonwood snag, it belonged to Bluejay.

60. gʷəɬ kaẏkaẏ tusqada xʷuʔələ tul̓ lil.

It probably was the thievery of Bluejay from far away. [Bluejay carried and dropped them below the snag.]

61. xʷiʔ gʷəʔabs(s)qawc.

Nobody (around here) had potatoes.

62. ʔu dxʷgʷəgʷədalus tiʔiɬ sqaẁc, x̌ičəc, hikʷhikʷ.

Oh, these big, red potatoes grew in abundance downward.

63. ʔəsʔistəʔ ʔə ti.

Like this [high].

64. ʔa tiʔəʔ diʔəʔ gʷəl diɬ čəd ʔuʔux̌ʷtxʷ.

These were there and they were what I took (to plant).

65. huy čəd pədalikʷəxʷ ʔə ti pədəxʷ wəxʷsus.

Then I planted now in the season of the frog.

66. d̓zəlabacəxʷ.

The season [February] had changed now.

67. x̌ʷul̓ ƛ̓ud̓zəpil čəɬa ƛ̓uc̓əbidup.

When it changed, then we would clear land.

68. čəda ʔuʔuladxʷ ʔuʔuʔuladxʷəb čəd.

And then I fished, fished in order to catch fish.

69. huy qa ti sʔukʷədgʷiʔ tiʔiɬ qiwẋ.

Because the steelhead were plentiful to get.

70. ƛ̓uʔuq̓ʷictub ʔə tiʔəʔ dxʷʔal tiʔiɬ camp tiʔəʔ sʔuladxʷ.

This one took them down to the camp, the salmon.

71. kʷi bads, shuyubs əlgʷəʔ.

His father, he sells them.

72. dəxʷʔukʷədxʷ čəɬ tiʔiɬ səpləl, tiʔiɬ ləpəskʷiʔ, šukʷəʔ.

This was how we could get flour, the pilot bread, and sugar.

73. ʔa čəɬ, gʷəl diɬ təsətitəyil ʔə tiʔiɬ lux̌luẋ, cəbagʷiɬ.

We were there for a long time, suddenly two canoes of those old folks water traveled.

74. tsiʔiɬ tudsqaʔ ʔə tiʔiɬ tudbad bəɬ tsiʔiɬ tuʔəpuss, suq̓ʷaʔ ʔə kʷəsi sk̓ʷuys tsi sk̓ʷuy ʔə tsə diɬ.

The older cousin of my father, offspring of his aunt, younger cousin of his mother, was the mother of that person.

75. tiləb ʔucut tsiʔəʔ diʔəʔ, tsiʔəʔ wʔis

Right away this one [called wʔis] said:

76. "bəł ʔə sʔuladxʷ tsi dstaləł.

"My niece is full of salmon.

77. šubaliʔəxʷ čəł təš stagʷəxʷ."

We are dying of hunger."

78. ʔəstixǎdiʔ čəł ʔə tiʔił qiw̌x̌.

We had steelhead spread out [drying].

79. ʔa cutəb ʔə kʷi dsx̌aʔx̌aʔ, xʷiʔ kʷi gʷədx̌əč.

Then my inlaw said, (because) I had no sense.

80. "łuʔəłtxʷ čəxʷ łuʔəłtxʷ čəxʷ tadʔəpʔəpus."

"You will feed, you will feed your aunts."

81. ʔəx̌ tiʔiʔəʔ diʔəʔ.

They came.

82. ʔəx̌ tsiʔəʔ, tsi sdiʔəʔx̌ał, ʔi tsiʔəʔ šisəbulicʔəʔ.

She came, tsisiʔəʔx̌ał and this šisəbulicʔəʔ.

83. k̓ʷəd, bəł ʔəstixǎdiʔ ti dəxʷšubəxʷ təš stagʷəxʷ.

(They) observed, so many (salmon prepared for drying while all of us were on the verge of starvation).

84. "gʷaadil łi, gʷaadil łi."

"You folks seat yourselves, seat yourselves."

85. p̓ax̌ax̌ kʷi dəxʷ ʔal tiʔił sgʷistalb.

It matters not (that they have been invited to sit on the ground.) [laughter from SSP]

86. "gʷaadil łi."

"You folks seat yourselves."

87. gʷaadil tiʔiʔəʔ.

They seated themselves.

88. ʔukʷədatəbəxʷ ʔə kʷi dsx̌aʔx̌aʔ tiʔił qʷəłayʔulč.

My inlaw had taken this wooden container.

89. huy cilcilidəxʷ tiʔəʔ salsaliʔułəd dxʷʔal tiʔiʔəʔ diʔəʔ.

Then he dished up two plates for them.

90. huy čəd q̓ʷatyidəxʷ əlgʷə ʔsəliʔułəd ti diičuʔ, ti diičuʔ.

Then I placed two plates, one for each one.

91. huy tiʔił sʔəʔəłəds əlgʷə gʷəl šuucəb ʔə tsi dʔəpus tiʔił dsəsʔuladxʷ bašabəxʷ, šabəxʷ tiʔił qiw̌x̌, bəkʷ tiʔił x̌aq̓ʷuʔs ləšəqəd čəd.

When they finished eating then my aunt saw the fish I had been catching. They were dry now, the steelhead were dry, including the backbones I had lifted (hung up high to dry).

92. ʔəxʷʔulusbid čəd, p̓aƛ̓aƛ̓ gʷəxʷiʔəs kʷi adsubəq̓əd, ƛ̓ucutəb ʔə tiʔiłəʔ ƛ̓uʔuxʷiʔxʷiʔ, p̓aƛ̓aƛ̓ gʷəxʷiʔəs gʷadsubəq̓əd kʷi stab tuxʷ čəxʷ ləcušabad, dił gʷəsʔaʔs gʷədahadxʷ čəxʷ gʷəʔəstagʷəxʷ.

I respected it (all food), it mattered not that you didn't eat it, those who were hunters would say, it matters not that you yourself are not going to eat some things, yet you should preserve it, there might be someone who is hungry that would benefit from it.

93. huy c̓əx̌əłdalbəxʷ tiʔiʔəʔ.

Now these (people) provisioned themselves (with my food).

94. xʷiʔ gʷədsəshaydxʷ gʷədsuhuyubtxʷ kʷi sʔuladxʷ.

I didn't know about selling [bartering for] salmon.

95. ʔəx̌tub ʔə tsiʔəʔ ʔiłlux̌ tiʔəʔ dču? ləšal, ʔi tə kuut.

The eldest one brought one shawl, and one cattail mat.

96. ʔəx̌tub ʔə tsiʔəʔ ʔiłtisuʔ tiʔəʔ kuut ʔi təsc̓ayəp ʔi tə sil dču? sʔistəʔ, ʔaʔəd gʷəl ʔəsqʷat.

The youngest one brought a cattail mat and a skirt and some cloth, one (portion), put it there where it lay.

97. "ʔəshaydxʷ čəxʷ ʔu ʔəsʔəx̌id gʷadstayi(d) kʷi adʔəpʔəpus."

"Do you know how much you should (offer, charge) your aunts?"

98. "ʔu, xʷiʔ gʷədsəshaydxʷ, dəgʷiʔ kʷi ʔutugʷugʷud yəx̌i čəxʷ ʔəshaydxʷ."

"Oh, I don't know, you should be the one to figure it out because you know,"

99. cuucəxʷ čəd tsiʔił diič̓u?.

I said now to one of them.

100. huy kʷədatəbəxʷ xʷətadəxʷ čəd ti bəkʷəł x̌ituł, x̌aq̓ʷuʔ.

Then it (salmon) was taken, I took it down (lowered it), including the ___, the backbone.

101. huy t̓ugʷudəxʷ t̓ugʷudəxʷ ʔəsʔəx̌i(d), yəlac tiʔəʔ cił p̓itus ʔəsšab, ʔi tiʔəʔ cił bəkʷ tiʔəʔ x̌ic̓usəd, bəkʷ tiʔəʔ t̓alus, ʔi tiʔəʔ baʔəsq̓ʷəl dił stayids tiʔił ʔiišəds, gʷəl balətayid tiʔił diič̓u?, ƛ̓al baʔəsʔistəʔ.

Then someone figured – figured how much, six of the dried, and also this, along with spread out dried salmon, and this that was also cooked – was what was offered his friends, and also made the same amount available to that other one.

102. hay, ʔəx̌txʷ tiʔił sgʷaʔs.

Then, (she) brought her own.

103. ʔəx̌tub ʔə kʷəsiʔ dʔəpus tiʔəʔ sgʷaʔs.

My aunt brought her own (things).

104. dču? sqəlikʷ ʔi tiʔəʔ puʔtəd ʔi tiʔəʔ siqiw̓s, ʔi tiʔəʔ bakuut ʔi tiʔəʔ basc̓ayəp, sil, sil.

One blanket, and this shirt, and these pants, and also this cattail mat, and also this skirt, cloth, cloth.

105. "ʔu, cukʷ kʷiʔ sil kʷi łudsgʷaʔ' dxʷscutəb čəd.

'Oh, only the cloth will be mine,' I thought.

106. 'ługʷəłtxʷ čəd tsi dsk̓ʷuy tiʔəʔ.'

'This will be for my mother.'

107. ʔa tiʔəʔ gʷəl ṭugʷugʷugʷəd, ṭugʷugʷugʷəd, ṭugʷugʷugʷəd, ʔəsʔəx̌id.

He was there and he figured, figured, figured, how much.

108. x̌ʷiʔ gʷədsəshaydxʷ gʷədsʔuhuyub.

I didn't know about selling (my work effort).

109. qʷəʔuhuyubtxʷ čəd ciɬ tiʔəʔ q̓ič sʔuladxʷ dxʷʔal tə pastəd.

I usually, though, did sell treasured salmon to white people.

110. tuhuyub čəd gʷəl ƛ̓udc̓aʔilc ʔi tə kʷatəʔ tiʔiɬ dc̓uʔ ʔə tiʔiɬ qiw̓x̌, hikʷ.

I sold, and one dollar and a quarter (was what I got for) one large steelhead salmon.

111. gʷəl gʷəɬ ʔaciɬtalbixʷ shuyub gʷəl x̌ʷiʔ gʷədsəshaydxʷ.

But as for selling ~ bartering to (my own people) I didn't know how to do that.

112. cuuc čəd kʷsi dʔəpus swiʔs.

I said to my aunt *swiʔs*.

113. x̌əw̓s tə ciɬ puʔtəd, diɬ ƛ̓al baʔəsʔistəʔ tiʔəʔ siqiw̓s ʔi ti ___.

The shirt was new, and also the pants and the ___.

114. ɬəčil.

(Someone) arrived.

115. ʔatub ʔə tsi dʔəpus tiʔiɬ sgʷaʔs gʷəl huy.

My aunt brought out her (bartering things) and finished.

116. ʔu čəda bakʷədyidəxʷ ʔə tiʔəʔ qəlx̌ tuəspačtxʷ čəd gʷəɬ qiw̓x̌ p̓ip̓itaɬ, huy čəd c̓əc̓əxʷusədəxʷ əlgʷəʔ.

And then I got for them some salmon eggs from steelhead that I had put aside, and then I added to what I had already given to them.

117. "gʷəɬtxʷ čələb sqaw̓c tiʔəʔ qəlx̌.

"The salmon eggs will be for (eating with) potatoes.

118. gʷəɬtxʷəxʷ čəɬ.

That is what we shall have them for now.

119. diɬəxʷ kʷadsdahadubuɬ ɬuləʔuluɬəli."

You will have done us a great favor when we are water traveling."

120. ʔux̌ʷ tiʔiʔəʔ, gʷəl ʔa ʔəsqʷat tiʔəʔ tudəʔubad.

They went, and the things they had given to me were laying there.

121. ʔa ʔəsqʷat gʷəl ɬčil kʷi bad ʔə ti tudstətudəq, tubaʔəsqʷic.

They were laying there, and the father of my children arrived, he had been downriver.

122. ʔa gʷəl ləwiliq̓ʷ, "ƛ̓ub čəxʷ ʔu ʔux̌ʷuyub ʔə kʷi tadsʔuladxʷ tassab."

He asked, "You decided to sell the salmon that you had dried?"

123. "ʔu, ʔutagʷyib ʔə tiʔəʔ ʔal tiʔəʔ, tux̌ʷ čəd ʔəsd̓aƛ̓əb ʔəsʔəx̌idəs kʷi dc̓u."

"Oh, the folks bought it, only I was mixed up about (how to charge) for each one."

124. "ʔulub ʔi ti saliʔ ti dxʷʔal tsi sdiʔəxaɬ ʔi tsi sq̓ʷəluliċəʔ bək̓ʷʔaɬ xaq̓ʷuʔ k̓ʷaʔɬtaluʔ qəlxq̓ʷəluɬəd."

"Twelve went to sdiʔaxʷaɬ and sq̓ʷəluliċəʔ, including the backbone, the eggs."

125. "ƛ̓ubʔas tsi siʔab."

"That was all right, honorable female one."

126. gʷəl diɬ gʷəɬ wʔis tiʔəʔ dču sqəlikʷ ʔi tiʔəʔ siqiẃs, ʔi tiʔəʔ puʔtəd, ʔi tiʔəʔ kuut, ʔi tiʔəʔ sʔil.

And this was from *wʔis*, this one blanket and the pants, and the shirt and this cattail mat, and the cloth.

127. tiʔiɬ gʷəl gʷəsčayəp ʔə k̓ʷi gʷədalqʷuʔ [rest spoken too fast, inaudible].

That could be a skirt for underwear.

128. "x̌ʷuɬ adsx̌ədyid tiʔiɬ adsx̌aʔx̌aʔ tiʔiɬ sqəlikʷ ʔi tiʔiɬ siqiẃs ʔi tiʔiɬ puʔtəd, gʷasƛ̓altxʷ čəxʷ." cutəb čəd. "gʷasƛ̓altxʷ čəxʷ ʔu tiʔiɬ siqiẃs ʔi tiʔiɬ puʔtəd.

"You just pass that on to your [male] inlaw, that blanket and the pants and that shirt, would you wear them, I was told, would you wear the pants and the shirt?

129. x̌ʷuɬ adsx̌ədyid tiʔiɬ ƛ̓uʔuxʷiʔxʷiʔ."

You just pass that on to those who are hunters."

130. ʔabyid čəd k̓ʷi dsx̌aʔx̌aʔ gʷəl ṫiwiɬ,

I gave (these things) to my inlaw and he prayed:

131. "huy čəxʷ dahadubšəxʷ tsi dsx̌aʔx̌aʔ gʷə xʷiʔəs gʷədsəsx̌aƛ̓il."

"You have indeed done me a great good deed, my inlaw, so that I might not be having a hard time (without warm clothing)."

132. ƛ̓uƛ̓ax̌ʷəxʷ čəd ʔə tiʔəʔ səxʷəsx̌ətqad.

I grew then (out of my immaturity).

133. huy, huyəxʷ tiʔiɬəʔ suyayus čəɬ, huy tiʔiɬ sušabalikʷ čəɬ.

Then, we finished working, we finished drying [salmon].

134. gʷəl lə ʔa tiʔəʔ tuswatixʷtəds ʔal tiʔəʔ ʔal tiʔəʔ ciɬ ʔal xʷəɬq̓ʷalič q̓ixʷ.

And he had some land there at that place, upriver.

135. ʔu ɬuʔux̌ʷ čəd ɬuʔaplsac čəda gʷəʔəƛ̓txʷ čəda gʷəpəd čəd.

Oh, I would go and get apple trees and bring them and I would plant them.

136. "ʔu xʷiʔ, xʷiʔ gʷadsʔəƛ̓txʷ, xʷiʔ gʷəshaʔls gʷədiʔəʔəs, gʷəƛ̓ək̓ʷutəb ʔə k̓ʷi pastəd, xʷiʔ gʷadsəsk̓ʷədiʔdup, xʷiʔ ləʔadswatixʷtəd."

"Oh, no, do not bring them, it is not good for them to be here, the white people would chop them down, you do not have ownership of land here, it is not your land." [her husband argued]

137. ƛ̓ub čəɬ x̌ʷuɬ gʷəʔa ʔal ti ʔal tiʔiɬ swatixʷtəd, hiqəbəxʷ haʔɬ.

It is best that we just remain there at that land, it is excellent.

138. yaləxʷ čəd ʔu tuʔupədpədaʔ ti ʔal tiʔiɬ qəlbsaʔc, ʔi ti ṫəbxʷaʔc, ʔi ti raspberries.

I vainly planted the ___, and the ___, and raspberries.

139. qatiʔił tupədəd čəd.

I planted lots.

140. qa tiʔił tupədəd čəd sq̓ʷəlaɫədac huy ba.

I planted lots of berries because there was a great expanse of cleared land.

141. huy x̌ul ̓ ʔiɫx̌ix̌q̓ gʷatəs gʷasx̌ik̓ʷəbcut ʔal tiʔił li(h)ilil.

He [SSP's mate] continued to argue, asking Who would isolate themselves to an area so uninhabited by others?

142. xʷiʔəxʷ gʷəgʷat gʷəčit gʷəʔaciɫtalbixʷ.

There were no other people living near by.

143. tiʔił ʔaplsʔac gʷəl pədəd čəd.

Still I planted those apple trees (though warned).

144. gʷəƛ̓ək̓ʷduptub ʔə tiʔəʔ pastəd ʔuqʷəlayʔ.

The white people cutting wood would chop them down.

145. x̌ʷuləxʷ čəd ƛucuuc, "xʷiʔəxʷ k̓ʷi ads x̌icil, x̌ʷul ̓ čəxʷ huy ʔu adsgʷaʔ adsəsqəp."

I would just say to him, "Just don't get angry, you can just indulge in a decision [of mine] that is wrong."

146. xʷiʔ gʷəsʔəsʔəx̌ids ʔal tiʔił tudəxʷʔaʔs tudskʷədiʔdups gʷətuʔacac čəł gʷətuʔuʔux̌ʷ čəł, x̌ʷul ̓ čəł gʷətuʔugʷəčəd gʷətuʔuʔəɫəd čəł.

He was doing all right where he was, where he had land, we could have been living there, could have gone there, we could have just looked (elsewhere) for our food, our livelihood.

147. huy ʔisʔistaʔb, huy gʷəčədəxʷ gʷədəxʷyayuss.

[He] then did that, he then looked for something to work at.

148. huy čəłəxʷ hud ʔal tiʔəʔ dəxʷʔa ʔə Ben Gage, ʔaʔəxʷ tiʔił suyayuss, suyayuss, gʷəl ləlux̌il tiʔił dsəxʷstudəq.

Then he cut wood where Ben Gage was, that was where he worked, he worked and my (beloved child) grew older.

149. čəłaʔ hop hops.

Then we picked hops.

150. d̓ixʷbid ʔə July tiʔił swəliʔ ʔə tiʔił dsəxʷstudəq.

It was just before July [4th] that my beloved son was born. [Martin Sampson, born 3 July 1888]

151. huy čəł hop hopsəxʷ.

Then we picked hops now.

152. xʷšəqaɫdəł tiʔił hophops.

The hops [grew upward, high].

153. gʷədəxʷtuk̓ʷəxʷ čəł ʔal tiʔił huy ʔə hops čəła ɫčil dxʷʔal tiʔiłəʔ Stanwood, yəx̌i čəł ʔahaʔkʷgʷił.

Thus we would go home when the hop season was finished, and we arrived at Stanwood, because our canoe was there.

154. ʔa tiʔił basəsk̓iɫtxʷ čəł tiʔił q̓ilbid, ʔaʔutx̌s.

It was there that we had our seagoing canoe hung up.

155. baɫuləx̌əlayʔalgʷił čəł.

We will be now using our river canoe.

156. tiləb ʔutəqdub tiʔəʔ ʔə tiʔəʔ t(u)absʔələdalʔtxʷ tuʔal sqajət siti.

Right away [he] met someone who had an eating place in Skagit City.

157. "ɬudiʔəʔəxʷ čəxʷ.

"You will stay here now.

158. dsx̌aƛ gʷəčəɬ hud ʔə kʷi qa.

I want (someone) to cut lots of wood.

159. dsx̌aƛ kʷi q̓iʔq̓iqxʷuʔ, dču̓ʔ jəsəd ʔi kʷi buus inch."

I want short ones, one foot and four inches."

160. "ʔu, ƛub, ʔa ti ʔaʔutx̌s.

"Oh, all right, there is a salt water canoe.

161. x̌ʷuɬ čəxʷ ʔuq̓ilq̓ilid, ɬugʷiid čəd.

You just load it up, I will call it.

162. ʔu ʔal ti dəxʷʔa ʔə Mr. Dance tiʔiɬ dsəxʷɬič ʔi ti dšəqači."

Oh, my saw and axe are there where Mr. Dance is." [her mate replied]

163. "u x̌ʷuɬ čəxʷ ʔuʔuxʷc."

"Oh, you just go after them."

164. diɬəxʷ həlhəliʔ čəɬ tədiɬ.

That was what kept us alive [that source of income].

165. ʔux̌ʷ čəɬ, čəɬabaxʷaacəb ʔə kʷi dqəsi.

We went, and my uncle was reluctant to have us leave.

166. ʔuxʷaabid, x̌ʷaacəbəxʷ čəɬ ʔə tiʔəʔ Johnny, bad ʔə tiʔəʔ Davy John.

He wanted [him, us] to stay, Johnny, the father of Davy John, didn't want us to leave.

167. "ʔu, ʔaciɬ čəxʷ q̓əlbic, x̌ʷaligʷədəxʷ čəd.

"Oh, why don't you stay and camp with me? I'm failing now.

168. ɬuq̓əlb čəxʷ dʔiʔibac, ɬuq̓əlb."

You, my grandchildren, will camp (here with me)."

169. ləqʷicəxʷ čəɬ gʷəl x̌iʔdubuɬ.

We were traveling downstream when he observed us.

170. ʔabil x̌ʷiʔ gʷəsčəgʷalətxʷs čəɬ x̌ʷuɬ ləbəlx̌ʷ.

If he hadn't been outside then we would have just gone on by.

171. q̓əlb čəɬ, čəɬa baqʷic ʔal tiʔiɬ dadatuʔ.

We camped, and we again went downstream in the morning.

172. tuʔux̌ʷəxʷ kʷəsi ʔayx̌ʷaɬ, tuʔux̌ʷəxʷ dxʷʔal kʷədi ʔal di tugʷiid kʷədi sčistxʷs ʔəsƛiqabac həwəʔ ʔə kʷi saʔ.

ʔayx̌ʷaɬ went now, she went to call her husband, it seemed though that he was broken out with something bad [smallpox ?].

173. ʔahəxʷ čəɬ, ʔučələxʷ hud tiʔəʔ, bək̓ʷabacəxʷ ʔučəɬ hud, ʔučəɬ hud, čəɬ hud, čəɬa ʔacac.

We were there now, they (cut) stovewood, all hands turned to deal with creating a wood supply, made wood, made wood, and we were there.

174. ʔuɬčil tiʔiɬ paspastəd, ʔəsɬaɬlil.

The white people arrived, they lived here now.

<table>
<tr><td>175.</td><td>"čaʔ tiʔadsutabyi."</td><td>"What are you doing for them?"</td></tr>
<tr><td>176.</td><td>"qʷəłay tiʔił dsułičid čəd, x̌aƛ̌tub ʔə Johnny."</td><td>"Wood is what I am cutting, Johnny wants it."</td></tr>
<tr><td>177.</td><td>təyilalikʷ, łix̌ʷalič ti ƛ̌uʔəsq̓iltub ʔə ti cił ʔaʔutx̌s, dčax̌ʷ gʷəl buusalič.</td><td>They carried it by water, the family ocean going type canoe could be loaded with three cords (of wood), once in awhile it could carry four measures.</td></tr>
<tr><td>178.</td><td>p̓əq̓ʷaʔəb łup̓ilabəs, gʷəl ləhaʔł.</td><td>When the water is high it is floated, and that is good.</td></tr>
<tr><td>179.</td><td>xʷiʔ gʷəsuqʷuʔqʷaʔs xʷiʔ.</td><td>He doesn't drink, no.</td></tr>
<tr><td>180.</td><td>x̌ʷul̓ ʔal tiʔił sx̌ʷul̓s didiiču̓ʔ.</td><td>While he is just by himself, alone.</td></tr>
<tr><td>181.</td><td>haʔł ʔaciłtalbixʷ, xʷiʔ gʷəsuqʷuʔqʷaʔs.</td><td>He is a good person, he doesn't drink [alcohol, booze].</td></tr>
<tr><td>182.</td><td>ʔa, ʔacac ʔəsłałlil, xʷiʔ kʷi sgʷaʔgʷatəgʷiʔ, ʔu xʷiʔ kʷi adsʔux̌ʷ xʷiʔəxʷ kʷi ładsʔux̌ʷ dxʷʔal sqajət siti.</td><td>He was there, living there, no one talked to him. Oh don't you go, don't you go to Skagit City now [in warning].</td></tr>
<tr><td>183.</td><td>"ʔuhədiw̓səb kʷəł kʷədi t(u)adʔalʔal ʔə kʷi tukʷədxʷ kʷi saʔ sx̌əł."</td><td>"Someone with a bad illness went into your house."</td></tr>
<tr><td>184.</td><td>c̓əx̌ kʷi sx̌əł ʔukʷədub ʔə tiʔiłəʔ tuMr. Ball, smallpox.</td><td>Was the illness that (the late = tu-) Mr. Ball got smallpox?</td></tr>
<tr><td>185.</td><td>tušubali bəkʷ kʷi ʔal tiʔiʔił tuʔacac, xʷiʔəxʷ kʷi diiču̓ʔ tuhəliʔ</td><td>Everyone who was there died, there was not one who lived.</td></tr>
<tr><td>186.</td><td>gʷəl ʔuhədiw̓cut d̓əł, kʷəł ʔal tsi ʔal tsiʔił ʔalʔalləb.</td><td>And they went in, so it seems, into the little house that belongs to you folks.</td></tr>
<tr><td>187.</td><td>ʔušuucəb kʷəł ʔə kʷi Mr. Dance, ʔudxʷəq̓yax̌adid gʷəl šuuc, kʷəł tiʔiłəʔ piʔpiʔt diʔaličup, diʔaličup tiʔił lələwasəd, gʷəl ƛ̌aləxʷʔəsƛ̌aʔtxʷyitəb tsi ʔal tiʔił xʷhudaliʔləb.</td><td>It is said that Mr. Dance opened the door and he saw [inside], it seems the little beds on the other side of the fire, the sleeping beds were on the other side of the stove, and it seems they also liked your little cook stove.</td></tr>
<tr><td>188.</td><td>"ʔəsčal kʷi ładx̌əčbid."</td><td>"What do you think about that?"</td></tr>
<tr><td>189.</td><td>"ʔu, łuwiliq̓ʷid čəd tsi dčəgʷas."</td><td>"Oh, I will ask my wife."</td></tr>
<tr><td>190.</td><td>łčil tiʔəʔ sdiʔduukʷ, diduukʷali.</td><td>? ___.</td></tr>
<tr><td>191.</td><td>Ben Gage tiʔił ʔułčiltxʷ gʷəl baʔux̌ʷʔalikʷ, baq̓ilab.</td><td>Ben Gage got there with it and he, he loaded up.</td></tr>
</table>

192. "ʔu, x̌ubʔas x̌ʷuĺ ʔuhudutəb ʔə ti Mr. Dance, x̌ʷiʔəx̌ʷ kʷi ɬubasʔux̌ʷ čəɬ paʔtab, hudud, x̌ub ʔuhudud.

"Oh, Mr Dance, can just as well burn it down, we will never be going there, ever, burn it, it is best if he burns it.

193. p̓aƛ̓aƛ̓aƛ̓ tiʔiɬ stab, x̌ʷiʔ ləłəqalgʷas ʔə gʷəšubali.

The things are unimportant, not worth dying for.

194. k̓ʷəɬijəd ʔə kʷi coal oil gʷəl hudud."

Pour coal oil over it and burn it."

195. "ʔu, x̌ʷuĺ ʔuhilibəɬ tsi dčəgʷas, ɬuhudutəbəs, x̌ub ʔuhudud, hudud, x̌ub."

"Oh, my wife said to just go ahead and burn it, let them burn it, burn it, that will be all right."

196. baɬčilalikʷ, x̌ub k̓ʷəɬ.

(Someone) came back with the answer, that, it is said, will be all right.

197. k̓ʷəɬijtəb tiʔəʔ tuʔalʔal čəɬ.

They poured over what was our house.

198. yəx̌i kʷa ʔa ʔal tiʔiɬ dəx̌ʷʔaʔs tiʔiɬ x̌uʔiqs, abstab čəɬ.

Because, though, the box (trunk) was [safe] where he was, where our things were (stored).

199. gʷəl cuukʷ tə ciɬ pipiit tiʔiɬ ʔa ʔi tiʔiɬ sqəĺqəlikʷ čəɬ ʔi tiʔiɬ c̓əx̌ʷc̓əx̌ʷ stab čəɬ, tiʔiɬ čawc̓awayulč, x̌ʷtiʔhaliʔ.

And it was only our little bed that was there and our blankets, and our worn things, our dishes, teapot.

200. x̌ʷiʔ kʷi sd̓uq̓ʷuds əlgʷə tiʔiɬ x̌ʷtəq ʔə tsiʔiɬ ʔalʔal, tux̌ʷ batəqʷ tiʔiɬ səshuytəgʷiʔ.

They didn't remove (break apart) the door of that little house, yet it was good and strong the way it had been made.

201. tuʔukʷax̌ʷax̌ʷ ti ciɬ Mr. Dance.

That Mr. Dance was helping.

202. x̌ʷuĺ d̓əɬ ʔiɬsikʷid k̓ʷəɬ ʔəlgʷəʔ gʷəl x̌ʷiʔəx̌ʷ kʷi basqʷibids əlgʷəʔʔ huy ləsɬuyab dəx̌ʷšubalis bək̓ʷ.

They just ripped it, it seems, and they didn't fix it because they were scared because it had caused so many deaths.

203. tiʔəʔ Jack Moore, bədaʔs, tsiʔiɬ jid, bədbədaʔs, čəgʷass.

This Jack Moore, his children, that Jid, children, his wife [died ?].

204. tiʔəʔ ciɬ tuJimmy Snohomish, čəgʷass.

This Jimmy Snohomish, and his wife [died].

Murder of Indian Doctors.

1. AS: x̌aƛ̓tub ʔə tiʔəʔ pastəd gʷadsgʷaagʷədbid tiʔiłəʔ tadyəl̓yəlab, tiʔiłəʔ tadskʷədatub ʔə tiʔəʔ xʷdaʔəb.

   AS: This white man [LM] wants for you to talk about your parents (ancestry), about when the Indian doctor took you.

2. gʷəl x̌aƛ̓txʷ kʷi gʷəbadsʔilid ʔəx̌id kʷi tubasgʷəlaltəbs kʷi adbad ʔi tiʔiłəʔ badsuq̓ʷa.

   And he also wants you to talk about your father and your younger brother being killed.

3. x̌ʷul̓ ɬuləhuy kʷi ɬadsyəcəbtxʷ, ɬadsʔaʔəd ʔal tiʔəʔ diʔəʔ gʷəl ɬubatəčəd ʔəsʔəx̌id tubasgʷəlaltəbs tiʔił adsuq̓ʷaʔ, dxʷʔal tiʔiłəʔ tuxʷdaʔəbs əgʷəʔ, dxʷdaʔdaʔəbs əgʷəʔ adyəl̓yəlab, dił sx̌aƛ̓s gʷadsʔilid.

   When you finish telling him that, putting it here, again add how your younger brother was killed, [go on then] about their Indian doctors, your ancestor doctors, that is what he wants you to talk about.

4. ʔəsxʷəlxʷəlkʷ kʷa, tuxʷ tiʔił ʔugʷəlaltəb kʷaʔ, adscapa, tuxʷdaʔəb tiʔił tubad ʔə tiʔił dbad.

   They were intoxicated though, yet they killed your grandfather ___ [ƛ̓əlax̌ədbid]. The father of my father was an Indian doctor. [SSP whispers these words in confidentiality]

5. tučaʔčas gʷəl tuʔiʔixʷədil.

   He was yet a child and he became (an orphan?).

6. ʔəsq̓ʷibtxʷəxʷ ʔu.

   Does he have it [recorder] fixed (ready) now?

7. AS: ʔa.

   Yes.

8. tučačas tiʔił tubad ʔə tiʔił dbad, ƛ̓əlax̌ədbid tiʔił sdaʔs.

   The father of my father was still a child, ƛ̓əlax̌ədbid was his name.

9. ck̓ʷaqid ƛ̓učəsaʔtəb dxʷʔal stititəb, dxʷʔal stititəb, gʷəl tuhaydxʷ tiʔił xʷdaʔəb.

   He was always sent out to bathe spiritually, to spiritually bathe, and he understood the doctoring power.

10. ʔal kʷi səlux̌ils gʷəl ƛ̓ubaɬəd.

    When he got older, he doctored.

11. p̓aƛ̓aƛ̓ tiʔił subaɬəds tiʔił ʔaciɬtalbixʷ dxʷʔal tiʔəʔ dčagʷadxʷ.

    For one year he doctored people freely.

12. tuxʷ tux̌ƛ̓gʷas tiʔəʔ dᶻətgʷadacac gʷəl dᶻak̓ʷuʔ ɬuqəlx̌ad, tiʔił subaɬs, tiʔił subaɬs, tiʔił subaɬs, gʷəl tulux̌il.

    Only after the salmonberry season was halfway over would he finally (put aside), his doctoring, his doctoring, his doctoring, and he got older.

13. gʷəl tiʔəʔ ciɬ tusuxʷadᶻətəgʷəl ʔə kʷədi tuhaʔkʷ tuʔaciɬtalbixʷ tutaycəgʷəls. šuʔ ʔəsʔistəʔ tiʔiɬ tudəxʷgʷəlalti tiʔiɬ tudscapa ƛalal ʔa ʔal tiʔiɬ swatixʷtəds.

And this thing that the people in the past used to indulge in, killing each other, going to war on each other. You see that was how my grandfather was killed, right there on his own land.

14. tutəyil tiʔiɬ tubšədəʔ, diɬəxʷ tudəxʷ ʔətabəds.

The warriors water traveled, and that was how he died.

15. gʷəl xʷuləxʷ tuluƛil tiʔəʔ diʔəʔ bədbədaʔs gʷəl bagʷəčəbəxʷ ʔə kʷi sxʷədaʔəb.

And as his children grew older they looked for doctoring power.

16. bahilitəbəxʷ əgʷəʔ ʔə tsiʔəʔ skʷuys ɬutiʔtəbəs, ɬuxʷiʔəɬdalbəs gʷəl haydxʷ əgʷəʔ tiʔəʔ xʷdaʔəb tiʔəʔ səsaliʔ.

Their mother instructed them to bathe spiritually, to fast and the two of them found their doctoring help.

17. tiʔiʔəʔ ʔiɬluƛ ʔi tiʔəʔ wəɬ ʔiɬtisuʔ.

The eldest and the very youngest.

18. ʔi tiʔiɬ ʔiɬʔəgʷsadᶻəʔ gʷəl ləxʷiʔ ləsqəlalituʔ gʷəl xʷuɬ dxʷsxʷiʔxʷiʔ tiʔiɬ Charley suʔyius, ʔiɬʔəgʷsadᶻəʔ.

And that middle one did not have (doctoring) power, it was only a power for hunting that Charley suʔyius [Vi's GF at Slox], the middle one, had.

19. gʷəl tiʔəʔ ciɬ Dr. Dickəxʷ tiʔiɬ sdaʔs ʔal tiʔəʔ gʷəɬ pastəd, yələxacuʔ tiʔiɬ sdaʔs ʔal tiʔəʔ gʷəɬ ʔaciɬtalbixʷ.

And this Dr. Dick now is his white man name, yələxacuʔ is his Indian name.

20. gʷəl ʔa tiʔəʔ gʷəl luƛəb kʷaʔ.

And he was there for a long time and he got older, of course.

21. gʷəl ləʔuxʷ kʷi dbad, ʔuxʷ kʷəsi dskʷuy dxʷʔal tiʔəʔ ʔal sqajət siti.

And my father went, and my mother went to this Skagit City.

22. gʷəl ʔa tiʔəʔ ləcuqʷuʔqʷuʔqʷaʔ, ləcudᶻəkʷəkʷ ɬixʷixʷ.

And there were these who were drinking, traveling about, three of them.

23. tiʔəʔ Johnny Price, ʔi tiʔəʔ Ed Moses, ʔi tiʔəʔ Sam Price.

This Johnny Price, and this Ed Moses, and this Sam Price.

24. gʷəl ləʔəydub ʔə tiʔəʔ cədiɬ tiʔiɬ sqaʔs, tiʔiɬʔ sqaʔ ʔə tiʔəʔ Johnny Price, gʷəl xʷuɬ dičuʔ, gʷəl ləcugʷaagʷəd kʷi lcuqʷuʔqʷuʔqʷaʔ ti Johnny Price ʔi ti Ed gʷəl dxʷčadəs kʷi sgʷaxʷs əgʷəʔ.

And he [her father] found his older cousin, elder cousin of Johnny Price; he was alone, and those who were drinking were talking together and they walked somewhere.

25. ʔa gʷəl ləʔuxʷ ʔuxʷ tsiʔəʔ dskʷuy dxʷʔal tiʔiɬ dəxʷʔa ʔə Willie Bo gʷəl kʷədalikʷ ʔə tiʔiɬəʔ suyayuss, kʷədalikʷ čəɬ (yəxi xʷuɬ tuləsxʷiltab).

There, and (she) went, my mother went to where Willie Bo was, and she took [along] from her work, we took [because we were owed money].

26. čəda cut, "x̌ʷul̓ čəxʷ iɬkʷədad k̓ʷuyəʔ k̓ʷədiʔ dsgʷaʔ, ɬudəxʷk̓ʷədaliɬəd ləb," gʷəl x̌ʷul̓ ʔugʷəʔuʔəd ʔal tiʔiɬ sʔux̌ʷs əgʷəʔ.

And I said, "You just go ahead and take mine, Mother, use it for buying your food," and she agreed as they left.

27. tab, ʔəsxʷəlxʷəlk̓ʷəxʷ k̓ʷi dbad gʷəl badxʷq̓il tsiʔiɬ dsk̓ʷuy.

What! My father was drunk and my mother got on board his canoe with him.

28. gʷəl lə "x̌ʷul̓əxʷ čəxʷ ʔu dᶻəɬ ʔu ƛuʔiɬq̓ʷuqʷ̓a."

And [she said to him] "It seems that you just went ahead and drank."

29. kʷaʔwa k̓ʷəɬ ləʔəƛ̌əxʷ tiʔiɬ caadiɬ dəxʷtəšs ʔa.

Now it seems, that those who would be responsible for his misfortune were on their way, coming now.

30. huy gʷədgʷaacəbəxʷ tiʔəʔ ʔəsxʷəlk̓ʷ, ʔə tiʔiʔəʔ.

Then they talked away to those who were drunk, they did.

31. čəɬtubəxʷ tiʔtuʔsulč huy, ƛ̌al baʔəsxʷəlxʷəlk̓ʷ dəxʷsəsaliʔbids əgʷə tiʔiɬ dbad, dəxʷgʷəlalds, bək̓ʷ tsiʔiɬ dsk̓ʷuy.

They made drums [metaphorically] of them, then they were also drunk and they ganged up (the two of them) on my father, thus they killed him and abused my mother also. [They beat my father like a drum and hurt my mother.]

32. tuƛ̌ipəbsəbtub ʔə tiʔiɬ tuJohnny Price tsiʔiɬ tusqaʔs.

Her older cousin, Johnny Price, choked her.

33. gʷəbək̓ʷs gʷətušubali gʷətuxʷiʔəs tiʔiɬ tusp̓alils.

Thus all of them might have died had she not revived.

34. dəxʷk̓ʷid k̓ʷi səsləxʷ ʔə k̓ʷi dbad gʷəl kʷaʔtəb, yəx̌i čiq̓icutəxʷ k̓ʷəsi dsuq̓ʷa wiʔwiʔədəxʷ, gʷəl sasaxʷəbəxʷ tiʔəʔ papapstəd, x̌ʷuʔələ x̌ʷiʔ lətib luƛ̌luƛ̌.

That, how many times was my father stabbed and they let him go because my younger sister hollered, and the little white kids ran, maybe they were not very old.

35. šudub ʔə tiʔəʔ gʷəl saʔsaxʷəb, dəxʷʔaʔs ʔal tiʔiɬ gʷəl tul̓aʔəx̌ gʷəl ʔa gʷəl ʔux̌ʷtub dxʷʔal tiʔiɬ ʔa.

They saw them and they ran, that was why they were there, and they took him over there.

36. ʔux̌ʷəxʷ tsi dsk̓ʷuy dxʷʔal tiʔiɬ dəxʷʔa ʔə tiʔiɬ ʔi sqʷax̌ʷəbqəd huy tutəyiltəbəxʷ k̓ʷi dbad.

My mother then went to where sqʷax̌ʷəbqəd (and others were), then my dad was taken up the river.

37. huy čəɬ tuyəcaladitubəxʷ yəx̌i čəɬ lil.

Then we were informed about what happened, because we were far away.

38. ʔux̌ʷ tsi dsk̓ʷuy gʷəl səɬax̌iləxʷ gʷəl ɬčisəbuɬ, x̌ʷuʔələʔ t̓at̓əgʷt.

My mother went and it was night when she arrived to us, maybe midnight.

39. huy čəł ʔəλ̓axʷ, ʔulułəxʷ ʔə tiʔił lil.

Then we came, we water traveled for a long ways.

40. gʷəl ʔal tiʔił ʔal Lyman tiʔił dəxʷčaʔkʷ čəł, čəłaʔ təyil.

And it was at Lyman that we came down to the water, and we water traveled upstream.

41. təyil čəł čəłaʔ q̓il dxʷʔal tiʔił ʔal x̌ʷix̌ʷalič gʷəl ʔa tiʔił dʔəpus ʔa tsiʔił sk̓ʷuy ʔi Johnny Buck, ʔacac ʔəsʔasəbuł.

We traveled a long way upriver and we arrived at Lyman, and my aunt was there and mother and Johnny Buck, they were there waiting for us.

42. huy čəł təyiləxʷ, yəx̌i čəd x̌ʷul̓ diičʷu ləcəq̓aʔəb.

Then we traveled, because I was the only one poling (the canoe).

43. ʔuk̓ʷačil tiʔił dəxʷʔux̌ʷ čəł gʷəl x̌əł kʷi bad ʔə ti dsəx̌ʷstudəq.

It was morning where we went and the father of my son became ill.

44. x̌ʷiʔəxʷ gʷəsucəq̓aʔəbs x̌ʷuləxʷčəd diičʷuʔ, huy baləsd̓uq̓ʷd̓uq̓ʷil tsiʔił dsk̓ʷuy, ʔəsčəłq̓ʷidgʷas, x̌ʷiʔəxʷ gʷəsgʷəd̓akʷads.

He no longer poled, I was now alone, because my mother was also broken, her middle was separated [probably had broken ribs], she no longer moved around.

45. ʔa, təyil čəł, čəłaʔ ʔalil tiʔił q̓ix̌ʷ, ʔałx̌adbid ʔə Lyman čəłaʔ łalil čəłaʔ gʷax̌ʷ, ləgʷłəxʷ čəł tiʔəʔ ləsx̌əł.

We traveled a long way upriver, below Lyman we beached and walked, we left the ones who were sick.

46. λ̓ub łuʔibəs liłlaq.

It would be best if they walked later.

47. łax̌əxʷ čəłaʔ dxʷq̓il dxʷʔal tiʔił dəxʷʔa ʔə tiʔił ʔəsłałlil.

It was night when we arrived to the place where they were living.

48. kʷačil gʷəl pədtəb tiʔił tudbad.

When morning came, they buried my father.

49. čəłaʔ bał̓ukʷ.

And then we again went home.

50. bagʷiidəxʷ tiʔił tustaʔtəb čəł.

We (collected our few belongings).

51. kʷi dsəx̌ʷstudəq tiʔəʔ cədił baʔugʷəlaltəbəxʷ kʷa, ʔaləxʷ tiʔił diʔabac tiʔił sgʷəlalti.

My dear one (brother), was, however, killed, he was on the other side (Canada) when he was killed.

52. x̌ʷiʔ gʷədsəshaydxʷ ti dəxʷgʷəlalti.

I don't know why he was [revenge] killed.

53. λ̓aləxʷ badxʷdaʔəb, gʷəl λ̓uʔubaład tiʔiʔił kʷaʔ ʔal tiʔił tusʔaʔs ʔal tiʔił diʔabac.

He was also a medicine man, and he was doctoring them, those where he was, on the other side.

54. gʷəl tuλ̓ubil tsiʔəʔ sładəyʔ tuʔubaład, gʷəl ʔuʔəx̌idəxʷ kʷi badəxʷ x̌əłs gʷəl tiləbəxʷ ʔuʔatəbəd.

And this woman was getting much better as he doctored her, until what happened to her that caused her to relapse and right away she died.

55. šuʔu, gʷəl ʔəscutəbəxʷ dił kʷi dsuq̓ʷa tiʔił tux̌icis tiʔəʔ dił.

Trouble, and they said that it was my younger brother who got angry and caused this.

56. diłəxʷ tudəxʷ čalčaləti gʷəl tuʔucutəb.

That was why they chased him, and they shot him.

57. dəxʷhaydxʷ čəł čəłaʔ tuʔux̌ʷc čəłaʔ tuʔəx̌txʷ dəxʷłčiltxʷ čəł txʷdiʔəʔ.

That was what we found out, and we went after him, and we brought him here.

58. xʷiʔ gʷəsəshaydxʷ čəł gʷat kʷi dəxʷtəšsʔa, p̓aƛ̓aƛ̓ tiʔił sgʷaʔgʷəd ʔucutəb, ti dəxʷtəšsʔa tadi ti dəxʷtəšsʔa.

We didn't know who was responsible for doing him in (his murder), it was only gossip that was sounded, that one was responsible for his death.

59. x̌ʷuĺ p̓aƛ̓aƛ̓ ləcugʷadgʷəd tiʔił caadił ləcugʷaagʷəd, dəxʷ xʷiʔ gʷəsəshaydxʷ čəł gʷat kʷi tudəxʷtəšs ʔa ʔə tiʔił diʔabac ʔaciłtalbixʷ.

It was merely gossip spoken by those who were talking, thus we did not know who was responsible on the other side for the act (that did him in).

60. gʷəl tuĺʔa gʷəl xʷiʔiləxʷ gʷəxʷdaʔəb.

From that time, the Indian doctors became no more.

61. xʷiʔəxʷ gʷəgʷat gʷələcugʷəčəd gʷəxʷdaʔəb.

No one was looking for doctoring power.

62. xʷiʔəxʷ ʔə tiʔił tudbədbədaʔ, xʷiʔəxʷ.

No one among my children, not anyone.

63. tuĺʔa gʷəl xʷiʔiləxʷ kʷi gʷəxʷdaʔəb.

From that time there were no more Indian doctors.

64. tuĺʔa gʷəl tux̌əł tiʔił tudqəsiʔ, tiʔił ʔiłluƛ̓, laqbi(d) ʔə tiʔił suq̓ʷaʔs, kʷədəxʷ ʔə tiʔəʔ sx̌əł, ʔəsq̓əpaʔdup, qəp.

From that time my uncle became ill, the eldest one, after his younger sibling (or cousin), he took on this illness, a craziness, crazy.

65. qəp tiʔił sx̌iʔuss.

His head became crazy.

66. ʔuʔibʔibəšəxʷ dxʷʔal p̓aƛ̓aƛ̓, dxʷʔal tusʔatəbəds, təš tiʔił sx̌əł.

He wandered around for no reason, until he died, afflicted by this illness.

67. tiʔəʔ cədił, tiʔiʔił tuʔəgʷsad̓ads əgʷəʔ, tiʔił dəxʷʔatabəds, x̌əł.

This one, the one in the middle from them, died from illness.

68. ƛ̓al baʔəsʔistəʔ ti ʔiłtisuʔ.

It was that way also with the youngest one.

69. yubil tiʔił łəq̓aligʷəds tudəxʷacacs.

Relatives, where he was, on one side, died.

70. diłəxʷ, shuys tiʔił suhuyhuyucut ʔə tiʔił tudyəlyəlab.

That finishes what my ancestors did.

71. huy lətəš sx̌əł ti?ił ?iłkʷəlq, x̌ʷul̓ lətəš sx̌əł.

The rest of them died of illness, only from illness.

72. cugʷukʷ ti?ił dbad ti?ił ?utəš lab, ?ugʷəlaltəb ?ə ti?i?ił.

It was only my father who died because of liquor, they killed him.

73. tux̌ʷ bək̓ʷiləx̌ʷ ti?ił tucaadił tugʷəlald x̌ʷul̓əx̌ʷ tušubali, x̌ʷi?əx̌ʷ gʷədiič̓u? gʷəhəli?.

But all of those who killed him are finished, they just died, there is not one of them alive.

74. huy gʷəł ti?ə? lab suyayus, p̓aƛ̓aƛ̓ gʷətəlix̌ʷəł addč̓agʷł tux̌ʷ ?ugʷəlald.

That was the work of liquor, it mattered not that you belonged to one (and the same) house, yet you killed them.

Big Windstorm

1. AS: xʷiʔu gʷadsgʷaʔgʷəd k̓ʷuyəʔ gʷadsyəcəb, gʷaslax̌dxʷ čəxʷ, xʷiʔu gʷadsgʷagʷətxʷ ʔə tə təčaʔkʷ tusupuʔalikʷ, tushikʷ tuspuʔalikʷ.

AS: Mother, won't you talk about, tell about, what you remember about, won't you talk to him [LM] about the windstorm offshore, the big windstorm.

2. SSP: ʔu tiʔił tuləcuxʷiʔxʷiʔ, ʔu.

SSP: Oh, what about those who were hunting? What?

3. AS: dił gʷadsgʷaʔgʷətxʷ k̓ʷuyəʔ, tiʔiłəʔ.

AS: That is what you would talk to him about, Mother, that.

4. ʔa gʷəl ləcuuc tsiʔiłəʔ sk̓ʷuy ʔə tiʔiʔił, bad ʔə tiʔił tustətudəq.

There and (somebody) said to the mother of those, the father of the children.

5. AS: x̌ʷuĺ čəxʷ ləʔux̌ʷtxʷ k̓ʷuyəʔ x̌ʷuĺ, ʔa ʔəshuy tiʔəʔ diʔəʔ.

Al prompts his mother saying: Just go ahead with your story, Mother, just go ahead with it, this one has it [recorder] ready for you.

6. ʔacac gʷəl ləcut, "ʔuʔəƛ̓ ti šəxʷəb.

He was there and he said, "The wind is coming.

7. cikʷ ʔugʷəq̓ʷəsšad tadi dxʷcaʔkʷ.

Offshore is getting very (threatening).

8. təx̌ʷudłi ti q̓ilq̓ilbid dxʷʔilusəb čələpa łasłidłidtxʷ."

Pull up your canoes toward the houses, and you folks have them tied."

9. huy dxʷšišəqtəbəxʷ tiʔəʔ stiwatł, dxʷšišəqtəbəxʷ tiʔəʔ sdəxʷił gʷəl łidłiditəb, dxʷʔal gʷəspuʔitiʔ.

Then they tied them up this large canoe, they tied up the hunting canoe, to keep them from being blown (away).

10. huy čəbaʔədəxʷ tiʔəʔ tustabs dxʷt̓aq̓t, tusʔələds.

Then their things were carried upland, their food.

11. k̓ʷədatəbəxʷ ʔə k̓ʷəsi ʔal tiʔəʔ sqəlqəlikʷ gʷəl k̓ʷədatəb ʔə k̓ʷi bad ʔə tiʔił dsəxʷstudəq ʔi tiʔił tusuq̓ʷaʔs gʷəl x̌ac̓x̌ac̓ič̓təb əgʷə, ləx̌ʷləx̌ʷijtəb ʔə k̓ʷədi sulič, xʷi ləłubadiʔdtiʔ k̓ʷi juĺčuʔ.

She there took the blankets to the father of my beloved son and his younger brother and they covered them, put cattail mats over them, the waves will be fierce (and dangerous).

12. tiləb ƛ̓aq̓t kʷi sʔa ʔə tiʔəʔ sʔəɬəd čəɬ, tiʔaʔ stab čəɬ, x̌ʷuləx̌ʷ ʔuɬičitəb tiʔəʔ sʔulič, x̌ʷuləx̌ʷ ʔuɬič̓yustəb gʷəl čubčubaʔ.

Right upland then was where our food and our things were, the cattail mats were cut, they were just cut off [the tent frame] and carried upland.

13. qəlalčti ti ʔal x̌ʷatqʷəb.

The people (living) at Whatcom had bad luck.

14. d̓uq̓ʷil ti tuq̓iq̓ilbids.

Their canoes were all broken ~ smashed up.

15. ʔa kʷi ƛutəx̌ʷədxʷ kʷi q̓ilbids dxʷʔilusəb ʔal tiʔiɬ, x̌ʷulb ʔəsčəd̓k̓ʷil.

There were those who managed to pull their canoes up against the [buildings ?] there at ___ they were just smashed to smithereens.

16. gʷəl tiʔəʔ cədiɬ ʔal bibəlqʷaʔb gʷəl bək̓ʷ ʔukʷədxʷ tiʔiɬ sgʷaʔs əgʷəʔ, x̌ʷiʔ gʷəd̓uq̓ʷil.

And those who (lived) at [an area between Chuckanut Drive and Bellingham] all took care of their canoes, none were broken up.

17. təx̌ʷudɬi ti q̓ilq̓ilbid dxʷʔilusəb čələba ɬasɬidɬidtxʷ.

You folks, pull your canoes close to your houses and have them tied up.

18. huy dxʷšišəqtəbəxʷ tiʔəʔ stiwatɬ, dxʷšišəqtəbəxʷ tiʔəʔ sdəxʷiɬ gʷəl ɬidɬiditəb dxʷʔal gʷəspuʔitiʔ.

Then they lifted them up, the large ocean vessel, they pulled up the smaller hunting canoe, and they tied them to keep them from being blown.

19. huy čəbaʔədəxʷ tiʔəʔ tustabs dxʷƛ̓aq̓t, tusʔəɬəds.

Then they packed their things upland, their food.

20. kʷədatəb ʔə kʷəsi ʔal tiʔəʔ sqəlqəlikʷ gʷəl kʷədatəb tə gʷəq̓ilbids əgʷə.

She took their blankets and their canoes.

21. gʷəl ʔa tsiʔəʔ k̓ʷəlwass əgʷəʔ, qaləp ʔə tiʔəʔ tutaktəd, bad ʔə tsiʔəʔ Betsy.

And there was their inlaw, (widow tidišəʔ) of the late doctor, the father of Betsy.

22. gʷəl ʔa ləcuhudičup ʔal tiʔiɬ čaʔkʷ huy laq̓ʷus.

And there (she) was building a fire down by the water because she was there.

23. huy dukʷtxʷəxʷ tsiʔəʔ k̓ʷəlwass, "x̌ʷuɬ ləcuʔəx̌ix̌əd tsiʔəʔ x̌ʷiʔ ləhaʔɬ.

Then he [taktəd ?] got (irritated) at his inlaw, "What is this (crazy thing) doing?

24. ɬuhud d̓əɬ ʔu kʷədi huds."

Will her fire burn?"

25. kʷədad tiʔəʔ hud ʔə tsiʔəʔ kʷəlwass gʷəl saxʷəbtxʷ dxʷɫaqt dxʷʔal tudʣaq̓ cić̓kʷ liɫgʷəd gʷəl cikʷʔəxʷ ʔəsx̌il tiʔəʔ q̓aliɫ q̓ʷuʔq̓ʷuʔ sč̓əbid kʷi tuʔuq̓ʷuʔəd, dʣixʷ ssuxʷils.

He now took the wood of his inlaw and he ran it upland toward it, [landed] right under and it was very ___ this pitch, lots of bark, (she) had gathered when it first began to blow.

26. huy hudič̓upəxʷ.

Then (someone) rebuilt a fire.

27. wiwiʔadəxʷ tsiʔəʔ lux̌.

Now this old woman hollered.

28. wiwiʔacəxʷ tiʔəʔ bədaʔs.

She hollered to her son.

29. "ʔusaxʷəbtubəxʷ ti tudhud ʔəsšalqidiš gʷətuÌ̓čadəs, ʔuʔəx̌ix̌ədəxʷ čəd ti dbədaʔ, ʔuʔəx̌i[d] ti ʔitək̓ʷbixʷ ʔuʔəx̌iʔx̌ədəxʷ čəd dəbədaʔ, ʔusaxʷəbtubəxʷ šə tudhud."

"___ ran off with my wood, wherever he was from. What shall I do, my son, what have the Suquamish done. What shall I do, my son, what have the Suquamish done. What shall I do, my son, my firewood has been taken." [SSP uses Southern Lushootseed]

30. tuÌ̓čad kʷi tusaxʷəbtxʷyid ti kʷəlkʷəlwass kʷi tuʔuxtxʷ dxʷʔal kʷi gʷədəxʷ hudud, cutəb ʔə tsiʔəʔ Aggie.

Where did they run away with it, her inlaws took it so that they could burn it, Aggie [?] said.

31. hududəxʷ tiʔəʔ salagʷəp, hudud kʷi tusč̓əbid, kʷi tusč̓aʔč̓ast, q̓ʷatədəxʷ, huy sq̓ʷuʔq̓ʷuʔ sč̓aʔč̓ast, hudud ʔə kʷi hikʷ gʷəl x̌əcəd tiʔəʔ liɫč̓it, huyud təqad ʔə kʷi gʷədəxʷ ʔəx̌ ʔə kʷi sšəxʷəb.

Someone now burned the tree side, someone burned the bark, burned tree limbs, spread them all over, because there was lots of bark, made a big bonfire and snatched the nearest (brush) and made a (barrier) that would keep the wind out.

32. x̌əɫəxʷ tisq̓əsəd swawˀtixʷtəd ʔuxadʣx̌adʣəx̌əd.

It was now kind of like a partition island (bunched, jammed, crunched against).

33. gʷəl ləcuuc tsiʔəʔ č̓əbass, "ʔəshudəxʷ di hud."

And he said to his inlaw, "The fire is burning now."

34. č̓ubəstxʷ kʷədad tsiʔəʔ stab ʔə tsiʔəʔ sk̓ʷuys gʷəl saxʷəbtxʷ, saxʷabtxʷ.

He took it upland, he took his mother's things and he ran with it, ran with it.

35. č̓əbč̓abaʔədəxʷ ʔəgʷəʔ tiʔəʔ sqəÌ̓qəligʷss tiʔəʔ diʔəʔ, tiʔəʔ, tiʔəʔ, təlixʷ suʔsq̓ʷaʔ, q̓ʷiq̓ʷiÌ̓əxʷ əgʷəʔ.

They packed their blankets, these, these, married to siblings, they were strong now.

36. huy ɫəgʷɫəgʷidəxʷ tiʔəʔ bəbədaʔs, gʷəl q̓əsidid.

Then they left their children, they partitioned them [off].

37.	tab, gʷəq̇iq̇ilbid ʔə ti tutxʷləbiʔ, huy ʔupix̌ʷəb.	Where were the canoes of the Lummi, because it had flooded?
38.	tab šəšəq̇ʷaluʔ dᶻuq̇ʷil.	What ___, smashed up ___?
39.	ʔa kʷi ƛutəx̌ʷədxʷ kʷi q̇ilbids, ʔa kʷi ƛutəx̌ʷədxʷ.	There were some who managed to pull their canoes, there were some who managed to pull them up.
40.	ʔa kʷi x̌ʷiʔ gʷəsukʷədxʷs kʷi q̇ilbids.	There were some who were unable to get their canoes.
41.	x̌ʷuləx̌ʷ dčaʔgʷił kʷi ƛutəx̌ʷdub.	They were able to pull up just one canoe.
42.	x̌ʷuləx̌ʷ dčaʔgʷił gʷəł diičuʔ.	There was only one canoe that belonged to someone.
43.	tux̌ʷəx̌ʷ ləsaxʷsaxʷəb tiʔiʔəʔ ləkʷax̌ʷatəgʷəl.	They just ran around, helping each other.
44.	kʷi tusʔələds ʔəgʷəʔ, saxʷsaxʷəbtxʷ dxʷʔilusəb.	Their food, they hurried it up to higher ground.
45.	bək̇ʷ dəxʷʔuƛuq̇ʷuds ʔəgʷəʔ, huy hikʷ tuṗix̌ʷəd.	They stuffed things in everywhere, because the water was all over everywhere.
46.	x̌ʷiʔ gʷəʔuʔatabəd, x̌ʷiʔ.	No one died, no.
47.	x̌ʷuł tustabs ʔəgʷəʔ kʷi ʔudᶻuq̇ʷud, q̇əsq̇əsəds, hikʷ tuhuyutəb sʔušəbabtxʷ ʔə ti šəxʷəb tiʔił ʔaciłtalbixʷ.	It was just their things that were broken, barrier partitions, the people were caused much misfortune by the wind.
48.	ʔa kʷa tiʔəʔ cədił luƛ ləcučiq̇icut, ʔa tiʔəʔ luƛ, ʔučiq̇icut, ti saxʷəbtəgʷiʔ ti tuhuds.	There was, though, this old person hollering, there was this old one hollering, (when) someone ran off with the wood that belonged to (the old one).
49.	huy bałčiləxʷ tə cədił kʷəlwass tusaxʷəbtxʷ, tiʔił.	The inlaw again arrived who had run off with that.
50.	x̌ʷuł ʔəgʷəʔ ləcux̌acx̌acəb.	They were just quarreling.
51.	bagʷəgʷədgʷətxʷəxʷ tsiʔəʔ kʷəlwass, "x̌ʷuł ʔuʔəsgʷədil tiʔəʔ tidišəʔ x̌ʷiʔ lə ʔux̌ʷ hiwiləxʷ čubəʔ, čəbaʔigʷsəb čəxʷaʔ čubəʔ."	He scolded his inlaw, "Is tidišəʔ just going to be sitting there, not going, go on now, go upland, pack your things upland and climb."
52.	x̌ʷuł ʔəsgʷədil ʔugʷəgʷədgʷəʔ tsiʔəʔ tidišəʔ.	tidišəʔ just sat there talking.
53.	qəp šə ƛubaṗalil.	Crazy, she ever used good sense.

<table>
<tr><td>54.</td><td>čəbaʔigʷsəb tsiʔəʔ tidišəʔ baʔuxʷ ʔə kʷədi ʔəshud.</td><td>tidišəʔ packed her things upland and went to the fire.</td></tr>
<tr><td>55.</td><td>"diɫ tiadqʷəlxʷ kʷi ʔuʔəƛ̓txʷ tiʔəʔ tadhud, čadəxʷ ʔəshudəxʷ ʔə tiʔəʔ.</td><td>"It is you who brought what had been your firewood, where is it burning now.</td></tr>
<tr><td>56.</td><td>ʔal tiʔəʔ kʷi ɫadsʔa," cutəb ʔə tsiʔiɫ bədaʔs.</td><td>You will be here," her daughter said to her.</td></tr>
<tr><td>57.</td><td>xʷiʔ ləʔəsčubəʔ ʔə tsiʔəʔ tidišəʔ.</td><td>tidišəʔ hadn't climbed upland.</td></tr>
<tr><td>58.</td><td>x̌ʷuɫ ləx̌acx̌acəb ʔi tiʔəʔ kʷəlwass.</td><td>She and her inlaw were just quarreling.</td></tr>
<tr><td>59.</td><td>huy x̌ʷuɫəxʷ ʔa gʷəl q̓əsq̓əsəbəd ʔəgʷəʔ, q̓əsq̓əsəbəd.</td><td>They were just there and they partitioned themselves, partitioned off.</td></tr>
<tr><td>60.</td><td>ʔəbiləxʷ xʷiʔ tsiʔiɫ gʷəl šubaliʔ ʔəgʷəʔ.</td><td>If it had not been for her (tidišəʔ) they would have perished.</td></tr>
<tr><td>61.</td><td>tab gʷətukʷədxʷ ʔəgʷəʔ šudxʷs kʷədiʔ x̌ʷəlč ʔugʷəkəlšaad.</td><td>They wouldn't have been able to (save) anything, when it was seen how the salt water was acting up.</td></tr>
<tr><td>62.</td><td>təx̌ʷtəx̌ʷutəb tiʔəʔ q̓ilq̓ilbid dxʷʔiluss čəbčəbaʔigʷsəb əgʷəʔ.</td><td>They pulled their canoes upland, packed their belongings upland.</td></tr>
<tr><td>63.</td><td>gʷəl bək̓ʷil tiʔəʔ tusʔəɫəds, bək̓ʷil tiʔəʔ stabs ʔəgʷəʔ ʔilusəb.</td><td>And their food was finished, their things were finished upland [All of their things were removed to higher ground].</td></tr>
<tr><td>64.</td><td>liləxʷ.</td><td>Far away.</td></tr>
<tr><td>65.</td><td>huy ƛugʷəqʷšaad kʷədi q̓uʔ, x̌ʷəlč, ɫaq̓əs dxʷʔal tiʔiɫ ʔilgʷiɫ.</td><td>The water churned, the salt water, when it landed on shore.</td></tr>
<tr><td>66.</td><td>kʷaʔ ʔəsɫidɫidəxʷ tiʔəʔ cədiɫ q̓ilq̓ilbid dxʷyələbids ʔə kʷədi sƛaʔƛakʷtxʷ.</td><td>Their canoes, though, they now had tied.</td></tr>
<tr><td>67.</td><td>sɫid kʷədi ʔilaqs, dxʷyəlalgʷiɫs ʔəsɫid kʷədi šədᶻts dxʷyəlalgʷiɫ, xʷiʔəs gʷəsgʷədᶻakʷads puʔutiʔ.</td><td>The rear was tied, the right side, the front ends were tied, to the right, so that they wouldn't move when blown.</td></tr>
<tr><td>68.</td><td>gʷəxʷiʔəxʷ gʷəčit gʷədəxʷəsx̌əcs ʔəgʷəʔ gʷədᶻaq̓, xʷiʔəxʷ.</td><td>There was nothing near that they need to be afraid of falling (crashing down), no more.</td></tr>
<tr><td>69.</td><td>hudhudičup ʔəgʷəʔ.</td><td>They built fires ___.</td></tr>
</table>

70. kʷədi tučačas, kʷədi tučačas, kʷədi tusčədi(d), gʷəl lələx̌il.

The children, the children, __, and daylight came.

71. xʷiʔ gʷəsx̌ax̌s ʔəgʷəʔ, huy ʔuqəsqəsəd.

They didn't get cold, because they had partitions.

72. x̌ʷuləxʷ ʔuhuy tiʔəʔ cədił ʔučubčubaʔigʷsəbs qəsqəsədəbs gʷəl k̓ʷask̓ʷasəbəxʷ ʔəgʷəʔ ʔə kʷədi x̌ax̌yəƛ̓.

When they had finished packing their things upland, making partitions, then they toasted some bone dry salmon.

73. "tagʷəxʷəxʷ čəł tsi siʔab, tagʷəxʷəxʷ čəł."

"We are hungry now, dear, we are hungry now."

74. huy k̓ʷasəbəxʷ tsiʔəʔ ʔə kʷi dčuʔ.

So she toasted one now.

75. ʔabyid tsiʔəʔ sčəłsbədaʔəb ʔə tiʔəʔ dčuʔ.

She gave her stepdaughter one.

76. k̓ʷasəbtxʷ tsiʔəʔ dʔəpus, huy ʔəłʔəładəxʷ ʔəgʷəʔ.

She toasted for my aunt, then they ate.

77. ʔu tusx̌ax̌ax̌ayəbəxʷ tiʔəʔ ʔi taktəd ʔi tsiʔił k̓ʷəlwass.

Oh, how taktəd and his inlaw laughed.

78. x̌uləxʷ ʔux̌acx̌acəbilb tiʔəʔ təlixʷ, x̌ʷul ʔux̌acx̌acəbilb.

These people [married to relatives] just quarreled, they just quarreled.

79. ʔuʔəx̌iʔtub ʔə tsə ʔal tidišəʔ šə tuba ___.

What did they – there at (or with) tidišəʔ – do with ___?

80. bačəgʷsəb tsiʔəʔ k̓ʷəlwass gʷəl bagʷəgʷadgʷatxʷ.

Her inlaw came to her and she was scolded.

81. tsiʔəʔ tidišəʔ xʷiʔ ləčəbaʔigʷsəb, "čəbaʔigʷsəb čəxʷa čubəʔ."

This tidišəʔ doesn't bring her things upland, "Carry your things upland and climb up."

82. ʔux̌ʷ ʔə ti čəbaʔigʷsəb kʷəsi tidišəʔ gʷəl čubəʔ.

She went, carried her things upland did tidišəʔ, and went upland.

83. dił ssač̓ ʔə tiʔił shuy ʔə tiʔił shuy ʔə tiʔiʔił tutukʷtukʷ, huy tup̓ix̌ʷəb, ʔi tuhigʷil tiʔəʔ x̌ʷəlč.

That is the end of what happened to those who were submerged, because of high waters as the sea became very big.

84. xʷiʔəxʷ gʷəstab sq̓ilbi(d).

There were some who did not have canoes.

85. baʔəxʷ kʷi ƛ̓absq̓ilbid, ʔabslaʔ.

There were a few isolated ones who had a canoe.

86. gʷəl x̌ʷul̓ ʔušudxʷ tiʔił gʷəl təytəyiltxʷ kʷədi sgʷaʔs tuq̓ilq̓ilbi(d) txʷq̓ixʷ.

When (someone) saw this (lack) he traveled his own canoe upland.

87. p̓əq̓ʷ txʷq̓ixʷ ʔə tiʔəʔ cədił stuł̓tuləkʷ.

Floated upriver of the rivers.

88. tuʔuxʷtub ʔə kʷi diičuʔ ʔə tə cədił txʷləbi tiʔił cəbaʔgʷił q̓ilbids dxʷʔal kʷədi gʷədəxʷʔaʔs, dəxʷhəliʔs, xʷiʔs kʷi łusd̓uq̓ʷils.

One of the Lummis took two canoes so that it would be there, that he might survive, that they would not get smashed.

89. xʷuləxʷ dčagʷił q̓ilbids tiʔił badəxʷʔuxʷs.

Only one canoe did he use to go with.

90. xʷuləxʷ lədxʷtəxʷud, gʷəl bała?c, tiʔił ʔiišəds.

He just pulled it, and he arrived at his people.

91. t̓aqtəxʷ.

They were now upland.

92. xʷuł d̓əł ƛ̓ułəgʷəldxʷ tiʔəʔ q̓ilbids gʷəl tuləd̓aqič si dxʷʔal tiʔił q̓ilbids tiʔił ʔud̓aqs tə səkʷəbac.

Just as they left their canoes, it seems then something fell over them, right toward their canoes, did the alder tree fall.

93. xʷulb ʔəsgʷəbiƛ̓əd.

They were just crushed.

94. ʔucut kʷəł ʔəsƛ̓ubil ti dəxʷʔa ʔə ti dq̓ilbid, ʔəsƛ̓ubil, cugʷəxʷ tiʔəʔ cədił tuʔuxʷtxʷ tubadəxʷ ʔuxʷ dxʷʔal tiʔəʔ ʔiišəds.

It was said that my canoe was all right where it was, it was all right, only (using) that one that went toward his people.

95. bədbədaʔs kʷi həliʔ sʔəxids kʷi dəxʷʔuxʷtəgʷi kʷi q̓ilbid gʷəl xʷuł ʔutəxʷutub ʔal ti, čədaʔ dxʷcutəbid łud̓uq̓ʷil.

He had living children was the reason he pulled the canoe, it was just pulled here, and I thought that it would get smashed up.

96. dił shuys tiʔił shuhuyucut ʔə kʷədi tuʔaciłtalbixʷ.

That finishes (what I have to say) about what the people used to do.

97. d̓ixʷ ʔaciłtalbixʷ, tuxʷ ƛ̓utusʔugʷaʔgʷəd tuxʷ, ƛ̓usugʷaʔgʷəd ʔə tiʔəʔ cədił ʔi taktəd, sʔugʷaʔgʷəds ʔəgʷəʔ, lələlalx̌bids ʔəgʷəʔ kʷi suhuys.

First people, it was only conversation, only, what this taktad (doctor) and them talked about, they told about what they used to do.

98. dił sšac̓s tiʔił dču? sʔəyəhub hayəxʷ.

That finished that one legend, that does it.

AS asks SSP to talk about selling feathers and stealing sheep

1. AS: gʷaagʷətxʷ čəxʷ k̓ʷuyəʔ ʔə tiʔiłəʔ tuhuyub ʔə tiʔiłəʔ tustuq̓ʷ diʔabac gʷəl tuʔuqadəʔ əgʷəʔ ʔə tiʔiłəʔ ləbətuʔ.

AS: Mother, tell him about selling feathers on the other side [of the water, Vancouver Island] and about stealing sheep.

2. SSP: ʔuʔəx̌iʔ.

SSP: What happened?

3. AS: tiʔiɬəʔ tuʔuhuyub ʔə kʷi sťuqʷ dxʷdiʔabac tuťukʷtub gʷəl tuqadaʔəxʷ əgʷəʔ ʔə tiʔiɬəʔ ləbətuʔ.

[AS rephrases his request] Those who sold feathers to the other side were brought home and they stole the sheep.

4. SSP: tuťuċudəxʷ ʔəgʷəʔ.

SSP: They shot them now.

5. AS: ʔa.

AS: Yes.

6. SSP: tagʷtagʷəxʷ.

SSP: They became hungry now.

7. AS: ʔux̌ʷtxʷ, ʔux̌ʷtxʷ kʷuyəʔ.

AS: Go ahead and tell about it, talk about it, Mother.

8. SSP: ʔu, tuʔugʷitəb ʔə kʷədi ʔal bitoliʔəʔ kʷi stə kʷi sťuqʷ, kʷi buʔqʷ, huy ʔux̌ʷəxʷ tiʔiʔəʔ diʔəʔ, ʔux̌ʷəxʷ tiʔəʔ tuɬʔal dxʷʔaha.

SSP: Oh, someone from Victoria called for feathers, from ducks, so they went, those from dxʷʔahaʔ [Samish].

9. ʔux̌ʷəxʷ gʷas ʔə tiʔəʔ tuɬʔal swədəbš qaʔhalgʷiɬ kʷi gʷatgʷatəs ʔiišəds ʔəgʷəʔ.

They went now, these from Swinomish many canoes, whoever they were, their acquaintances [of the dxʷʔahaʔ].

10. ʔa gʷəl suxʷil.

They were there and a wind came up.

11. xʷiʔ dᶻəɬ kʷi tubaʔabssawəd, xʷiʔ gʷətuʔabssawəd, xʷiʔ kʷi baʔabsxʷəltəbalc, xʷiʔ.

It seems that no one had prepared lunch, no one had lunching food, no one had a gun, no.

12. huy ʔəƛ̕əxʷ tiʔəʔ ʔuťukʷ.

Then they came home.

13. gʷəl ʔal tiʔəʔ sčəgʷucid tiʔəʔ labatuʔ ʔə tiʔiɬ dxʷčaʔkʷ.

And it was on this island, where there were sheep of that one toward the water.

14. huy cutəxʷ tiʔəʔ diičuʔ.

Then one of them said,

15. "ʔu, gʷədxʷtəcaladiʔalikʷ čəɬ ʔə tiʔiɬ labatuʔ ɬustabəxʷ kʷi ɬusʔələd čəɬ."

"Oh, we could hit those sheep on the head, what else are we going to have to eat?"

16. xʷiʔ dᶻəɬ ʔu gʷəsċəx̌əɬdalbs tiʔiɬ ʔabsləpəskʷi.

It seems they had not provided themselves with food (other than) that pilot bread.

17. huy ʔəƛ̕əxʷ ʔəgʷəʔ, huy pusudəxʷ ʔəgʷəʔ kʷi dčuʔ.

Then they came, they threw at one. [Killed a sheep with a puck of pilot bread.]

18. huy q̓ilidəxʷ ʔəgʷəʔ gʷə liləxʷ xʷuʔələʔ gʷəl q̓əx̌ʷəd, huy gʷəl, q̓əlq̓əlałciʔ.

Then they loaded it on board and maybe they were far away before they butchered it, then they cooked their meat.

19. q̓ʷəb ʔəgʷəʔ, yəx̌i huy təlč ʔə kʷi dəxʷʔululuł ʔə kʷi pastəd.

They did, because they missed where the white people water traveled.

20. huy, huyucid ʔəgʷəʔ gʷəl bahiqicut.

Then, when they finished eating, they again shoved off in their canoes.

21. ʔix̌ʷduptub, dxʷbəčduptub kʷədi šawšaw ʔal kʷədi čaʔkʷ.

They threw them, sunk the bones in deep water offshore.

22. ʔa huy tiʔiʔəʔ diʔəʔ gʷəl ʔəx̌ gʷəl cugʷəxʷəs kʷi stab kʷi ʔa yəx̌i qaha ʔəgʷəʔ, huy cickʷəxʷ ʔəstagʷtagʷəxʷ.

There they were and they finished and they came, leaving whatever [was already] there because there were lots of them, and they had been very hungry.

23. tux̌ʷ tusugʷahəgʷəʔ, suləlaləlalx̌.

It was just what was talked about, reminiscences.

24. diłəxʷ kʷi bəsłəčisəbs tiʔəʔ swədəbš.

Suddenly someone arrived at the Swinomish.

25. baləcuq̓ʷəlq̓ʷəlab, gʷəčadəs, gʷəgʷatgʷatəs.

They were roasting food, wherever it was, whoever it was.

26. tulabatuʔ, diłəxʷ sšubaliʔ čəł təš stagʷəxʷ, tiʔəʔ dəxʷgʷəlalalikʷ tə ləbatuʔ ʔə tiʔəʔ ʔayədləb.

The sheep were there, when we were dying of hunger, so sheep were killed by your acquaintance.

27. x̌ʷuləxʷ ʔəgʷəʔ ləʔukʷukʷbitagʷəl.

They just made fun of each other.

28. huy huy kʷi gʷəsx̌ayəb, xʷiʔ ləgʷədəxʷtucdupəd čəł, hiwiltxʷ łi.

Then when the laughing was over, we weren't guilty of shooting them, go on with it.

29. gʷəl ləlaʔtəb čəł ʔə tiʔił swədəbš dibəł kʷi gʷəgʷəlald tiʔił ləbatuʔ, kʷa cił x̌uhuydxʷ həlgʷəʔ tiʔił sgʷaʔs gʷəl bəkʷil.

And the Swinomish accused us of killing the sheep, however, they ate theirs and finished it up.

30. ʔa łčil dxʷʔal tiʔəʔ swatixʷtəd, ʔəstagʷtagʷəxʷ.

There they were, they arrived to the land, hungry.

31. xʷuʔələʔ ʔušayil kʷi ʔiłčaʔkʷ, dəxʷtucils ʔə kʷi dču sqigʷəc.

Maybe someone hunted downland, was the reason that one deer was killed.

32. xʷuʔələʔ xʷiʔ kʷi sq̓ʷəlałci ʔə tiʔəʔ cił sqigʷəc gʷəl ləʔululł kʷi pastəd, huy łalisəbəxʷ ʔəlgʷəʔ.

Possibly the deer meat was not cooked and the white people were water traveling and beached near to them.

33. čad̓isəbəxʷ tiʔəʔ cugʷəxʷ tuʔa ləbatuʔ.

Then the one sheep that was there was hidden.

34. xʷiʔ ləcukʷ caadiɬ, bəkʷ tiʔiɬ paspastəd tuʔuhuy ʔəsʔistəʔ, ləcugʷəlald tiʔəʔ labatuʔ ʔə tiʔiɬ ʔəsɬaɬlil.

It was not them alone; the white people all did the same, they were killing the sheep of those who lived there.

35. lil ti sʔatəgʷi tiʔiɬ labatuʔ ʔal tiʔiɬ dču sčəgʷucid kʷəɬ gʷəl x̌ʷuɬ ƛuʔiɬugʷəlali ʔə tiʔiɬəʔ paspastəd, gʷəl tubaʔabyitəb tiʔiɬ ʔaciɬtalbixʷ ʔə tiʔiɬ labatulqiʔ, cukʷ tiʔiɬ biʔac tiʔiɬ ƛusuʔələd ʔə tiʔiɬ pastəd, tiʔəʔ cədiɬ tuʔugʷəčəɬ swatixʷtəd.

The sheep were kept far away on this one island, it was said, and the white people killed them, and they gave the Indians the wool, only the meat (they kept) for their food of the white people, those who were out looking for land [homesteading ?].

36. ʔugʷəčidup, ʔudᶻəkʷdᶻəkʷ.

Traveling about searching for land.

37. čadəxʷ tiʔiɬ tuʔəxʷqalqaligʷəd dxʷʔal sʔələd dxʷʔal sʔələd dxʷʔal sʔələd.

Where are those who were worried about food, about food, about food.

38. tugʷəɬ sʔux̌ʷləb tassawədəxʷ čələb gʷəl lətucduptub čələb.

That belonged when you went, you would have provisions of food, and shooting would take place for you folks.

39. cugʷəxʷ ʔubasʔələd, ʔa ʔu kʷi sʔələd čəɬ gʷədəxʷ təsaladiʔəd kʷi labətuʔ, xʷiʔəxʷ gʷəstabəxʷ gʷətusʔələd čəɬ.

Was that the only food [available]? Did we have any food that we needed to hit sheep over the head? We had no [other] food.

40. liləxʷ, liləxʷ kʷa tiʔiɬ ʔal bituliʔəʔ gʷəl ʔəẏdxʷ kʷi suxʷil ʔə kʷi šəxʷəb gʷəčadəs,

Far away, they were far away at Victoria before they found the wind when it blew, wherever it was.

41. kʷi dəxʷʔaʔs dxʷʔal buusaɬdat.

Thus they were there for four days.

42. suxʷil gʷəl ƛupuʔalikʷ gʷəl gʷəʔuləx̌il, puʔalikʷ gʷəl ƛuləx̌il, puʔalikʷ gʷəl gʷəʔuləxʷil.

There was wind and it blew and it became light, blew and it became day, it blew and it became night.

43. stugʷaq̓ʷ.

South wind.

44. ʔutagʷtagʷəxʷ.

They became hungry.

45. ___ cut ʔəgʷəʔ ʔə kʷədi dəxʷdxʷʔas təciɬ kʷi dəxʷ ʔələɬads ʔəgʷəʔ gʷəl baʔəẏdxʷəxʷ ʔəgʷəʔ tə ciɬ baləcuq̓ʷəlq̓ʷəlab.

___ themselves where they were that they ate and they found some who were roasting food.

46. ʔu. cikcikicut dxʷʔal stagʷəxʷ tiʔəʔ ƛuʔuʔux̌ʷ dxʷdiʔabac.

Oh, the hunger pains they had, those who went to the other side (to Vancouver Island).

47. tuʔəx̌id, tuʔəx̌id kʷi dəxʷxʷiʔs gʷətuxʷəltəbalcs ʔəgʷəʔ.

Why, why was it that they did not have guns?

48. cickʷ baʔəsq̓əččut ʔəgʷəʔ ʔə kʷi stəḱstəḱiʔ.

They were also (in great danger) from the enemy stəḱi.

49. ʔa tubax̌ʷad̓ətəb.

There were some who were murdered.

50. bad x̌ʷuʔaləʔ ʔə tiʔiʔiɬəʔ ʔiɬidusbiʔ kʷi tuʔutucutəb təš ti stəḱiʔ gʷəl tuʔatəbəd.

It was the father of the Cladoosby who was shot by the stəḱi and he died.

51. gʷəl batuʔukʷədubu ḱʷəɬ kʷi dyəl̓yəlab yəx̌i tuyəcəbtub ʔə kʷəsi stəḱi.

And one of my relatives managed to save himself because a female stəḱi warned him.

52. ʔuʔux̌ʷad̓ətəb ti stəḱi ʔə ti ʔal swədəbš, ɬušubali čələb.

The Swinomish killed the stəḱi, you folks will perish.

53. tiʔiɬəʔ tud̓əḱʷd̓əḱʷ, ləcugʷəčalikʷ, huy bəlkʷəxʷ tiʔiʔəʔ.

Those who were traveling about, looking, then they returned.

54. bəkʷ ʔəsʔəx̌id suhuy ʔə kʷi ʔaciɬtalbixʷ.

The Indians were doing everything.

55. hay masi diɬ shuys tiʔiɬ dsuləlalalx̌.

Praises, mercy, that finishes my reminiscing.

56. LM: dayəxʷ haʔɬ, həbu.

Leon Metcalf says: That was very good, haboo.

---

1. At this point, taqʷšəblu discontinued transcribing this side of the tape. She fastforwarded to the end of side 2 to see what was on side one. Notes on the outside of the reel to reel box indicated there were stories on the tape. taqʷšəblu found no sʔəyəhub on either side. SSP continued on side number 1 of reel to reel tape number 60 [LM]. Here we find SSP's son AS talking to her. (P 26)

2. Dr. Andie Palmer – Lushootseed student, Canadian citizen, and anthropologist at the University of Alberta – says she has heard or read of an island in the Vancouver Island area where a farmer kept a herd of sheep that survived without any care from him and these animals were taken by one and all for their own use. (P 36)

Jacob

Jacob's Quests

Jacob Wahalchu, the Suquamish chief who died in 1911 at the reputed age of 112, gave Edward Curtis (1913: 97-100) a remarkable account of his own quests. Though he carefully denied that most of these powers were acquired by him, some of this rhetoric was pro forma protection of his spiritual partnerships.

Jacob did not begin questing until he was a young adult because he dreaded the ordeal. He began spontaneously when, returning from hunting deer by torch light, he found his mother opening a pit oven filled with fish and clams. Hungry from his night long hunt, he grabbed a steaming rock cod, which his mother slapped from his hands, scolding him that children should not take the best food until the elders have eaten. She called him worthless and insensitive. Hurt, angry, and ashamed, he began to cry and ran into the woods. That night he decided to undertake a quest and went to the cemetery at Eagle Harbor. There, he climbed into a burial canoe with the remaining bones. Nothing happened so the next morning, he removed the bones and tried to use the canoe to go across the inlet, but it was useless so he put it back.

Instead, he walked until he was opposite Old Man House, the extremely long house associated with Chief Seattle. Remembering a lake in the woods where others had quested, he made a log raft, crossed the channel, and went to find a marsh where the lake had been. Determined to succeed, he spent four days fasting nearby, tying himself upright to a fir tree each night so he would no sleep. The fourth night, a human voice called to him to look north, where he saw a light that directed him there.

The next morning he went north to Point No Point and on to the beach below Foulweather Bluff, where he saw a huge oncoming wave tossing logs before it. He turned to run, but was transfixed by the sound of howling wolves. He knew spirits were near and stood to receive them. Two ducks, on white and one black, approached him on the water. Unimpressed by what he took to be minor powers, he backed away, knowing that if he turned he exposed himself to their wrath. The ducks submerged. The howling continued, gradually changing into the words of a song that said he had made a mistake in refusing this power. Jacob knew the tune to be that of an important wealth spirit. Depressed, he tried for another five days to have the power return, but then gave up, too starved to continue. A short ways south, he met people camping, who gave him food and shelter. When he regained his strength, he borrowed a canoe and went home.

After a time, he decided to quest again, going to Fletcher Bay and walked along the beach. Nothing happened until a log drifted in, struck the point, and fire flashed toward him. Immediately, the gravel turned to quicksand and his feet sank. Three more flashes came toward him, but he dodged them, watching smoke rise from the spots were they struck behind him. A woman's voice called out in woe that they had missed him and failed. From the tune, Jacob knew that this was a curing power, but since his parents had advised him against this profession, knowing full well the life threatening dangers to himself and his family from rival doctors, he backed away and left.

A year or two later, Jacob went to Alki Point after fasting, ostensibly to hunt ducks. He paddled out to pick up his spent arrows and, while leaning over the side, saw a large house on the bottom of the Sound with many salmon resting on its roof. Herds of elk stood around the outside. Excited, Jacob went home to get his father to help with the hunt, but he was not there. His mother, understanding the situation, sent him back alone, but, by then the house was gone. A faint refrain told him that this was the greatest wealth power.

The next time, Jacob fasted at Deception Pass for eight days before he dreamed he was in the middle of a canoe between an old couple. The man looked back and the woman forward. The old man told Jacob that he would live to be very old, like this couple, and that no one could harm him because these elders could see in all directions. In this way, Jacob got long life power, confirmed by his advanced age.

Again, Jacob quested by swimming from Whidbey Island to a small island at the north end of Deception Pass. Exhausted, he crawled onto the beach and recalling that Cowlitz dug into the ground with their hand to make contact with "the other side," he did the same. All night he moved sand, praying for clams, mussels, elk, fish, and plenty. The next day, he walked the beach to stay awake. He dug all the second night until, just before dawn, a voice called out and he looked up to see a standing war spear, which began to dance. Then it changed into a stone war club, which also danced and sang that it was quick tempered and ate men quickly. This was a warrior power.

Jacob soon became prosperous and influential. Then he married and his questing came to an end because marital relations were not liked by the spirit powers because they reeked of mortality.

Auburn's Collector of Indian Myths
By Charlotte D. Widrig

Seattle Times 12 September 1952

STORIES of the Chinook Wind, the moon and the stars and the five mallard-duck brothers who brought the rain, and of the mythical origins of many natural Pacific Northwest landmarks are filed, indexed and cross-indexed in the home of Arthur C. Ballard of Auburn, a field-research authority on Indian life.

Although he began his absorbing hobby in middle age, Ballard's childhood memories and family background greatly sharpen his personal interest and understanding of Indian affairs.

Ballard's parents were among the early pioneers of this region, migrating in 1857 from the New England states, because they considered the soil worn out, to the Pacific Coast where crops were reputedly prodigious. The family took a circuitous route to the opposite side of the continent, crossing the Isthmus of Panama on a little train which moved so slowly that the children hopped on and off, picking flowers that grew along the way.

After a seven-year sojourn in Oregon, the Ballards traveled on by covered wagon to Washington and permanently settled in 1866 where the city of Auburn now stands. William Rankin Ballard, one of the boys who picked the posies at Panama, later became captain of the steamer *Zephyr* and the Ballard District of Seattle bears his name today.

Not even a wagon road had been put through the White River Valley when the family took up a homestead beside a river which flowed through the area at that time. Indian villages of the Muckleshoots were not far away. Ballard's father built a home and went about farming his land, growing potatoes mainly.

Arthur was born on the property in 1876. As he was the last child of the family, his parents liked to have him nearby and his world of adventure when he was a young boy was limited. Besides, he had plenty of walking going to and from school.

The Indians always were friendly and helpful. Men were employed to harvest the crops and some of the women helped with housework and washing. One of the incidents Ballard remembers best is his mother's account of sickness and sorrow when diphtheria, the scourge of that era, struck the family. One of his older brothers died and the Indians living nearby gathered beside the house to sing a mourning dirge of sympathy.

The pioneer mother in times of trouble would be worn and tired to the point of exhaustion. During another epidemic, Betsy Whatcom, the Indian woman who had mothered the King children after an early-day massacre, volunteered to come in and take over the care of the sick baby, Arthur Ballard, 2 years old. She forthwith stationed herself at his cradle, rocked it when he stirred and materially assisted in nursing him back to health.

As a young man Ballard attended Whitworth College in Sumner, one of several denominational colleges which were springing up in the Pacific Northwest. Later he attended the University of Washington, majoring in Latin. In 1901 he became a teacher at the Klickitat Academy at Goldendale, a Presbyterian institution.

This career did not last more than a few years, but Ballard's interest in education and civic affairs never has dwindled. The ground on which the Auburn Carnegie Library stands is one of his donations to the city.

Ballard's major hobby was born in 1911 when he overheard a chance remark to the effect that Indians in general were not understood. This remark piqued [2] his curiosity and started him on his research into a subject which was to become a lifetime pursuit. He learned the language of the nearby tribes and began to meet with a few of the old-timers and record their stories – stories of the origins of names, cosmic myths, ceremonials, tales of adventure and first-hand history of early days.

The deeper Ballard delved the more intrigued he became, until the subject overwhelmed his leisure and gradually became a romantic escape from the workaday world, a psychological effect not uncommon among those who "ride a hobbyhorse" and ride it hard.

"I've always been working against time," he explained, "with many a day lost on a wild-goose chase."

But all in all, Ballard feels that his achievement has justified the years of effort and the large sums of money he has spent on this subject, for the source of such material has been lost inexorably with the passing of the older generation. The Indians had no written language and Ballard regrets that the young folk know but little of the old traditional primitive myths. Many of these stories he has compiled in an anthology, as yet unpublished [and lost], entitled "*Listen, My Nephew!*"

In the Indian myths and ceremonials which Ballard has studied so painstakingly, he finds the germs of science, drama, art, music and history. The Indian yearning to understand the forces of nature – life and death, summer and winter, fire and water, flood and drought, rain, snow, hall, and such – mixed them up with magic, superstition and psychology in attempts to explain and influence natural and supernatural powers.

Indian friends among Ballard's acquaintance have been responsible largely for the success of his studies. Many have co-operated further by reproducing ceremonial objects used in the dim past.

The two boards illustrated on this page belong to a complete half-size set of six known as "swowsh" {swawawsh} boards, used in an imaginary journey to the under-world as practiced by the Duwamish, Skykomish and Snoqualmie Tribes. The medicine men would sing and put on a great act as the shaman went below, [3] crossed a mythical river on his way to the underworld and attempted to recover a wandering soul, stolen by the dead, and return it to the sick person on earth to whom it belonged.

The boards are of cedar, painted with ceremonial significance. The dots on them represent rain, symbolical of casting a fog so the dead couldn't catch them on their return journey. Other pictures represent mythical objects of magic to aid the shaman further.

When the boards were not in use they were kept hidden, for it was considered bad luck for anyone who disturbed them, even unawares. When they were in use people turned their faces aside and covered the faces of their children, for the magic was too powerful to be looked upon by ordinary human eye.

Of all the Indian legends, the one which appeals to me most is the Duwamish story of Quarry Hill, for this was the scene of many of my own childhood adventures. Often did we scramble, especially in the springtime, over the rocks and through the woods, lured on and on by flaming red-currant and dogwood blossoms that covered the hilltop. Little did we realize we were trespassing on the hallowed home of the Grandmother of the Chinook Wind! For, according to Ballard's story, that is where the Old Lady lived.

The myth is one of nature, a myth explaining summer and winter and, in a way, springtime and resurrection of life. It tells of a time when the North Wind claimed the valley with an icy breath until young and old perished in his relentless grip. But, the stalwart grandson of the Chinook Wind came to the rescue, battled on and on until he melted the snow in the mountains and poured the Duwamish River through the North Wind's frozen barrier. The proofs that are given for the reality of the myth are Quarry Hill, the Duwamish River and the outcropping of rock on the other side of the valley.

As an anticlimax to the story it may be noted that Quarry Hill, a familiar sight from Highway 99 southeast of the Duwamish Bridge, is being demolished slowly by rock-crushing operations. Contrasting the safe method used today, I recall the old crusher on the opposite side of the hill back in the years when I went to grade school. The long walk home was never dull, for plodding along between the river and the hill we always were alert to the cries of a blasting crew who shouted "FIRE!" three times before a fuse was touched off. Rocks at times would plummet clear across the field where we hid with pounding hearts pressed close against the nearest protecting stump we could find.

Shocked by the terrifying fright experienced, we could have believed easily the Indian's lament – "they're breaking up the Old Lady's bones!"

"SWOWSH" BOARDS, which were used by the Indians in ceremonies representing visitation to the underworld to retrieve stolen souls.

Ballard holds a natural spruce knot with Indian carved face and hair made from strands of cedar bark – a ceremonial representation of the "Spirit of the Earth."

Naming Culture
Among Lushootseeds of Puget Sound

Abstract

Hereditary *names*, today and in the past, bind together the Lushootseeds of Puget Sound. They crosscut considerations of culture history, gender, age, rank, descent, kinship, pedigree, residence, territory, and waterway. They are the focus of the basic institutions of *person*, *place*, *sept*, and *power* from immortal spirits. They are at the heart of the crucial factors of "blood" and of "mud" – kinship and landscape. By good fortune, examples of the renowned names who "begat" the present day world can be retrieved from fieldnotes and documents, and confirmed by living holders of these names. In sum, these data allow the fuller integration of the Salish into wider patterns and traditions so typical of the rest of the Northwest Coast.

Introduction

For the Lushootseeds of Puget Sound, *names*, above all, provide the nexus (lynchpin) intersecting their concepts of kinship, pedigree, territory, and culture history. Any full understanding of this ethnohistory of naming, however, has been obscured by a lack of available data, especially in publications. Indeed, most of the supporting information occurs only in fieldnotes provided by fluent speakers of high rank, who were themselves holders of crucial ancestral names.[1] Once these data were assembled, moreover, the relationship between these Coast Salish and other cultures of the North Pacific becomes much more clear. Salish is a language family distinctive of the Northwest, divided into Coast and Interior branches.[2]

Like the "begats" of the Judeo-Christian Bible, a sequence of names establishes family lines of descent which standout distinctly within these bilateral societies. Over time, these names are successively embodied in a person within a household which is anchored to a series of locales specifically keyed to needed resources. Today that household is conceptual, but until a century ago it was physical and multiple.

---

[1] The prime trove of these fieldnotes come from the amazingly productive years in the early 1950s when Sally Snyder, a graduate student of Melville Jacobs, worked on the Swinomish reservation and among landless ("unrecognized") Skagits and Sauks living upriver. Her life nor career was never easy so we are especially fortunate that copies of her notes are preserved in Special Collections at the University of Washington, though they are closed to the public and their use requires permission from a board of trustees. My admiration of her notes has been confirmed by thirty years involvement with these communities, where I am honored to be a friend of Goliah, Lahalbid, and Kwaskadub.

[2] Lushootseed (Puget) belongs to the Coast Salish Branch and, for English speakers, seems daunting because of its complex phonemes, the same sound often pronounced with four variants, and a confusion of the sounds of B and M, D and N that confounds the ethnohistoric record.

Unlike the Tsimshian with over a dozen chronological episodes in their ethno-ethnohistory (Miller 1997b), Lushootseeds recognize fewer eras.[3] Little is said about creation *de novo* of the world. Instead, successive recreations mark distinct eras, each following a global destruction caused by human arrogance, overcrowding, and disrespect for the world.

Elders now dead hinted that there was a local genesis which was known only to shamans, while the recreations were largely common knowledge. Key members of chiefly families, however, had much more detailed versions of these changes that included *dicta* – special words, spells, and formulae that profoundly affected all other beings in the world, and could be used to help or harm. Invoking the Creator in these *dicta* and prayers also suggests an original creation.[4] Though now mostly known as *shaq si'ab* "above lord" under missionary influence, the persistent use of *xa'xa* "taboo, sacred, forbidden" indicates great antiquity for this deification.

Because important names are eternal, all fieldworkers in the Northwest have disconcerting moments when it is unclear if an elder is speaking of a mythological person from the dawn of time, a protohistoric figure, or one of their current relatives – all with the same name.

The reformers, by convention, are known as Changers, sometimes Transformers, who set the world right and prepare the way for modern humans. In the past century, as natives have stopped speaking Lushootseed in favor of English, what seem to have been teams of siblings have now been individuated as a single named person. In Puget Sound, the major Changer has become identified with the Moon, while his less powerful brother became the Sun.

All of the standard cataclysms seem to be reported, firmly based in local geology, including destruction by flood (with canoes as escape arks), quake (viewed as the world capsizing), fire (easily correlated with volcanic eruptions like that of Mt St Helens), and plague (with survivors protected by special rituals envisioned by named prophets). Among Lushootseeds, at least one renowned name is associated with each of these destructions, as well as systems of power provided in compensation for the lost lives. In a later section, the famous name of Lehalbid provides an example of this close association with a crisis.

---

[3] This paper builds upon my prior work with Tshimshian eras (Miller 1997b) for the matrilineal north coast, and vastly improves the my prior discussion of kinship and naming among Lushootseeds (Miller 1997a, 1999). More recent effort has used native names from fieldnotes to reconstitute aboriginal villages burned out so the prime "vacant land" could be homesteaded (Miller 2000).

[4] The significance of high-rank names are better known closer to the northern coast. Wilson Duff (1952, 85) noted their importance among the Stalo of the Fraser River, while commenting that each researcher (Franz Boas, Diamond Jenness, Charles Hill-Tout) was given a different list and pedigree of these important hereditary names – indicating that the actual name was merely a marker for the crucial concept of rank. Creation epics are reported in some detail for the Stalo, from Old Pierre, a shaman, and for the Nuxalk (Bella Coola), as summarized in Miller (1999).

names

Institutions

Native Lushootseed society in Puget Sound involved concepts of territory, kinship, pedigree, and culture history. It was and is organized around practical considerations of gender, age, rank, descent, residence, and waterway. In more general terms, these are concerned with *person*, *place*, and *sept*, a kinship grouping traced through both maternal and paternal lines over at least four generations. Over all of these was and is the all-important fourth factor of religion, namely *power* from immortal spirits. Subsets conferring power focus on the high god (*xa'xa*), immortals (guardian spirits), ghosts, and *dicta* (special words). As appropriate for this rainy climate, the basic symbolic opposition underlying these factors is that of "blood" and of "mud" – kinship and landscape.

Culturally, the building blocks of this society, increasing in size, included notions of the individual person (composed of a gendered aging body, a mind, and souls with spirit allies), of the house (including hearthers, locals, and distant kin), of the canoe (transport across time and space, distinguished by habitat as forest, prairie, river, or sea), and of the world (the entire drainage, linked both to resident immortals through rituals and to more remote peoples and places through marriage, ritual, and trade).

Person ~ "blood" *stúlig^{w}əd*

Personhood was characterized by gender as male or female, by age as older or younger, and by ranking as freeborn or slave. The leaders of households and communities constituted the elite, "owning" (in the sense of holding and hosting) famous names and resource locations. Other members of the freeborn rank were commoners, valuable for their labor and support but otherwise undistinguished.

A few transgendered individuals are known from fieldnotes, but these did not constitute a "third gender". Instead each was identified anatomically since natives once wore few if any clothes beyond rain gear when necessary.

Lushootseeds along the coast emphasized rank and class, while those inland, upriver, and in the southern Sound held more Plateau ideals of a kin-based society. "Southern Puget Sound culture emphasized spirit quests and had a lesser emphasis on inherited privileges than the Northerners" (Roberts 1975: 32, 35, 77), and hence provided the birthplace for the more democratic beliefs known as the Indian Shaker Church, recognizing a universal, omnipotent God.

Space ~ Place ~ "mud"

In terms of the overall Puget Basin, Marian Smith (1940: 7), relying on her fieldwork among the Puyallup and Nisqually, devised a spatial model, based on units of decreasing size, for describing how native peoples related to their watersheds. She explicitly recognized that the greatest allegiance and loyalty coincided with the entire drainage system of Puget Sound. Take these units in reverse or increasing size, better indicates the progression.

Therefore, within each watershed, group cohesion, loyalties, and affiliations grew in terms of (a) hearth mates eating together at the fires within a household, (b) residents of all neighboring houses, (c) birthright locals – those born there as distinct from inlaws, visitors, and foreigners, (d) seasonal settlements, camps, and resorts, (e) wider community networks, (f) tributary waterways, and (g) the entire drainage of a river.

Each river constituted a "tribe", designated by the endings of *-bš* (-bsh) (if more cohesive) or as -bixʷ (-byuh) 'bunch' if more dispersed. The ending *-mish* in English (Snohomish, Skykomish) is the same as *-bsh* in Lushootseed. Rivers and streams with side trails linked all of these together, while trails along and across ridges gave access to separate tribes.

Membership within each drainage derived from the subtle, discerning, and valued appreciation of customs such that insiders, in contrast to outsiders, understood the complexities of "the feud, the snub, the verbal innuendo" and accordingly "were appropriate guests for a ceremonial feast" (Roberts 1975: 79).

Traditionally, the crux of the entire system and the basic reason for gathering people together was the display of bonds with particular immortal powers. No one could be successful without such help. For centuries, leading families had bonded with the most powerful spirits in their locales. Lesser family members, some commoners, and even a few slaves could also have spirit partners, but these were less powerful than those of the leaders.

Kin

In addition to considerations of space and place ("mud") within an overall drainage, Lushootseeds also traced kinship through the bloodlines of both parents. The immediate family grouping (derived from four grandparents) is technically called a *kindred*, while the huge extended family, which was and is transnational or intertribal (though eight great grandparents), is a called a *sept*.

Among ordinary kinspeople, a *nodal kindred* formed around its senior member(s), often the grandparents as a married couple. After the death of the last surviving spouse, the kindred regrouped around the marriage of their oldest child – if fit and able – and so on, through a generation or two. Leading families, however, formed a *stem kindred*, which continued across generations because the stem consisted of the line of holders of its famous, renowned name, conferring control ("management") of locations and resources that made up the "estate" of these nobles. Influence from Wakashans of Vancouver Island may have led to occasional *ramages*, descent based on birth order, especially a line composed only of eldest sons or eldest daughters.

Traced through all of the bloodlines of great grandparents, a sept had its own network that even now extends beyond space and time, as a "nondiscrete, nonlocalized, property-holding group" (Suttles 1987: 210). It existed wherever its members lived, and included ancestors from the past and children yet unborn. It had no fixed size nor place, except in family lore explaining the origin of its famous names. It was managed by the oldest able elder (male or female), who provided guidance and 'advice' about the proper use of resources and the transmission of names, positions, and artifacts within the kindred. If it held a famous name, stories about past holders of that name and their fea(s)ts served to specify places where the kindred indeed had a birthright through past actions, particularly on-going partnerships between the spirits of these places and family members. These most powerful spirits (conferring wealth, power, bounty) dwell in remote locations, either high up in the mountains or deep in the water, either ocean or river. Its most prized possession has been called 'advice' (xwdikw [x̌ʷdikʷ], also teachings, knowhow, wisdom), which included special formulae (*dicta*) to control activities for good or ill, genealogical details, and a body of stories from the beginning of time.

House *al'al*

Major nodes in this overall system were cedar plank houses, once located along the shore near spots rich in local resources, such as a salmon stream, berry patch, and hunting territory. Even spirit beings lived in such houses, though only special people could see them. Beyond this house node were and are at least three concentric rings occupied by allies, by competitors for regional status, and, third, by strangers (Roberts 1975: 82). During the late 1800s, officials broke up these communal homes. Instead, single family dwellings were built with milled lumber, though many people shared these rooms. Today, these households are conceptual and symbolic, though periodically reconstituted inside local school gyms, tribal halls, and ceremonial smokehouses when they host family namings, potlatches, and other displays of their generosity.

These community halls, sometimes inspired by styles of ancient housing, are still used for ceremonies, feasts, and gatherings, particularly in winter. These buildings and events continue such traditions. Regional networks also continue, now discussed according to modern reservations instead of former watersheds, though there is considerable overlap between these past and present locations.

The park-like old growth forests and the rugged terrain left few level spaces where people could live, so each house in every town had about fifty occupants, with placement within the house reflecting rank in local and regional society. Thus, with a door at the front or side, the owner of the house and his family had the best protected spot in a back corner, away from the drafts at the doorway. They constituted a nobility, providing leaders for varied community tasks (Miller 1997a). The hallmark of nobility was being hard working, steady, and reliable.

Along the sides were families of ordinary common folks, who contributed food and upkeep to the household in return for the prestige of living with wealthy relatives. The least desirable and most exposed places in the front of the house harbored slaves, who had either been captured in raids, purchased, or born to their lot. Each family had its own hearth fire along a side of the house, since eating together as a 'commensal unit' was what defined close, caring , trust relations. Nobles usually had more than one wife, but each seems to have had a separate fireplace hearth to feed her own children and their playmates.

On important occasions, particularly during winter, the head of the house hosted public events on behalf of all the residents. Accordingly, most families moved out to other accommodations, either nearby homes or mat tents, to make room for guests. Two or three large, public fires were lit down the middle (along the long central axis) of the big house. Huge amounts of food – gathered by slaves and housemates and prepared by women under the direction of the senior wife of the host – were served throughout the festivities.

Changes in social status – such as naming, puberty, marriage, or death – provided the occasions for hosting, for inviting in guests. The more prominent a family, the more people would be invited from furthest away. Important families had far flung networks of friends and kin, forged by marriage, adoption, gifts, help, trade, and social obligations. They also named their infants at the youngest possible moment, when it was clear the heir would live.

Today, all of the religions and sects of the modern world can be found among the native peoples of Puget Sound, but they co-exist with much more ancient beliefs and practices based in the landscape. Even the modern churches, however, have distinctly native features because families and communities continue to worship together. In the northern sound, Catholic for 150 years, cedar boughs freshly cut from the forest and flutes carved from cedar limbs are used during the Mass. Similarly, Protestant churches on reservations will feature native designs and concepts such as the "Great Spirit" in their services.

Two modern religious expressions, moreover, continue ancient beliefs and traditions associated with the spirits of the land. One is sometimes called the Smokehouse Religion because it uses public buildings in the form of ancestral, communal, cedar-plank houses. It continues the tradition of personal spirit helpers and special regard to certain places, often remote and sacred, on the land and in the water. The other is the Indian Shaker Church – founded near Olympia in 1882 by the death and revival of John Slocum – incorporated under the protection of Washington state law in 1910. It blends ancient beliefs with those of Christianity into a distinctive pattern of worship now spread from California to Canada and Montana (Miller 1999).

Resources

Lushootseed natives had an extremely complicated social life which was comparable to the complexity of farmers elsewhere in the world. Here, however, they largely lived by harvesting (without the effort planting) the bounty that nature provided for them. They did enhance plots and fields of plants with edible roots, such as wild carrots, onions, camas, and other bulbs; but this wise cultivation of nature was not the same as intensive farming (Miller 2005). When natives encouraged the growth of certain wild plants, they unobtrusively left seeds and roots in moist locales. After traders from the Hudson's Bay Company introduced natives to "Irish" [Andean] potatoes, these prior talents at tending wild foods allowed them to quickly raise such tubers as a cash crop (Suttles 1987: 137-151). Traditionally, people moved with the seasons to camps near available natural foods. The climate was mild, due to the offshore Japanese and California Currents, and rainy, so the region abounded with plants and animals.

Chief among these foods were five species of salmon which (more properly, who) spawned and died in the rivers each year, although some years the runs were more abundant than others. By working hard for a few weeks, a household could catch and dry enough fish to meet winter needs of the family and its guests. Yet people did not live by fish alone. After the summer fish runs, families went into the uplands and mountains to collect dozens of kinds of berries, which were also stored for winter use. Men hunted a variety of mammals, both sea and land, during the fall and winter, depending on where they lived. In the spring, fresh greens and early fish runs enriched the diet of stored supplies. By prudently and generously using resources which were locally "anchored," a household could add to their respected "radiance" throughout a larger region (Miller 1999) by sharing with the needy and hosting the great at public events where witnesses were called and gifted to remember and, if need be, testify about what had happened in terms of family names and privileges that had been publicly proclaimed.

K^w*askadub*

The best-known name from fieldwork, fieldnotes, and documents is that of Kwaskadub [$\overset{w}{\text{k}}$askadəb] "roasted, burnt head". Chiefly names are usually distinguished by the endings –*qd* [–*qn*] 'head' or –*qs* 'nose, point' indicating their duties as deciders or leaders (Bates, Hess, and Hilbert 1994: 127, 178, 179).

The lone appearance of this name in print is dramatic. In his dictated autobiography, John Fornsby, a shaman, told how, as boy picking berries near Skagit City, he entered the overgrown feasting house of his great grandfather, and found him still laid out on the rear platform. Later, the body was reburied behind this house and then moved to the Swinomish Catholic Cemetery. After this potlatch house washed away in a flood, one of its carved houseposts (3 x 4 x 8 feet) was later found and installed by Lummi workmen paid by Fornsby at a famous potlatch when graves from a nearby island were moved to the same cemetery.

That Kwaskadub was a famous trader with several homes at strategic locations. His winter and thus primary home was on Penn Cove at Coupeville on Whidbey Island. The home at Skagit City where he lay in state was at the lower end of a two-mile-long logjam that forced migrating salmon to pool before they wove their way upriver. Local garden grew huge nettle plants (some eight feet tall), processed into fiber for nets and other fabrics. These nets were specifically adapted to microhabitats. This logjam determined canoe travel on other rivers until it was dynamited away in 1878 (Collins 1974: 39).

Kwaskadub has several adult children who forged dynastic marriages. More famous and much better documented is the son named Sneatlum (*sditleb* in Lushootseed), who was a fur trade middleman for Ft Nisqually, founded in the south Sound in 1833. Sneatlum was also a Catholic lay leader. At least one of his wives was Makah, from the far northwest tip of Washington State. After Sneatlum died 16 December 1852, a carved wooden effigy dressed in his own clothes was set up on what became Sneatlum Point on eastern Whidbey Island (Gibbs 1877: 203). Another Kwaskadub son flaunted the rules of rank by taking up with a slave girl, who thereafter was named 'mistake'. One of his daughters married into Chehalis.

Kwaskadub's nephews (sibling unknown) included Goliah, a community spokesman drafted by Governor Isaac Stevens into signing the 1855 Treaty of Pt Elliot (Mukilteo) as "chief" of northern Sound tribes. As an official speaker, though not of noble family, Goliah, having the advantage of some English fluency, appealed to American authorities.

Goliah's brother, known only in fieldnotes, was sadsəhəbix^w [sad$^{\prime}$əhəbix^w], who maintained a fortified home at Quartermaster Harbor between Maury and Vashon Islands, an important portage in the south Sound. Both Penn Cove, the Lower Skagit homeland, and Quartermaster Harbor were sheltered bays deep into islands, providing portage shortcuts. Famous as a warrior and slaver, he also had crucial access to the fur trade at Fort Nisqually. Because he raided the nearby Duwamish for slaves, his fort was under constant threat so in old age "this village moved to Gig Harbor. The movement took place not long before the treaty" (Smith 1940: 11).[5] Throughout this region, competition took many forms, not all of them involving weapons and warfare.

---

[5] *The Puyallup-Nisqually* (Smith 1940, 11) is based on Marian Wesley Smith, Microfilm Roll #3 (Reel A1738), British Columbia Archives, MSS 2689: Box 6, Folder 9 (Houses 26); Royal

Moreover, a clearer view of the international and intertribal complexity of the region is shown by the ability of important families to set themselves up in foreign territory and to take advantage of slaving upon locals and trade at the British fort. Of especial note, via intermarriage among local chiefly families, these famous hereditary names thereby become legitimately claimed by heirs.

Both Kwaskadub and Sneatlum appear in the Fort Langley journal during June, July, and August of 1830 as "the two Scadchats Chiefs – Neetlum & Weskienum" (Maclachlan 1998: 150, 156). On Friday, August 10th, Sneatlum's son married the daughter of a Cowichan leader, variously known as Joshua, Josia, Old Joe, or Shashia. In 1847, Paul Kane painted portraits of him and his son Cul-chil-hum. At least one other son is mentioned, but the father died blind and heirless in 1870. Cowichans, then as now, had winter villages on Vancouver Island. After Ft Langley was founded by the HBC in 1827, its journal noted that these island villages had permanent camps on the mainland along the Fraser River to take full advantage of salmon runs.

Between 1780-1810, *Ba'da'ył* (*ma'na'ył* in Straits Salish), a granddaughter of Kwaskadub, was captured by Klallam raiders from Dungeness who quickly realized her rank and married her to a noble son. At the wedding, the groom wore an enormous rawhide mask. Kwaskadub gave his family ten slaves, a seagoing canoe, and many blankets, and, in return, received twenty slaves, a canoe, and other goods (Elmendorf 1993: 108-10).

Alice Campbell, married to the Upper Skagit chief descended from the famous prophet Captain Camel (Campbell), explained the upriver source for the name Kwaskadub.

> Long ago there were people who turned into rocks [in the Flood]. This Kwaskadub was the name of one [of them] way up on the Skagit. It is the name of one of Andrew Joe's relatives. They came up to ask the people there for a name (certain people used to go to certain places to obtain a name). If they had known, they could have asked the Sbalix here [Concrete, Wa] for a name (Sally Snyder, Box 108, Folder 5, Page 58).

What is noteworthy about her report is the transport of a renowned name from an earlier era into a later one. Kwaskadub survived the Flood by being carried upriver and then turned into stone, with his powers intact. When the renewed coastal family came looking for an ancient name, they were reminded of the upriver rock and so revived that name, neatly bracketing the all-important salmon runs between the downriver resource site at the lower logjam and the farthest point upriver where salmon came to spawn.

Elsewhere in the notes the "begets" of the name itself are listed, descended from the first being send down from Heaven to what became Sneatlum Point. As founders of the pedigree of human chiefly lines, these "renowned names" (Collins 1966) constituted the *hik^w si'ab* (highest rank), based on words for "big, high, most, very" and "wealth, rich, treasure, abundant" (Bates, Hess, and Hilbert 1994: 15, 109).

The first ancestor of the Lower Skagit, sent down by the Creator to this point, was named KeKedab [kəkədəb]. He sired had three families, each living within a compartment of a huge cedar plank longhouse inside a stockade. Like the Iroquois whose symbolic longhouse paralleled

---

the Mohawk River across central New York, the Skagit occupants of each section settled along the Skagit River, with those in the back of the house furthest upriver, as compared to those who stayed in the middle, and those in the prestigious front section who took over the river mouth, delta, and islands (Sally Snyder, Box 108, Folder 10, Page 33, AJ).

Each compartment took along or developed specialized artifacts and technologies appropriate to the ecology of their new homelands. Such distinctions are most clearly indicated by different types of nets. Those out in the saltwater used the reef net (*sxwalo*) named for the twisted willow bark that formed its tough cordage. In the lower river, the weir net (*ql'its*) also of willow bark was used, and upriver the trawl net (*shubid*) was woven from a grass that had to be traded from afar. Both river nets were suspended from a pair of canoes working together, but the weir also included a wide pocket to contain the fish. Today, native fishers, protected by federal and treaty laws, rely on commercially manufactured nets and motor boats to accomplish the same ends.

Of note, the plain straight net of the *shubid* was deployed effectively in the water, as well as in the air and on land. Set above the group in strategic locals, it caught flocks of waterfowl as they rose in flight, while set across game trails it took deer and other mammals. Sometimes, as on Whidbey Island, these nets were once set up before communal deer drives.

In the very beginning, other beings already lived on the earth, including an underwater Wealth spirit, who took on the appearance of an ugly, pitiful young man or of a tiny baby. Using mind control (probably through *dicta*), he compelled the family of KeKedab to adopt him. The daughter who nursed him eventually became pregnant, and he married her in the guise of a handsome, hard-working man. Again using dicta, he enabled his wife and son to live underwater with their affines until the boy was old enough the quest for spirit power on land. The son fasted for a year and received "help" at both Sneatlum Point and the bottomless lake across from Greenbanks, a portage. Arriving outside of his own home, he sent his fasting cousin to tell his parents to "clean out" their home so he could publicly dance and sing his newly acquired powers. As he did so, the beach filled with fresh foods (Sally Snyder, Box 109, Folder 2, Pages 12-13, 39-40 AJ). Thereafter the Lower Skagits were known as a wealthy, powerful, and generous tribe. Those inheriting the name *K^{w}askadub* managed all of the trade along the Skagit River through an upriver partner at Concrete also inheriting a single name through time.

Descendants of the first founder, with a bewildering set of names, marry into nearby communities, beginning with the Swadabsh [true Swinomish] and Samish to begat seven named grandchildren. These in turn marry further away into Lummi and other villages. Since these sons are wealthy, they have many wives, all of whose children stand to inherit their own renowned names. The names of daughters are equally renowned and pass to females along bilateral lines. The only bar to sharing a name within a kindred is proximity. Siblings and cousins who live far apart can share the same ancestral name as long as confusion about identities is kept to a minimum by distance. In time, these names pass to known historic personages, such as Goliah who signed the treaty. In the begats, the original name belonged to the son of a woman from Oak Harbor on Whidbey Island, married to a grandson of the founder KeKedab. Oak Harbor itself was founded by someone named *xachded* (Sally Snyder, Box 108, Folder 2, Page 96 AJ). Such ancestors might be preexisting beings, animals, or geological features changed into mere humans, and thereby in need of spiritual aid to be successful.

Among the many descendants of KeKedab were famous standouts, such as the boy who was an endurance warrior, who trained by spitting on a rock, running around Sneatlum Point, and returning before it had dried (Sally Snyder, Box 108, Folder 2, Page 97 AJ). He easily outran deer, elk, cranes, and eagles. Much later, as part of US Coastal defenses, the strategic lookout used by this warrior eventually became fortified by concrete encasements as Fort Casey.

The heirs of KeKedab suffered through many crises, including the periodic destruction of the known world. Four major eras include 1) a primordial one of real or semi spiritual beings who marry humans to create descent lines, 2) lawless times when humans and dangerous spirits are punished for damaging general wellbeing, 3) Changers who prepare the world for present conditions, and, most recently, 4) the world as now known. The high god system for transferring power goes back to the beginning of the world.

Specific communities have traditions of particular disasters. Northern Lushootseeds tell about Glacier Peak in the North Cascades – a volcano that erupted 6700 years ago. A flood of its ash and debris formed Sauk Prairie and rerouted the Sauk River itself from the Stillaguamish into the Skagit (Vance 1957: 309).

For Skagits, the earliest Changers were four brothers, oldest to youngest, named Shield {$sg^w\partial dili\check{c}$}, Knife, Fire, and Baby. Each taught ancestors along the river important skills, such as defense, butchering, cooking, and child care. The immortals (spirits) system of power was another result.

Starchild and Diaper Boy created orderly time by becoming Moon and Sun, while their heirs formed chiefly families across the region, receiving the first *dicta*. Before they settled in the sky, they incinerated the world and used the ashes to more evenly scatter resources for use in the next era.

Lower Skagits share the story of Robe Boy, whose family survived the Flood in a canoe. The many victims of the Flood probably established the ghost system of power. As the scoured landscape slowly revived, Robe Boy and his dog hunted for the meat of tiny animals, sewing these pelts into his robe. Later, a voice from above told him to gather up scattered animal bones and, using *dicta* while waving the robe, create new people. They arose dull and very cold, so he waved the robe over charcoal to recreate fire. Herring swarmed in the slough to feed them, and a mountain goat provided wool for warm clothing. They lacked sense until Robe Boy took up local dirt to make brains for them (Snyder ms, Tale 68, AJ). Eventually these dull humans wandered away, and Robe Boy discovered that his parents were alive and had taken refuge on Sneatlum Point where they were mourning for their children presumed to be dead.

Robe Boy married a human woman and had two sons, First Light and Daylight (Lehalbid). Much later when plague from the east threatened all the people, Lehalbid envisioned a protective song and dance. As a prophet, he led the community at LaConner in constant services until the pestilence passed over them. Holders of this name maintained at least four houses around Fidalgo Island – near the present Swinomish police station, in a fort on Sullivan Slough, on Pull And Be Damned Road along Martha's Bay, and at Snee-osh Point. They shifted by season to these "resorts" to benefit from local foods as these reached peak conditions for harvesting.

The founding of the Indian Shaker Church in 1882 provided the most recent system of power, which was linked with the universal on of Christianity. As such, it renewed the primordial power from the high god, closing the loop that began at creation.

Conclusions

The very mention of King Arthur, Brunhilde, El Inka de la Vega, King Philip (Matecom), Jesus, Malinche, Wovoka, Fatima, Panini, Slocum, and so on identifies these famous names with a place and a time, as well as a gender. Each represents a moment in world history, with the understanding that namesakes partake of the qualities and personalities of their eponymous ancestor. Eskimos (Inuit) remain empathic on this concept.

Similarly, names, especially renowned ones, are at the very heart of Lushootseed culture. Regardless of the loss of language, of territory, and of community health, these names continue to be passed on to appropriate heirs. Associated with them are symbolic households, resource estates, art forms, and histories. Upholding these institutions on either side are the mainstays of "blood" and "mud". As a name serves to infuse a person with all the past, present, and future of prior namesakes, so Andrew "Span" Joe evoked the eternal fusion of mud and of blood when he said that Robe Boy made the "brains" of his revived people from the very earth of that place. Among Lushootseeds, as most other native peoples, the mind is located at the heart not the head of a person, at the very center of being, so these brains involved the core of a person.

Hereditary names have long been recognized as vital features of the complex matrilineal cultures of the North Pacific Coast, and regarded as distinct from the ambilateral and bilateral cultures to the south. Yet the regional elites consistently have intermarried, and continue to do so. The pedigrees established are based on the ownership of traditions based in hereditary names. Given this context, it is not at all surprising, in hindsight, that esteemed ancestors founding chiefly blood line on rich mud steeped in the past, were as crucial to the Salish as to their neighboring potential affines.

Ole Miss 10/17/07

house

The House of Salish
Noble Pedigrees, Privileges, and Names
Along the Skagit River between Logjam and Rock

Recurrent criticism has denied the significance of "house" (as House of Windsor, House of David) as a key factor of Salish kinship and society comparable to the all-important houses of the matrilineal cultures of the North Pacific Coast such as Tlingit, Haida, and Tsimshian.

A telling example occurs in one book, where the editors note [Levi-Strauss] "has also disagreed with Jay Miller's application of the notion of the "house" to the Salish". Yet Levi-Strauss himself lauds in its very first chapter "Reading a recent book by Jay Miller on the culture we refer to as Lushootseed, I found it gratifying that in order to characterize certain traits of the social organization, the author referred several times to aristocratic European houses" (Mauze, Harkin, and Kan 2004: xx, 3).

The counterargument pursued here is that while not integrated in Salish society to the degree of the north coast, claiming a house was an element of the coastal prestige system, especially among important families who could assert dynastic status. The Lushootseed language confirms its importance by the use of the suffix $-al'tx^w$ to indicate such a perpetual house ($si'ataltx^w$ House of Seattle), sometimes linked with the root $g^w\partial c$- / $g^w\partial\sigma^2$- "be born (for), originate" (Bates, Hess, and Hilbert 1994: 109). As such, this house is metaphoric and eternal, rather than merely physical. Indeed, the named house-holders may seasonally occupy a variety of built homes at strategic resource locations, easing the harvesting, preparation, and storage of that resource by members of the household and their guests.

Scholarly understanding of the features of this Salish House suffers from a lack of published data, much of it existing only in fieldnotes and, of course, alive within Salish communities. This article relies on the dense materials assembled in the early 1950s by Sally Snyder among the Swinomish and other Skagit River communities, and until recently under restricted access within the Melville Jacobs Collection at the University of Washington main library. The Saanich fieldnotes of Diamond Jenness (1935) also discuss the importance of the House for Canadian Salish.

The most vivid published account of the direct link between a great name and its house, here physical as well as metaphoric, involves John Fornsby's encounter with his great grandfather, $k^w\partial skad\partial b$, while picking blackberries with other boys. "There were lots of berries. We crawled around and got to the middle back of the house. The body of my [great] grandfather $k^w\partial skad\partial b$ was right there. We got scared. We went home. We never picked berries. I laughed [with relief] when we got back into the canoe" (Fornsby to Collins 1949: 295-96).

This $k^w\partial skad\partial b$ was a famous Skagit leader based on Whidbey Island around modern Coupeville on Penn Cove, still famous for its local oysters. Sneatlum Point is its southern end, and the landfall of founding ancestors (below). In time a namesake of founder $\underline{x}k'\partial k'ad\partial b$ /$\underline{x}\dot{k}\partial\dot{k}ad\partial b$/ married, among others, a Samish wife named $tsi\ ?ag^wat$ and one of their middle sons first received the name-title of $k^w\partial skad\partial b$. This historic holder of that name had commissioned half a dozen Lower Skagit carpenters to build him a potlatch house,[6] with a painted post holding up either end of the gable, at what briefly became Skagit City (Fornsby to Collins 1949: 295-96), the ancient site of a prime salmon fishery (below).

Later, the body of this *kʷəskadəb* was reburied behind his potlatch house, which eventually was washed away in a flood. By then *kʷəskadəb* had again been reburied, with proper ceremony, at the Swinomish cemetery. The flood settled one of his house posts – 3 feet wide, 4 feet thick, and 8 feet long – in the back of the bay at LaConner. Johnny Fornsby hired men from Lummi to help him move and set up this housepost at a potlatch when the dead were gathered up from a gravehouse on Deadman's Island and moved to the Swinomish community cemetery.

An earlier *kʷəskadəb* was father of the equally famous Sneatlam [*sniʔxəb*], and uncle to Goliah, the spokesman drafted as signer for the northern Lushootseed tribes at the 1855 Treaty of Port Elliot – Mukilteo. One of his daughters married among the Chehalis, to the south.

Sneatlam became renowned throughout the Northwest as an early Catholic prayer leader and an important broker in the regional fur trade based at Fort Nisqually. At least one of his wives was a Makah from Neah Bay. Yet one of his brothers flaunted the rules of nobility by being involved with a slave girl, who thereby became known as 'mistake' (*dʼaxəb*).

After his death on 16 December 1852, a carved wooden effigy of Sneatlam stood on a high bank on the eastern side of Whidbey Island, "dressed in his usual costume, and wearing the articles of which he was fond" (Gibbs 1877: 203). To this day, his family has remained important in intertribal and international trading, now brokering as far away as China, especially for fireworks sold at tribal stands before July 4th.

A granddaughter of a *kʷəskadəb* by the name of *ba'da'yɬ* (in Lushootseed, *ma'na'yɬ* in Straits)* was captured by raiding Klallams from Dungeness, who quickly married her instead, later returning with her for a formal marriage ceremony, receiving ten slaves, a seagoing canoe, and many blankets from her grandfather in exchange for twenty slaves, a canoe, and other goods from these Klallams. At the wedding, the bride was wrapped in "a big mountain goat hair blanket" and the groom appeared with an enormous "rawhide mask over his face, painted like a face, that he shows when they are landing. That is *sxʷay'ačusən*, the kind he showed, two or three feet on a side, a square of rawhide with long hair and a face" (Elmendorf 1993: 108-100 dates these events to 1780-1810).

(21.2) [Frank Allen narrates] What I'm going to tell is three or four generation ago. Before *č'u'ct* and *təna'taltq*, before their time [told to FA by his great-uncle *wa'xʷəlacuD*].

The Dungeness Klallam get ready to go to Skagit, the people from *c'ɑ'qʷ'* and from *sttiɬəm*, all one tribe, make ready. They're going to Skagit now for war. Going for women and slaves now. They go and get to Skagit, to the mouth of Skagit River, at night, and they land away from the village and haul their canoes into the woods and hide.

---

[6] Potlatch is a charged term in the Northwest Coast literature, derived from the local trade jargon (Chinuk Wawa) word simply meaning "to give". Among Lushootseed, the equivalent word is *sgʷigʷi*, meaning merely "to invite" but there are also three other words that can be applied (Miller 1999: 147 #5).

Next morning they see two little girls playing on the beach. The Klallam catch them and ask them, "Who are your people?" One of the girls says, "My grandfather's name is *kʷałqədəb*." That is the chief of the Skagit people. They ask the other girl, "Who are your people?" And she names her father and grandfather, but they're just common people.

(21.3) So the Klallam talk to one another now. "Now, what are we going to do?" And one man, *sxʷıla'cəm*, says, "I'm going to take this girl home, this grandchild of *kʷałqədəb*, and keep her for my wife." Now they say to the common girl, "You go now and tell *kʷałqədəb* that we are Klallam and we're going to take his grandchild. Tell him we're not taking her for a slave, but so-and-so is going to take her for his wife. They tell the common girl that they will come again next year to buy the other girl from her grandfather. So they sent that girl home.

The Klallam push their canoes off. They are going home now, and that girl, the grandchild of *kʷałqədəb* cries. They tell her, "Don't cry. You are not going to be a slave. That man is going to be your husband."

As they are going home with the Skagit girl, the Klallam ask her what is her name. The girl says, "My name is *ma'na'ył*." Well, they land home with the girl [later returning to Swinomish for a lavish marriage ceremony, when] ...

All the Skagit and Klallam exchange clothes now. Pull off each other's shirts, have a good time now. "We're going to be relations now!"

(21.6) *kʷałqədəb* says, "Stay with me for two or three days, you people! We're going to get mussels." So they send lots of young men to get mussels, the big rich mussels that are at Skagit. And they fill whole canoes with them and bring them back and cook them now, on hot rocks they cook them with leaves over them. And everybody eats and eats. Oh, those good mussels!

Next thing, *kʷałqədəb* says, "Now you get camas." And they dig camas, the women dig those roots on Skagit Island, and they steam them in an oven, underground, for two or three days. And so they keep eating for two or three days. And so it is done.

(21.7) They get through and now *sxʷıla'cəm* says, "Now, *kʷałqədəb*, you come to my country now. We're brothers and sisters now, and all you people come!" So the Skagit take lots of camas and mussels and all kinds of food and go with the Klallam.

And when they get to *c'α'qʷ'* they land and everybody goes to sxʷıla'cəm's house. They have a good time there, they dance and sing and have lots of food. And they exchange clothes with one another, men and women, and have a good time.

Now sxʷıla'cəm gets up and begins to sing: "*heyɔ• tisiyɔ• hɔ / ta•či tisiyɔ• hɔ•* [Klallam] (ha! my chief [power] / my power has come now)." [in spoken Klallam: *ha tacsiya'm', ta'či tiya' siyam'*.]

After he sings his tamanawis he goes and takes hold of a slave and takes him to *kʷałqədəb*. He takes a woman slave and he calls his wife *ma'na'ył*, "Come on!" His wife comes. He tells his wife, "You give this woman slave to your grandmother, *kʷałqədəb*'s wife." And now he gathers blankets and goods of all kinds and gives them to *kʷałqədəb*'s people, a little all around till everybody has some.

And now we're through with *ma'na'yɫ*. That is where we are from; my family is from that line on my mother's side. So we are related to the Skagit people from that time.

Extending their range of dynastic marriages, both Sneatlam, as *Neetlum*, and *kʷəskadəb*, as *Wheskienum*, appear in the journal of Fort Langley for June, July, and August of 1830 (Maclachlan 1998: 150, 156-6). This time, Sneatlum's son was marrying the daughter of a Cowichan leader, a chief variously known as *Shashia*, Joshua, Josia, or Old Joe. By luck, portraits of he and his son *Cul-chil-hum* were painted by Paul Kane in 1847. A brief biography, alas, mentions only two sons, leaving uncertain the fate of this daughter married among Skagits when he died blind and heirless in 1870 (Maclachlan 1998: 228-230).

While negotiations had been decided in the spring of 1830, the formal exchange took place in late summer after the Vancouver Islanders had moved across to their Fraser fishery. "This afternoon [June 17, Thursday] the two Scadchats Chiefs – *Neetlum & Wheskienum* accompanied by a half dozen of others & Sinaughten the Sinnahomes Came here – They have about 20 Skins Lar[ge] & Small…"

On June 29, Tuesday, Nanaimos and Cowichans arrived at the mouth of the Fraser, only to be attacked by Lekwiltok about July 4th, before the Nanaimo settled into their summer village on Friday the 16th. On July 10th, the Cowichan Shashia demanded 2 guns and 10 blankets for a dozen skins, but he left empty handed "for we have hardly So much property in the Fort." His concern was, of course, not the fur trade but his upcoming wedding responsibilities.

Neetlum himself visited the fort on August 7th, Tuesday; the Cowichan Shashia on the 8th, then on the 9th "In the evening two very large & three Small Canoes full of Scadchads made their appearance at our wharf – Their Chief (*Needlum*) was already in the Fort – he immediately embarked with them & pushed over to Joe's [Cowichan] camp – All the great men of the river are now assembled there – Our night watch is doubled & every thing in readiness in Case of the worst."

On Friday, August 10th came the culminating exchange in "A great Ceremony – going on the other Side solemnising a marriage that took place last Spring between a Boy of Needlum's and a little Girl of Joe's – Canoes – Guns – Blankets – Slaves etc. etc. are exchanged on the occasion.

On Saturday, the Skagit came across to propose trading, "for which they would have nothing but Blkts [blankets]" but were soon rebuffed. "They returned to the Cawitchin Camp in the evening & Spoiled Children they are." On Sunday afternoon, August 12th, the Skagits left for home.

Clearly, through pedigree and alliances, *kʷəskadəb* and his family held and hold high rank, meeting the criteria by having a wealth spirit power (below) and by inviting (to at least four potlatches) (Sally Snyder Box 108 Folder 2: page 17 Joe Joe). Accordingly they kept affirming it with generosity, as indicated by the specially built potlatch house where he was entombed.

This location just above Skagit City served to remind everyone of a major source of his bounty, namely the dense fishery at the lower end of a logjam, two miles long, that blocked the Skagit River from above Mount Vernon to Hamilton. Spawning salmon clumped there before managing to weave their way upriver. They were so abundant that harpoons and gaffhooks could be used along with nets.

house

Until the jam was dynamited away in 1878, peoples along the Skagit had extensive contacts with their neighbors because voyagers either had to drag a canoe through the brush around the jam, or, more readily, portage over to the lower Samish or the Stillaguamish rivers to reach salt water (Collins 1974: 39).

This fishery, potlatch house, and generous leader, therefore, account for the logjam in my title. They also, as it happens, account for the rock since, according to notes from Alice Campbell:

> Long ago there were people who turned into rocks [because of the Flood]. This *k^wəskadəb* was the name of one [of them] way up on the Skagit. It is the name of one of Andrew Joe's relatives. They came up to ask the people there for a name (certain people used to go to certain places to obtain a name). If they had known, they could have asked the *sbalix* here [around Concrete, Baker River and Lake] for a name (Snyder 108 5 58 AC).

Even before the Flood, with the founding of human society, the holders of these name-titles were not limited to one place because these ancestors married widely and dynastically.

Ancestors

These few ancestors were the primary founders for this region, the first strictly human generation of the Skagit world. Their names indeed were and remain mighty.

While most native people lived common, uneventful lives, those with what June Collins (1966) called "renowned names" – which acted more like titles – formed a set of famous chiefly leaders who owned several big cedar-plank houses in various richly endowed locales. That he (or they) could coordinate the building of more than one large home further spoke to his (their) leadership abilities. Indeed, in Lushootseed, such a person or family is called *hik^w siʔab*, in the sense of a grandee who is "big, great, high, most, many, very" (Bates, Hess, and Hilbert 1994: 109) in terms of authority, respect, ability, and, above all, presence.

According to Lower Skagit, *k'ək'ədəb* /kək'ədəb/, the first (Lower) Skagit man, was send down to *čuba'ałšəd* /čuba'ałšəd/ (note bene: Sneatlum Point) by the Creator to found three ancestral families who each first lived in one of the three compartments within one huge plank longhouse set inside a stockade, with those highest in rank in the middle and the eventual colonizers of the Skagit River in the one furthest back (Sally Snyder, Box 108 folder 10: page 33 AJ).

Once this first family was established, they found themselves lured into adopting a new member with vast consequences. Taking the shape of a young man, the Underwater Wealth Spirit (*tiułəbaxad* /tiułəbaxad/), who was usually both ugly and pitiful to humans, mentally compelled the family of *k'ək'ədəb* to adopt him after he made himself look presentable as a baby. A daughter took him to raise, then became pregnant by him. Since he appeared handsome and hard working, to avoid scandal, they were quickly married, before their son was born. The husband fixed it so his family could live underwater and took them back home. But this son was never happy there, and the family came back when he was old enough to quest for a spirit power.

He quested for a year. Times became hard and famine loomed when the son went to Sneatlam Point and to the bottomless lake across from Greenbanks. There he got power from the sea and a pair of powerful cedar shields. On his return, he told his cousin, who was also "pure" from fasting, to have his own parent's home cleaned up and renewed in four days in time for his return. Everyone worked hard and all was ready when he came into the house with the shields and sang the middle part of his song, which immediately filled the beach with food. From then on, aided by all these spirit powers, the Skagits grew mighty (Sally Snyder Box 109 folder 2: page 12 -13 AJ, cf Wealth married daughter of *k'ǝk'ǝdǝb #I* Sally Snyder Box 109 folder 2: page 39-40 AJ).

Eventually, trade up and down the Skagit River was managed by *k'ǝk'ǝdǝb* at Coupeville for everyone on Penn Cove and by a *daxalxʷǝd* – a *sbalixʷ* near Concrete on Lake Shannon at present Baker River – for those above (Sally Snyder, Box 109 folder 1: page 42 AD).

One of these later *x̲k'ǝk'ǝdǝb* /x̲k̓ǝk̓adǝb/ married both a Swinomish wife and the Samish wife named *tsi ʔagʷał*, having four boys and three girls. The next oldest son was the first *kʷǝskadǝb*, who had two daughters by one wife, and a son by another – who became a 1855 treaty signer and father of a chief, while another son who had a daughter and a son, who also signed the treaty. His second wife left no descendants (cf Sally Snyder, Box 108 folder 10: page 71 AJ, Box 109 folder 2: page 2 AJ).

One *kʷǝskadǝb* also had a famous warrior son *t'ax̲tał* /t̓ax̲tał/ who was an endurance runner and athlete. He would test himself by spitting on a rock and running around Sneatlam Point and back before it dried. He could outrun deer, elk, cranes, and eagles, killing them with his bare hands (Sally Snyder, Box 108 folder 2: page 97 AJ). Later young warriors trained by running from Sneatlum Point to Coupeville and on to Fort Casey, a strategic lookout (Snyder Box 108, Folder 2: page 10) now marked by a US defense bunker.

The half-Swinomish namesake son *x̲k'ǝk'ǝdǝb*, in turn, had 5-6 wives, with many descendants. The children of an Oak Harbor women included Goliah, designated a head chief in the 1855 treaty. From a half-brother descended the woman who married Johnny Fornsby, who as a boy to saw the body of his great grandfather lying in state. (Sally Snyder Box 109 folder 2: page 31 AJ; sons of *x̲k'ǝk'ǝdǝb #III*, Sally Snyder, Box 108 folder 10: page 43 AJ; Box 109, folder 2: page 3 AJ).

Overall, the name of *k'ǝk'ǝdǝb* seems to first occur shortly after the very beginning, going even "deeper, really, from the Flood. That's why it was hard to tell the history, because the Indian only had one name [over generations]" (Sally Snyder Box 109 folder 2: page 57 AJ).

Other founders were sent by the creator to specific locations, either at the founding of the world or to repopulate it after the Flood. For the Swadabsh proper on Swinomish slough, the important founder lived a third generation after the Flood, the son of Robe Boy known as *lǝx̲albid*.

lǝx̲albid

Gender equality permeates Salish culture, as shown by the pedigree of the name of the mother of *kʷǝskadǝb*. The family of the woman named *tsiʔ ǝgʷał* came into their own after the Flood (Sampson 1938: 14-16, Matson 1968: 29-38), and thereby came to "own" the story about a man who sensed the Flood was coming, and so tied four seagoing canoes to the top of a mountain with four long ropes that stretched out as the waters rose higher. When the waters receded, the mooring ropes broke off the high top of the mountain broke and three canoes drifted away. From the fourth, a man, his wife, son, and daughter landed safely. They quickly built cattail mat houses for use as a dwelling and storage.

house

Slowly, life returned. Little fish came into Swinomish slough and the girl went to play with them, until, one day, a great fish took her away. Saddened, her brother and his dog wandered away. He began to shoot small animals, prepare their pelts, and eventually sewed them into a blanket robe. When he finally came home, his parents were gone to Coupeville and the mat houses burned down as a sign of mourning because they thought both their children were dead.

In great despair, the boy wept until a voice told him to gather up and match all the animal bones he could find, lay them out, and wave his robe over them four times. Immediately, all these bones became people, but they were chilled. The voice said to gather charcoal from the burned houses, wave the robe over them, and thus fire was recreated.

Next he waded into the slough, where herring swarmed as soon as the hem of his robe touched the water. These fed the people. A mountain goat appeared to give everyone wool blankets as clothing to keep them warmer. These reformed people had no sense, however, so the boy made brains for them from the very soil of that place (Andrew Span Joe, Snyder ms.: Tale 68).

Eventually, his own human relations returned and these impromptu beings wandered away. Ever after known as Robe Boy (*xuyałič'a* /x̌uyałiča/, "made from a robe"), he married a human woman and had two sons, *tux̌ʷiqədəb* /tux̌ʷiqədəb/ (first daylight) and *ləxalbid* (daybreak), who, withstanding snide criticism like their father, seemed to refuse to quest and had a hard time in the community until they revealed successful quests and founded several houses and villages near resource locations and fisheries, celebrated with appropriate rituals.

ləxalbid had at least four houses around Fidalgo Island, located in modern terms on the east side near the Swinomish tribal police station, further east at the fort on Sullivan Slough, on the southwest near Martha's Bay and Pull and Be Damned Road, on the northwest at Snee-oosh (*sdiʔus*) Point.

Among the Lushootseed, importantly, socio-cultural institutions were arranged as concentric circles, from the most restricted of food economics to the most expansive of religious expressions in what I have called an "anchored radiance," with everything situated with the drainage of a major river draining into Puget Sound (Miller 1999).

Drainages

In terms of the overall Puget Basin, Marian Smith, after fieldwork with Puyallup and Nisqually, outlined a comprehensive spatial model with expanding components for each watershed, the maximum extent of allegiance and loyalty for most Lushootseeds. These units were (a) hearth mates eating together, (b) within a cedar plank household, (c) among houses of all neighboring residents, (d) of birthright locals – those born there in contrast to inlaws, visitors, and foreigners, including (e) all seasonal houses, settlements, towns, and resorts, (f) inter-community networks, (g) tributary drainages, of (h) the entire drainage of a watershed or basin. Integration was enhanced by distinctive styles and hereditary names given to canoe, which transport across time and terrains on mountain, forest, prairie, river, or sea.

Membership within each unit was based on well informed understandings, both subtle and discerning, of local customs such that insiders, in contrast to outsiders, fully appreciated the complexities of "the feud, the snub, the verbal innuendo" and accordingly "were appropriate guests for a ceremonial feast" (Roberts 1975: 79). To be involved in Lushootseed culture required formal training in and experience with the complexities of oratory, rank, and proper public expressions. Those of great prestige could also claim diffuse membership in a named House.

Every drainage had customs that set it apart, made obvious by dialect subtleties and by different styles of making fire or using nets, for example, as well as in venerating certain spirit powers and abilities. The most complex example, for the entire length of the Skagit River, involved net use.

Throughout the Northwest, nets – placed underwater, on land, in the air, or hand held in canoes – were used to capture fish, fowl, and other foods. Three major types of fish nets were once used along the Skagit, each instituted by the decree of a Changer~Transformer preparing the world for human arrival. Out in the saltwater, the reef net (*sx^walo*, literally 'willow' using its twisted bark for cords), developed by Straits Salish speakers, was deployed. In the lower river, the weir net (*qəlʔits*) was developed, and used by Swinomish and others. Upriver, the trawl net (*šəbəd*) was featured, made of a special mountain grass. The success of the net, however, relied on special *dicta* (formula, spells, power words) closely guarded by the leaders of a family and household because they guaranteed an abundant food supply.

Lushootseed Ethno-Chronology

Based on this background and comparisons,[7] then, a Lushootseed chronology must start with the creator high god (*xaʔxa*) who empowers (often mentally) other immortal spirits (*sqəlalitut*) who dwell in the sky, on and in the earth, and under the water. Foremost among these spirits were four brothers who traveled up the Skagit River, placing pairs of men and women at various locations to create future generations (Collins 1974: 158-59, Snyder Tale 73, Amoss 1978: 66-70, Miller 1999: 60-62). These brothers, oldest to youngest, were Shield (*sg^wədiləč*), Knife, Fire, and Baby, each with sustaining powers and abilities appropriate to their names. Shield protected and foretold. Knife taught the proper ways to butcher and prepare game. Fire showed how to cook it. Baby told these couples on how to fix family talents, skills, and abilities on their children, as well as limiting access to *dicta*.

The others went away upriver, and Knife may have stopped at the ancient Hozomeen Quarry, but Shield became a rock in the upper Skagit near Portage where he can be heard singing about 3AM by those who had fasted and prepared to learn his song so as to be able to hunt and fish successfully.

This era ended with the time of Starchild and Diaper boy, begat by Stars married to human women. After they had rescued their mother from slavery and married industrious wives, they gathered up everything useful on the earth and burned it in a great conflagration, then scattered these ashes everywhere so the essence of these materials, resources, and abilities could be more easily found by future generations.

Their children became the chiefly families throughout Puget Sound, each leader learning and guarding the special *dicta* to benefit his family and community. Powerful *dicta* were

---

[7] The best descriptions of Salishan cosmological worlds represent the Nuxalk (Bella Coola, McIlwraith 1948), Katzie (Jenness 1955), and Twana (Elmendorf 1960).

specifically given in compensation for the renewal of the world at the time when mortals and immortals were moving away from the bodily contact of marriage toward the immateriality of adoption (as described for Wealthman and the Sneatlum family).

The land repopulated and thrived until people failed to respect the proper rules, regulations, and avoidances needed for proper living, so a Flood set things right again. The few survivors included Robe Boy, his son *ləxalbid*, and their many descendants at Swadabsh, as other ancestors refounded communities in other locales. Though unstated, the host of dead from the Flood must have provided the incentive for the Ghost system still important today since the deluge obviously left behind more refuse and remains than did Fire.

The occasionally references to those few who "drifted away" during the Flood also suggests that one of these Flood casualties was one of the *kʷəskadəb* who ended up a petrified rock far up the Skagit. Thus, resolving the conflicting attributes and locations of this name, the Lower Skagit who went upriver to ask for this name were actually showing respect for the people among whom this *kʷəskadəb* ended up lodging. That is why they did not ask more important tribes around Concrete and elsewhere for a name. Presumably, that *kʷəskadəb* revealed his location to a descendant in a dream that was followed up by this delegation.

Most recently, the Creator has again asserted his priority by empowering John and Mary Slocum to establish the 1882 Indian Shaker Church, legally incorporated in Washington State in 1910, and still thriving. As Martin Sampson, Swinomish leader, noted, the advantage of Shakers was "worshipping God direct, they increased their healing over much greater distances." Unlike shamans, whose spirits remained localized, Shaker spirits could expand into the world as far as needed since they were affiliated with a universal God. Moreover, though a shaman's spirits deserted him or her at death, the Shaker Spirit led a member "home".

Simultaneously, immortal spirits remain active among initiates of modern *Syowin*, the so-called Smokehouse Religion that allows modern members to "inherit" family spirit powers in the context of this organization.

In modern Lushootseed beliefs about immortals or guardian spirits, such a power attaches itself to a person at birth, but only reveals its presence at puberty through at least two aspects, a being and a song, along with a personifying of the vision itself. Some or all of these aspects "travel" during the year and only join together during the winter when the person becomes "sick to sing" with the return of his or her spirit partner. For a woman, her spirit power was regarded as a personal friend, while for a man it was an impersonal force that infused his entire body when it returned (Amoss 1978: 51).

The song, at least, came from the east in the fall, moved slowly south and westward during the winter, and, in late April or so, headed east again. As a group, spirits came to the Nooksak on Mt Baker before they reached Vancouver Island, where they lingered until spring.

In contrast to these lay or career powers, shamanic curing powers were available at all times. According to Joyce Wike (1941), while the song traveled, the spirit itself stayed close to the human partner. Fierce black paint spirits traveled more widely than did those of calm red paint, who stayed nearby and could be used to cure or help others.

During the day, spirits also move around, hovering in the air (rather than treading on the ground), lower in the early morning then higher in the afternoon. They are constantly aware of human actions and leave if their partner becomes ritually impure or disrespectful. Then the spirit was said to "lift off" until it could be coaxed back by a shaman. Spirits liked daylight but,

house

lacking form or substance, were truly ethereal. Marian Smith (1940a:) reported that spirits had
the most nebulous of existences, with their appetites and pleasures supplied vicariously through
their links with humans, especially relatives who were kind enough to remember them and send
food and treats through an open fire.

Comparisons

The role of the *House* (*al'al*, *-altx^w*) among Coast Salish has been much debated by
academics, with some denying it entirely. Physically, this cedar-plank building served as "food
processing and storage, workshop, recreation center, temple, theatre, and fortress" (Suttles 91:
214, Kennedy 2000: 76). Among the matrilineal northern tribes, the house is the pervasive unit,
and its influence was felt in the south, where some communities strove to assert claims to a
similar but unique house as an aspiration rather than a routine feature. Thus, standout examples
include the Whale House (*saɬuɬtx^w*) comprised of five high ranking Comox communities near
Cape Mudge (Kennedy 2000: 52, based on Barnett 1955: 25), and Painted House of the
Snoqualmies east of Seattle.

Salish houses, repeatedly, have been called "similar in many ways to a 'House' in the
sense of European nobility [holding] property, tangible and intangible, names of heaven-born
First Ancestors, confidential knowledge (*sniw'*), ritual property (*ts'uxwten*), legends, songs,
dances, secret words (*dicta*), medicinal remedies, and ceremonial prerogatives (Barnett 1955:
141, 191; Jenness 1935: 52; Thom 2005: 85). All of these are place-based, as inalienable
patrimony, such that "senses of place focus attention on the connections and interrelations
between myth, legend, ancestor, spirit, song, identity, language, property, territory, boundary and
title" (Thom 2005: 409).

In his unpublished notes, Jenness (1935), closely attending to his elder interviews,
carefully distinguishes between corporate ownership and the commons.

> The real political unit was therefore not the village, but the big house occupied by a
> number of kinsfolk – an enlarged or genealogical 'family' to which the Saanich
> applied the term *hunit's'lakum*, and we in speaking of the similar European nobility
> use the term House. Each Saanich House, as we many call it then, possessed its own
> long shed-roofed dwelling,[1] its own camas beds on Galiano and neighboring islands,
> its own set of ancestral names or titles, and its own stock of legends, songs, and
> medicinal remedies (Jenness 1935: 29).

The accompanying footnote expands on such privileged property:

> #1. Almost any departure from established custom might become the privilege of a
> House, heritable by later generations, and by them alone, provided the public had
> ratified it; and the public ratified it when during some potlatch it heard the statement
> of claim without demur and accepted the gift that followed the statement. All such
> privileges or rights, however, hinged upon proof of lineal descent, and the most
> obvious indication of such descent was the possession of an ancestral title (Jenness
> 1935: 29 #1).

At Duncan, Cowichan Houses owned nearby weir sites along the river, but

house

"On the other hand, the sea near the villages, the hunting grounds and berry patches
round about, were common property; any villager, whatever his station in life, might
fish and hunt wherever he wished within the village territory" (Jenness 1935: 29).

Elite families owned property that included several houses occupied throughout a year at
seasonal resource sites, famous art works, and claims to epics, songs, displays, and rituals.
Senior members, both men and women, of elite families doubled as religious and political
leaders, depending on the season. Summer was devoted to economy, and winter to religion (cf.
Kennedy 2000: 7, 160, 326). The lowest class was largely immobile and marked by a strict
provincialism (Kennedy 2000: 125, from Smith 1940: 410).

An apt comparison to Nuchahnulth or Nootkan distinctions between kinship and noble
descent indicates "The situation among the people of the West Coast is not unlike that of
medieval Europe (a comparison suggested to me [a Welsh national] by a Toquaht chief) where
the descent principle was fully utilized only by the elite of society and where the common people
neglected to trace their genealogies the further they were removed from aristocratic rank.... In
addition, both principles need not be of equal importance for all members of the group (Kenyon
1980: 85-86). Emphasizing *ramages* of first-borns, Nuchahnulth differed from Salish
bilaterality, yet high families in both made claims to hereditary Houses.

tribal trade habitats

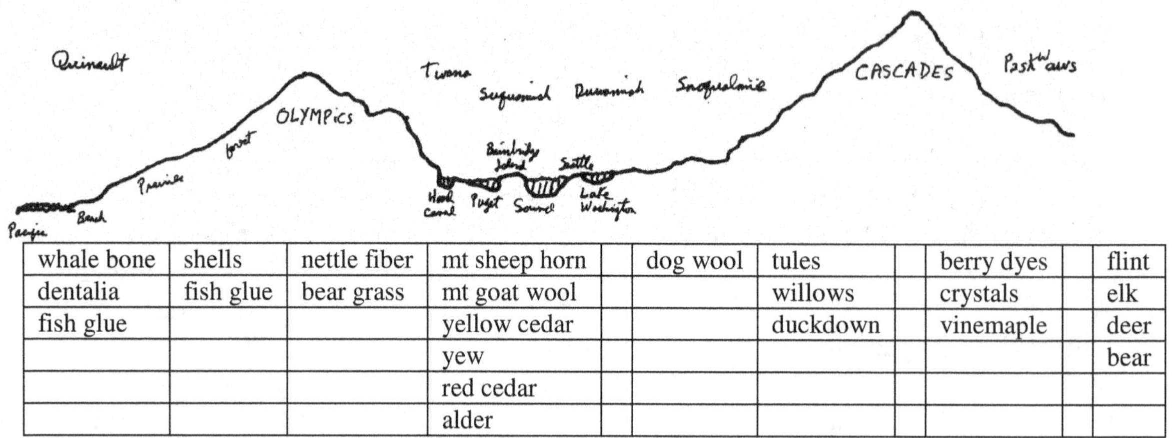

whale bone	shells	nettle fiber	mt sheep horn		dog wool	tules		berry dyes		flint
dentalia	fish glue	bear grass	mt goat wool			willows		crystals		elk
fish glue			yellow cedar			duckdown		vinemaple		deer
			yew							bear
			red cedar							
			alder							

Cascade Mt Passes

Pass	Height	Tribe
Hannegan	5082k	Nooksack
Harts	6191k	Methow
Washington	5477 ~ 5453	Methow
Cascade	5392 ~ 5351k	Skagit Chelan
Kaiwhat	5860k	Sauk
White	4501 ~ 5873	
Linsley's	5459k	Sauk
Indian	4977k	Skykomish
Wards	5705k	
Cady	4291k	Skykomish
Wenatchee	4236k	
Stevens	4061 ~ 4111	
Snoqualmie	3022 ~ 3015	
Yakima	3579k	
Stampede	3672 ~ 3688	
Tacoma	3540k	
Naches	4931k	
Carlton	4153k	Cowlitz
Cowlitz	5190k	
White	5873 ~ 4478	
Cispus	6394k	

Cascade 5392 ~ 5351 Chinook 5430 ~ 5440 Satus 3107 ~ 3130
Cayuse 4675 ~ 4833 Rainy 5475 ~ 4862

Another Plateau for Totemism
in Native America:
Interior Salish Tribal Emblems

Abstract

The following paper began as an only child but has developed into a twin, based on commentary given me after the first paper was finished. In presenting both papers, original and revision, emphasis can be added to the familiar injunctions that the best analysis is that supported by new data; the best fieldwork involves recurrent visiting, and the best data comes from close and conscientious cooperation, with mutual trust and sensitivity, among researcher and native teacher-advisors over a long period.

The original paper started when a person gave me information that no one else could duplicate. It took form as I found comparative data to support the lone report and required a second revision after other Salish elders commented on the first draft. The first was not so much wrong as it was incomplete, missing entirely one of the major dimensions of a culture: the spatial one linking humans with their land.

I

While working for the Colville Confederated Tribes of north-central Washington, comprised of Interior Salish who ranged both sides of the international border, 1 was given information by a reliable source which other Interior Salish were unable to confirm or to deny because they had never heard of it. Initially, therefore, I doubted my source and returned to question her more closely on the subject, only to learn that she had learned her information from a much more exalted person, one of the last hereditary chiefs. By its nature, this would have been public knowledge since it involved group identification, but it now appears that the historic disruption of the Intermontane Plateau peoples brought this system to an end over a century ago, making this system useless for modern transactions after everyone had congregated together on reservations and reserves. Comparative research from other areas of Native America, however, restored my confidence in the data and led me to discuss it more thoroughly here.

Fragmentary though it is, the information does specify a link between a particular tribal group and a particular animal in such a way as to suggest strongly the use of totems by several Interior Salish groupings on the American side of the Plateau. Most of these tribes have now gathered on the Colville Reservation, established by executive order in 1872, near or upon their aboriginal homelands. Linguistically, these tribes formed a chain of Interior Salishan dialects with at least two divisions. Along the southerly section of the Middle Columbia River were the Moses-Columbia, Wenatchi (Psq^{w}aws), Chelan, and Entiat village clusters. Further upriver were the Okanogan (Okanagan), Nespelem, Sanpoil, Colville proper, and Arrow Lakes Clusters. In an intermediate position between these two divisions were the villages of the Methow drainage, which had both a dialect particularly their own and a growing tendency historically to shift between Chelan and Okanogan vocabulary.

plateau

According to my advisor, each of these tribes had a particularly close relationship with an animal. While all of these bonds were not remembered, some were. Among members of the Okanogan chain, the Nespelem animal was the turtle; the Sanpoil a blue-ish lizard; and the Colville a frog. The Moses-Columbia identified with the bear and people camped at the upper end of the Grand Coulee (who may have spoken a Moses dialect) used the Eagle. In and of themselves, these data were vague and problematic. Yet, when placed within the more general context of Native North America, they conform to a widespread pattern of tribal totems.

Comparative Data

After I began to realize that this bonding of tribe and animal was not idle speculation and that my source was very sincere, I gave much thought to interpreting her statement. At first, the discussion of Shuswap totems by James Teit (1909: 373-381) came to mind, but closer inspection proved that this was a different phenomenon. Briefly, Teit found important social differences between eastern and western bands of Shuswap of the Canadian Plateau. By 1850 the Canyon Band and those bands (Lake, Dog Creek, and Pavilion) living north of Dog creek on the Fraser River had social classes of nobles, commoners, and slaves like coastal tribes. The freeborn were divided into totemic groups such as Grizzly, Raven, Wolf, Eagle, and Bear which were inherited bilaterally. Initially, the founders of these groups trained and fasted to join one of them, with that membership then passing to descendents. This primary means of recruitment was handled much like a guardian spirit quest since the guardian spirit complex continued to exist simultaneously with the crests. Of the two, the shamanic-guardian spirit complex was much the older.

Comparing the two lists of totems and spirits, Teit showed that the spirits were ecologically appropriate to the Shuswap territory, while the totemic crests pointed to the coastal tribes. The totems were listed above, while the list of possible spirits included Wolf-Dog, Cannibal, Corpse (mostly for shamans), Bear-Thunderbird, Frog. Wind, Rain, Arrow, Moose, Caribou. Elk-Deer, Buffalo, Snow (to aid hunters in tracking), and Serviceberry (for women).

Accordingly, Teit was able to propose three routes from the coast to the interior for such totemic crests:

1) Tsimshian to Carrier, 2) Bella Coola to Chilcotin, and 3) Squamish to Lillooet.

As neighbors of the Shuswap, these Interior Athapaskans (Carrier, Chilcotin) and Salishan (Liliooet) tribes interact with them through intermarriage, joint fishing, and ritual cooperation. Strengthening his argument for these routes is the greater elaboration of the crest system of the intervening tribes. This was not a wholesale adoption, however, since the Shuswap molded the new crests to their older cultural forms by making them conform to bilateral descent, rather than the matrilineality or ambilaterality of the coast.

In contrast to the Colville evidence, the Shuswap used the totems to establish internal distinctions within their tribe, rather than having a single totem to express their tribal unity. Further, Goldman (1941) detailed the diffusion of crests from the Bella Coola to the Alkatcho Carrier, who treat them as bilateral honorifics, and Miller (ms.) explored a similar transmission among the Coast Tsimshian, Upriver Gitksan Tsimshian, and the Carrier, who adopted crests progressively by increments involving trade, intermarriage, and the assumption of prestigious patterns of clothing styles, cremation, and potlatching. Most commonly, these borrowed crests were Grizzly, Wolf, Raven-Crow, Beaver, and Eagle, adding further confirmation to the argument that the similar Shuswap totemic groups also had a coast origin.

Looking much further afield, moreover, we can find a system more analogous to that of the Interior Salish among the tribal totems in the Northeastern Maritimes, where it functioned independently from a system of matri-clans with animal names among the Iroquois, and from the bilateral demes of the Wabanaki Algonkians, who may have also been more matrilineal in the aboriginal past before severe depopulation struck. Among the Wabanaki, these tribal totems function outside of the systems of personal guardian spirits and of family nicknames related to economic specializations.

The Wabanaki tribal emblems are scaled, in terms of the intensity of identification with each, from the highly explicit Passamaquoddy, whose tribal name means "those who pursue the Pollock (a fish)", to a more vague but nonetheless profound pervasiveness. Among the Malecite (now Malaseet) the associated animal is Muskrat, with the Micmac (now Miqmaq) having Deer, and the Penobscot Otter (Speck 1917: 13). Speck interpreted these emblems as game totems, expressing the most important staple of each group. In hindsight, however, this interpretation is overly functional, aligned with the famous thesis of A.R. Radcliffe-Brown that animals become totems because they are good to eat.

The work of Claude Levi-Strauss (1962, 1966) supplied a corrective to such gastric determinism by suggesting that totems are much better to think (or think with) than to consume; since humans living closely with nature utilize the full range of their ethological observations in their symbolism.

It, therefore, seems most appropriate to view these game totems as expressions of the land/water opposition so important in these cultures, with each member acting as an amphibious mediator within the system (recalling that deer are efficient swimmers and that pollack have a diverse salt water habitat since they "can be caught from breakwaters as well as out to sea" (Ursin 1977: 111)). In addition, perhaps indicating the beginnings of an overall inter-tribal integration for the various Wabanaki tribes, these mediators show an internal progression from usually aquatic to usually terrestrial species:

> pollack, muskrat, otter, and deer <

While the Wabanaki lack this national totem, the existence of such can be seen among the confederated tribes known as the Iroquois, where "Bald Eagle ... is the totemite of all the Iroquois. The eagle perches atop the great tree of peace which is symbolic of the Confederacy" (Fenton 1953: 117). There were other such tribal or national emblems in the Americas, but the Iroquois will serve to illustrate the type.

The development of this type can be seen among the historically created tribe called the Mohegan of Connecticut. According to Gladys Tantaquidgeon (1973), herself both a Mohegan and an anthropologist, after the defeat of the Pequot and the ascendancy of Uncas as the leader of the survivors, the native name of his own Bear clan became extended and rephrased to name the Mohegan, with the Bear as their special emblem.

The evidence of such unifying symbols provides further insight into the character of tribalism in Native America. It is presently fashionable to presume that such tribes have been the historic creations of federal interference, of treaty making, and of catastrophic dislocations due to epidemics and warfare. Wherry (1979: 34) stated that tribes existed more in the heads of Europeans than in the interactions of natives, although "The inhabitants of various river systems may have been gradually distinct culturally and politically."

His observation accords well with other evidence that indicates that river drainages or watershed often coincided with linguistic, community, and ritual groupings (Miller 1981). Certainly, this is the case for both the Wabanaki and for the Salish. Each of the Interior Salish "tribes" named above occupied a major tributary of the Columbia River. In the aboriginal period, which lasted until a century and a half ago, each drainage defined a tribe in that all of the camps and settlements shared a common language, territory, economy, and series of rituals. Moreover, the village nearest the confluence with the Columbia was invariably the largest and most dominant. Its chief and ritual leader were given the most deference and the name of this village was extended to include the entire drainage and the people dwelling along it. While lacking coercive powers, save for the ostracism of community offenders and the discipline of children with the approval of a council of distinguished citizens, the chief and priest did lead by setting the example, by marital alliances with other tribes, and by moral suasion.

In practice, the chief and the Salmon priest acted as regulators for all or most of the interactions among the inhabitants, neighbors, and the environment* In the event of community disruption or of malfeasance in office, these leaders had only to relocate in another settlement or river valley to become distinguished citizens there without any obligation to assume a leadership role.

During much of the year, people were scattered in temporary camps located at resource areas, so the full ceremonial organization or congregation did not emerge until everyone (or almost everyone) returned with their stored surplus foods to the winter village along the river.

More than anything else, the chiefs and priests served as the foci of and for the sentiments of each community congregation, serving to define the Salish as members of a moral community composed of all forms of life. In nightly council sessions and periodic First Foods Rites, these sentiments were given public expression, but, from moment to moment, however, they were acted out in terms of personal orientations to a series of overlapping foci. Among these were the chief, the priest, the sacred space of the council house and of ritual sites, cemeteries, a geographical feature important in mythology(like Moses Mountain), and, most of all, the water course that served/serves as the tribal lifeline.

The larger inter-tribal community was similarly defined by common residence along the Columbia and its tributaries, joint use of bountiful fisheries and attendance at the First Salmon Rites at the Dalles among the Wishram-Wasco Chinook and at Kettle Falls among the Colville, and shared mythic sagas relating to the adventures of Coyote finishing off the creation of the world, especially bringing Salmon up the Columbia to the different fisheries.

Given the tremendous amount of tribal interaction through fishing, ritual, and marriage, it seems likely that some means was developed to express these different tribal memberships in some obvious way. The most ready answer, of course, would be the use of emblem based on a pseudo-speciation among humans like that among animal species. These distinctions were not based on economic considerations, however, but rather on the need to express wide-ranging symbolism among these tribal cultures.

Thus, while my original data came from only one source, comparative information and the inter-tribal milieu of the Plateau provided a context for accepting their creditability. More to the point, such information has been passed down through a chiefly family line where the decision to share it with outsiders could be readily made without greater consultation with other elders. In all, it suggests the on-going importance of focal chiefs and totems for regulating the continuity of the tribe as an inter-meshed moral community interacting with the members, environment, neighbors, and the greater society of sapient beings of the biotic community.

II ~ Tribal Totems Revised

After the previous pages were written, more information came to me from another source that served to place everything in proper perspective.

While I had interpreted the totemic identifications as an expression of social solidarity, with comparative evidence for similar cases across the continent to support this, a single sentence from a Moses-Columbia elder provided the missing piece to the puzzle. Of course, I could not have readily understood her meaning if I had not already spent five years among the Colville and written the previous section.

When I asked her if she had ever heard if the Moses people ever had a special association with Grizzlies or the Bear, she flatly said "no." A few minutes later, she added "Those Ellensburg people were mixed up with Bears." Ellensburg is a town in central Washington, located on traditional Wenatchi land, but close enough to have received joint use by the Moses-Columbia and by the Sahaptians now on the Yakima reservation.

This reference to Bears at Ellensburg refers to the story of a Bear family who lived, in the Timeless Age, where the water tower now stands near the Rodeo Grounds. The place name in Salish for that knoll is "Bear's House" and it called to my mind several other places, especially hills, along the Columbia which are named as the House of a particular animal. Among these are Otter's House at Orondo and Coyote's House near Bridgeport, although Coyote has more than this one House because he traveled so widely. While not all of the tribal totems have been positively linked with Houses in those areas, the tradition does hold for the larger area.

The result of this addition data has not been the rejection of the past analysis, but rather a considerable amplification of it. What I said about tribal solidarity and overlapping foci continue to hold true, but it does not go far enough. Instead, the reference to mythology provided the means to ground a tribe within its territory, to locate them in space with a charter from the Myth Age. While the animal emblem of the tribe does express its commonalities during inter-tribal gatherings, it more importantly links the tribe to its land, making the tribe a united membership, an interacting congregation by virtue of occupying the same area where a humanoid spirit-animal or family lived in the primordial period when all the rules for human conduct were instituted. The Myth Age was the timeless period of what some Salish call the Animal Kingdom, when distinctions were minimal and the inhabitants shimmered simultaneously between spirit, human, and biotic forms. When all was ready for humans, this previous age changed instantaneously into the present age, permitting human ancestors to establish special relations with characters and places of the Animal Kingdom for the benefit of local descendents. This is what happened at Ellensburg between a Wenatchi ancestor and the Bear family.

plateau

The creditability of the earlier analysis, then, stands with modification provided by the new data. Seldom is an analysis so fortunate as to have new evidence, or previously unconsidered data, lend confirmation and amplification to a previous model. Such instances are particularly unusual in the human sciences like anthropology.

Moreover, this analysis goes considerably beyond professional considerations to underscore with great emphasis the vital role that land and territory play in the definition and orientation of Native American identity, on personal, community, and tribal levels. As a generalization of these findings, we can see that mythology maps people to their land, making it theirs from time immemorial, but, more than this, it indicates that, at least on the Plateau, a House is a home.

Five Language Families
and
Chinuk Wawa Trade Jargon

A substantial portion of the linguistic history of the Northwest involves Coastal Washington, which saw the spread of five language families, each of which was quite distinct (Kinkade 1990b: 197-212). The four main ones are Salishan, Oregon Penutian, Wakashan, and Chimakuan. Key to understanding their complex prehistory is the role of the "Salishan Funnel": the valley of the Chehalis River broadened by the outflow of the glacier that towered over Puget Sound, passing from the Black River to the coast. The fifth language family arrived in recent centuries, when tiny offshoots of the Athapaskan family based in central Alaska came to settle in the hills above the Columbia River as the Willapa, Swaal, and Kwaliokwa, with the Oregon offshoot known as the Klatskanie (Clatskanie, Tlatskani). A sixth form of speech was the trade jargon now known as Chinuk Wawa, an amalgam of words from northwest, European, and Hawaiian natural languages.

Salishan probably spread from the Boundary Bay region on the border of the United States and British Columbia, with the Coast branch moving north and south and the Interior branch moving east up the Fraser River before expanding on the Plateau (popularly known as the Inland Empire). The expansion of fir forests about 5500 years ago has been suggested as the habitat or ecological context for this Salishan diaspora. Kootenay, now considered an isolate, may have been the forerunner of this Salishan move into the interior. Nuxalk (Bella Coola), although now the farthest north on the coast, lacks marine vocabulary that indicates time in the interior (in the Chilcotin-Cariboo). Localized adaptations encouraged subgroupings of the Salishan family, such as Straits Salish, which coincides with island homelands, and especially the deployment of reef nets for salmon.

Lushootseed or Puget Salish, as written by linguists and educated speakers, has separate letters for each of its 46 sounds. The first attempts to write down this language, as elsewhere, were by missionaries, particularly a learned French Oblate (Fr Eugene Casimir Chirouse). The complexity of its sounds is based on the stunning logic of providing up to four different pronunciations by using different parts of the mouth. Routinely, these are the back of the throat (as k, q, x = German ich), the nose (nasals) and the lips (labials). Lushootseed functions with many more consonants and fewer vowels than English because many of the sounds produced at the back or sides of the mouth continue to force air through the lips and so can take the place of the more open, free flowing sounds known as vowels.

Within Salishan, Lushootseed is characterized by an ancient reworking of the two sets of transitive person markers, regularization of the suffix system, and an elaboration of prefixes. Over a century ago, the shift from nasals (M > B, N > D) by Lushootseeds, Twana, Chimakum, and southern Nootkans (Makah and Ditidat, called Nitinat in English) may have been a counter-response to territorial expansion by Straits-speaking Lummi, Klallam, and Samish (Duwaha, Nuwaha, dx^{w}a'ha).

Densely inhabited for centuries, special words had to be invented during certain conditions, such as a taboo on a word resembling the name of the deceased during mourning,[8] neighboring communities usually did not share the same word for something. For simple exchanges, a pidgin called Chinuk Wawa [Chinook Jargon] was used.

Often a basic sound occurs in fourway sets such that it is plain (said much like ordinary English), glottalized (said along with a raspy pop of air released from the voice box or glottis in the throat), and labialized (said through rounded or pursed lips). Moreover, these articulated pronunciations can be compounded so that a sound is both glottalized and labialized.

As distinct soundings, they are indicated by an ordinary letter, a letter under an apostrophe (glottal), a letter beside a raised W (labial -^{W}), or by both the apostrophe and the raised W. For example, K is said unadorned like _k_in, K' is "harsh, explosive" sounding [cf gee_k_], K^W is said like _Qu_een, and K$^{W'}$ combines the last two.

$$\nearrow \quad k' \quad \searrow$$
$$k \qquad\qquad k'^w$$
$$\searrow \quad k^w \quad \nearrow$$

Other fronted sounds (like the raised W (-^{W}) indicating rounded lips) that are probably unfamiliar include _l_ (known as barred L), a sound used in Welsh and a letter (for a different sound) in Polish, said by pushing air around the tip of the tongue while it is pressed against the roof of the mouth – something like the middle sound in Ca_thol_ic or a_thl_ete, and L (a glottalized barred lambda) said with a click at the back of the throat while tapping the tip of the tongue against the back of the front upper teeth.

Within Coast Salish, the Tsamosan subgroup adapted to the abundant prairies (Lane 1973; Norton 1979, 1980, 1985) of southwestern Washington. Proto-Tsamosan speakers moved down the "Salishan Funnel" and along the coast, presumably pushing Tillamooks farther south onto coastal Oregon, across the Columbia River settled by Chinookans. This "Salishan Funnel," as noted by Chehalis people, has the potential for some of the oldest sites in the region. This route between the coast and Puget Sound provided a thoroughfare for many tribes, as well as later Euro-American traders and settlers. Among its earliest sediments is "gravel originated as glacial outwash of the Puget Lobe of the continental ice sheet … transported … by the Chehalis River" (Blukis Onat et al. 2007: 129).

Oregon Penutian seems to have developed in the Willamette Valley, with diverging Chinookans moving into the lower Columbia River and Sahaptians upstream. Members of this language stock are quite scattered, and may include Tsimshian (now Tsmsyan) in far northern British Columbia as well as languages in Mexico.

Wakashans diverged from the northern tip of Vancouver Island, with Nootkans spreading down the western coast to specialize in whaling and Kwakiutlans occupying the eastern shores.

Chimakuans, unique to the Olympic Peninsula, emerged along the northern coast of the Olympic Peninsula until Klallams moved in along the shore and Makahs, the southernmost Nootkans, took over the cape, about a thousand years ago, in a prime location for whale spotting. Quileute Chimakuans raided through the area.

---

[8] William Elmendorf, Word Tabu and Change Rates: Tests of a Hypothesis 1970b: 74-85.

In terms of time depth, Proto-Penutian seems to have emerged as the earliest and most widespread. It later gave ground to Proto-Salishans and Wakashans. Chimakuans developed in comparative isolation under the Olympic Mountains until split between Chimakum on the east and Quileute-Hoh on the west. Chimakums were eventually absorbed into Klallam, while Quileute retain their communities at two coastal river mouths.

Upper Chehalis call themselves *q̓ʷaẏayiłq*, based on *sq̓ʷaẏayił* as the name of Mud Bay at the head of Eld Inlet near Olympia, and the suffix -q indicating 'language.' Further, the familiar Kamilche is a place name that is only analyzable in Upper Chehalis as *ke•m-* 'narrow, slender' + *-či* 'water' with an *-ił-* connective to accurately describe this slim arm of Puget Sound. Another place name near Shelton on Oakland Bay is the Chehalis (and Proto-Salishan) word for red cedar (*catawi*), distinct from the name for this tree in Puget Sound Lushootseed (*xpaẏəc*) or in Hood Canal Twana (*q̓ʷili*). In this way, place names and other grammatical forms provide a linguistic window on the ancient history of this region. Place names, unlike excavations, say softly what is locally inherent in, on, and about the Earth.

Tsamosan

Tsamosan (from its names for the numbers 2 and 4, formerly called Olympic Salish) is a subgroup of the Central Coast Salish branch within the larger Coast Salishan language family. Its four languages have coastal and inland subgroups. Coastal includes Quinault-Queets and Lower Chehalis; inland includes Upper Chehalis and Cowlitz. Upper Chehalis included three dialects -- Satsop, as well as Downriver and Upriver splitting at Grand Mound. Upriver used back of the mouth sounds (*k k̓ x*), where downriver used front of the mouth ones (*č č̓ š*) in the same words. For example, the word root for "slender" is *čema* for speakers downriver and *k̓ema* for speakers upriver, producing variants for a 'narrow trail' such as *čemašuł* and *k̓emašuł* (Kinkade 1991a: 40 #502).

Over time, some sounds from proto-Salish (the ancestral or parent language) have changed in Tsamosan. For example, Quinault and Coastal Lower Chehalis (Copalis) shifted from protolanguage word-initial sounds of **y* to *ǰ* and of **w* to *gʷ*. The most distinctive feature of Tsamosan among the whole Salishan family is a contrast between long and short vowels, which carry grammatical information (like choose/chose indicate verb tense in English).

Pronunciation of these sounds is mostly the same as indicated by familiar English letters. The rule for linguistic or technical writing, however, is that each distinct sound have its own single distinguishing letter so what are double letters in English have a single linguistic character.

č = ch

š = sh

ə = is a neutral or midrange vowel like that in the middle of the word "but".

ʔ = glottal stop is the pause in the word uh-oh. It is more of a catch or space than a sound.

' = glottalization adds the constriction of the flap at the back of the throat (glottis) to make hard sounding versions of plain letters: t' instead of t.

[h] = raised H indicates a puff of air after the sound, as with Misp[h].

[w] = raised W means the lips are rounded when the sound is said, K[w] rather than plain K, with Q said farther back in the throat than K.

[y] = raised Y indicates the palate and raised tongue are used to constrict the sound, as in the name for the Moses Columbia, Snk[y]use, of the Columbia's Big Bend country.

More complicated sounds for English speakers are back X /x̣/, barred L /ł/, and glottalized barred Lambda /λ̓/.

The back X is said at the back of the throat; the barred L /ł/ is said with the tongue tip at the ridge behind the upper teeth making air flow around to the sides of the mouth, sounding like that in the middle of Catholic [kałək] or athlete; and the glottalized barred lambda combines a click sound against the roof of the mouth with a closed glottis.

Tsamosan Consonants

p	t	c		č	k	k̓[w]	q	q[w]		stops, afficates
p̓	t'	c̓	λ̓	č̓	k̓	k̓[w]	q̓	q̓[w]		glottalized
		s	ł	š	x	x[w]	x̣	x̣[w]	h	continuants vl
m	n		l	y		w			ʔ	resonants
m'	n'		l̓	ẏ		ẇ				glottalized

Tsamosan Vowels

Upper Chehalis has 9 vowels, plus consonants x and g.

i	e	a	o	u	ə	short
	ee	aa	oo			long

Quinault has 7 vowels, plus consonants ǰ and g[w].

i		a		u	ə	short
ii		aa		uu		long

Lower Chehalis uses Upper Chehalis consonants and Quinault vowels
Tsamosan vowel locations within the mouth cavity

front [i] to back [u]
high to low [a]

i	u
ə	
a	

languages

Chinuk Jargon (Wawa)

Well-born people were expected to speak fluently many of the native languages in the region. As children, they were sent to live with kin who spoke these other languages so as adults they could conduct far-reaching negotiations, trades, and exchanges. However, some interactions with foreigners and visitors from beyond the drainages were conducted in a trade language known as Chinook Jargon (Gibbs 1970; Gill 1909), now generally spelled Chinuk Wawa to distinguish it from the Chinook language within the Oregon branch of Penutian. Commoners and slaves who lacked the advantages and contacts of the well-born relied on this jargon to communicate. With its simple sounds and basic concepts, set in a rudimentary grammar, it facilitated contacts among the peoples of the Northwest and beyond.

When Europeans began trading in the Northwest, Chinuk expanded from the Northwest into Alaska, California, and even to Hawaii, adding terms derived from English and French (Thompson and Kinkade 1990: 41). In the 1855 treaty negotiations between the U.S. Government and the tribes, jargon was used, although it was not truly adequate to this task.

Comparison with neighboring languages shows that the earliest words in Chinuk are drawn from the Nootkan languages (Lang 2008) of the West Coast of Vancouver Island and from Lower Chinook, spoken near the mouth of the Columbia River, including Grays Harbor (Thompson and Kinkade 1990: 41). Both regions also used the same type of sea-going canoe, which enabled trade and other exchange. Later words were added from Chehalis, and then European languages, especially French and Spanish.

By the mid-1900s, Chinuk was rarely spoken anywhere. However, several dictionaries or vocabularies of *wawa* have been published (Thompson and Kinkade 1990: 41). Chinuk contributed words common to modern American English in the Puget Sound region such as *potlatch* (to give away), *tyee* (senior, chief), *tillikum* (friend), *tahmanawis* (spiritual power, being), and some food and clothing terms (Thompson and Kincade 1990: 50).

In the Twin Cities Study Area, *skookumchuck* is the most prominent Chinuk place name, meaning strong water or current, aptly describing this steep waterway. While named *the-a-woot-en*, in Tsamosan according to Gibbs (its residents = *the-a-woot*) and, more accurately, Kinkade (*té•wtń* "fording place"), the current use of its jargon name probably stems from its former occupation by Suwal Athapaskans who vacated it in favor of Oregon to become the C~K~Tlatskanie.

five ages

Five Ages of Chehalis World History

#1) >   The world already exists, inhabited by bird-like spirits with great powers, potentials, and wealth. They have a shiny hoop to play games with until the four Coyote sons of Fox and the bowlegged Grandson of Dog decide to steal it. The oldest Coyote boy watches; grabs the hoop; is chased after, and relays it to his next younger brother just before the oldest is caught and killed. The hoop continues in relay until finally Dog's Grandson gets it. Swan uses his own doctoring power to cure grandson's hip, and turns his own white feathers into a heavy fog that enables the boy to escape with the hoop and return to Dog, whose win over Fox results in the rainbow. Some spirits get lost in this fog and take on the forms of present-day animals, plants, and places.

#2) >   Flood destroys everything after inlaws wrongly keep insisting that a bird (Junco or Thrush) wash his discolored face, thereby treating everyone alike and the same. A white patch exposed by the washwater attracts clouds, rain, and floods. Some animal spirits escape in canoes from the flood, and take turns trying to bring up soil from the ocean bottom. Muskrat succeeds; creates a mountain nearby (Capitol Peak); and the world is remade by earth spreading from it.

#3) >   Two sleepy girls talk of marrying Star husbands and are taken into the sky by an old man Star (white color) and a younger one (with red color). The grumbling wife of the old man becomes pregnant, escapes from the sky, and, at Claquato gives birth to Starchild, a boy destined to be Moon who is tended by his blind grandmother until stolen by two lonely women (Age # 4) carrying him off in relays. The distraught mother wrings a twin son from a diaper left behind. That twisted brother and the mother suffer greatly until Bluejay gets Starchild to return. Reunited, he straightens out his twisted brother, and joins with him in remaking the world of today. The twins avenge their family; burn up the old ways; and establish chiefly blood lines before becoming Moon and Sun in the sky. Starchild's own children become fish and trees.

#4) >   X^{w}ane/ Changer/ Transformer/ Coyote/ Misp^h - originally a set of five brothers - travel through the land, mostly along rivers. They destroy cannibal women, provide regular foods, set rules for living right, and change things into their present forms and conditions - in preparation for the eventual world of today's humans. From salmon innards, X^{w}ane creates two girls, who flee from him and, running in relays, steal Starchild from his blind grandmother (Age # 3). Beings wanting to hurt Changer are turned into deer, beaver, and other helpful creatures.

#5) >   Human beings arrive in this prepared world by canoeing upriver. Each village and tribe receives special abilities as it settles along a namesake river branch with it own special foods and resources. Species of plants and animals become as they are now: Freshwater Clams were spirits whose canoes capsized, Spring Salmon and Silver Lamprey take shape from flesh and oil removed from Steelhead, and so forth. A piece of a visiting Star is left behind to become Grand Mound.

five ages

Background

Placing Chehalis epics in their proper chronological order is like doing a jigsaw puzzle, one that was put together over centuries and now has to be put back together with some parts missing. The starting place is the Abstracts at the back of Thelma Adamson's *Folk-tales of the Coast Salish*, where many stories in her collection are summarized and compared with similar ones throughout the region. In addition, there is the book *Honne* by George Sanders and Katherine Van Winkle Palmer, and now published stories collected in 1927 in the Chehalis language by Franz Boas, many from Secenas. The boiled down ethnographic notes by Thelma Adamson from 1927 have important clues, especially on page 41 under Origins that mentions the hoop at the beginning of the world. In addition, there is a lot of scholarly work on particular themes or events that help with understanding. The new collection *Salish Myths and Legends ~ One People's Stories*, by M Terry Thompson and Steven Egesdal helps with comparisons. All the abstracts referred to below come from Thelma Adamson's *Folk-Tales*.

#1) Hoop #1 / abstract is on page 390, but the context comes from a wider understanding of the world beginning at a time when land was scarce and spirits were more like birds. Animals became more important when they took the hoop, with the spirit power of Swan especially significant since its downy feathers created the fog that helped animals win the hoop. Swan helped shift power from birds to animals, beginning the settling process since some spirits got lost in the fog and stayed where they were to become sacred places.

According to Mary Eyley, telling in Sahaptin Cowlitz a story she heard from her father in Salish Cowlitz, each of Coyote's sons gained his guardian spirit while fasting on a prairie. By age, name, and prairie, these sons are #1 pa'tawaswai @ sa'lk prairie, #2 pa'x̣ɬa @ kuku'ɬm (Jackson Prairie), #3 pa'swiyatkas @ nawa'qum (Newaukum), #4 pa'tcikwn @ q'qa'ya, and #5 patawaswa'ipatawaswai @ waxa'lat. During the fatal relay race each son presumably positioned himself on his own prairie to advance the hoop until Grandson ran with it onto Cowlitz Prairie (na'wq) and Animals won. Coyote dies in grief over his lost sons, old and young winners go toward sunrise, rain stops, and Grandfather holds up the hoop, which shows everywhere as rainbow.

Mary called the grandfather Dog both Naha´ntci and t'əpit'ə´pi. His grandson quested at lapa´ləm, a creek near Newaukum, which explains his Swan power. He is mostly likely the Cascade Golden-Mantled Ground Squirrel (*Spermophilus saturatus*), which lives only in the mountains of BC and Washington state, a range distinct from the more common species across the West. Though acting much like a chipmunk, it lacks their white facial stripes and instead has the orange-red head and nape for which they are named. It favors open areas in wooded terrain, such as prairies, and has July litters of 2-8 young. Omnivorous, it now begs from hikers and campers. During the fall it can add 50% to its weight in preparation for winter hibernation (Bowers, Bowers, and Kaufman 2004: 72-73). Because its habitat overlaps that of humans, and its weight gain came make its movements awkward, it is the most likely to be Dog's Grandson of the first epoch.

Nora Bowers, Nick Bowers, and Kenn Kaufman 2004 *Mammals of North America.* NY: Houghton Mifflin Co.

Melville Jacobs 1934 *Northwest Sahaptin Texts.* NY: Columbia University Contributions to Anthropology XIX Part I ~ English: 168-169.

#2) Flood #2 / abstract is on page 413. There are lots, and lots of Flood stories, but the song in this epic is particularly important because it still brings on the rain. Certain families still have the right to sing it and they usually say the son-in-law bird is a Junco, though Thrush is also mentioned. Help here comes from Laurel Sercombe's 2001 PhD dissertation *"And Then It Rained: Power and Song in Western Washington Coast Salish Myth Narratives"*. Bird's still have great power so when Junco washes his face, exposing white places, which attract the dense white clouds that bring the rain that causes the flood.

The simplest model for Crescent [Metchosin Igneous Complex in Canada] deformation that fits the observations is a dome-like uplift [from a continental margin rift extrusion] with little or no overall displacement relative to North America (Suczek, Babcock, and Engebretson 1994: 1H-6).

Suczek, Christopher A.; Babcock, R. Scott; Engebretson, David C. Tectonostratigraphy of The Crescent Terrane and Related Rocks, Olympic Peninsula, Washington. IN Swanson, D. A.; Haugerud, R. A., Editors, Geologic Field Trips in the Pacific Northwest: University of Washington Department of Geological Sciences, vol. 1, p. 1H 1 - 1H 11, 1994.

#3 Star Husbands / abstracts are on page 379 and 418. This epic is a well known and widely distributed over North America, though in the NW it explains the origins of chiefly families, who come from the Stars. Vi Hilbert (Skagit elder and US National Treasure) and Jay Miller discuss it in 1996.

Jay Miller and with Vi taqwsheblu Hilbert Lushootseed Animal People: Mediation and Transformation from Myth to History. *Monsters, Tricksters, and Sacred Cows. Animal Tales and American Identities.* A. James Arnold, ed. New World Studies. Charlottesville: University of Virginia Press 1996: 138-156.

#4 Changers / abstracts are on page 379 and 384. *Honne* (1925) is good for this because it presents Changer stories as interconnected, weaving them together as they would have been told night after night during the winter inside the old cedar plank long houses. These Changer~Transformers have many names, varying by river, by tribe, and by language, but all try to set the world right because, in the title of a famous collection by Mel Jacobs, "The People Are Coming Soon". Many bad and dangerous beings were put in their places during this epoch, marking the land and water in ways that still have consequences for humans.

five ages

#5 Humans / has no abstract, but a representative story is on page 241, its abstract on page 420. This is the epoch when what can be called "history" begins, and houses, towns, rivers, and regions take on their distinctive characteristics in terms of the foods they eat, the clothes they wear, and the customs they follow. Representative stories are in *Salish Myths and Legends*.

Jay Miller
   An Overview of Northwest Coast Mythology. *Northwest Anthropological Research Notes* 23 (2): 125-141 1989.
   Chehalis Area Traditions: *A Summary of Thelma Adamson's 1927 Ethnographic Notes.* Northwest Anthropological Research Notes (NARN) 33 (1): 1-72, Spring 1999.
   Tsimshian Ethno-Ethnohistory: A "real" Indigenous Chronology. *Ethnohistory* 45 (4): 657-674 1998.

Vi taqwsheblu Hilbert *Haboo* ~ Native American Stories from Puget Sound. University of Washington Press 1985.

Time Line for the Salish Sea

Animal People worlds destroyed and recreated by Knife/Baby Star Child Fire, Dewi flood, capsized Robe Boy

14,500 Glaciation forms the Salish Sea

11,000 Fraser River forms as ice age ends; humans occupy emerging land Skagit River flows into Fraser, then into Puget Sound.

6800 Crater Lake (Mazama, Oregon) erupts, covering the region with ash

6500 Red and Yellow Cedar emerge in the Northwest, becoming forests by 2500

5000 plank houses, villages, and towns are settled; wooly dog bred; social classes marked by artifact qualities

4500 Fraser rock slide redirects the river flow, blocks salmon runs for years

2500 Salish and Wakashan languages spread through the region

1400-800 burials in cairn and earthen mounds mark status

1000 Forts and defenses are built through the region as the use of the bow and arrow spreads southward

500 Columbus ravages the Americas

Gregorian Calendar dates

1670 British Charter for Hudson Bay Company

1700 Tsumani in Japan caused by NW earthquake

1763 British Royal Proclamation protects rights of Native allies in North America

1775 Spanish explorers killed at Quinault

1778 Captain James Cook sails along coast, crew later trades sea otter pelts in China to spark the fur trade

1792 Captain George Vancouver maps the Salish Sea, naming the southern end after its surveyor Lieutenant Peter Puget; Captain Robert Gray enters the Columbia River, establishing US claims to the NW

1804-6 Lewis and Clark expedition

1808 Simon Fraser reaches the BC coast

1811 Fort Astoria

1814 Oblates (OMI, Catholic Order of Mary Immaculate), Catholic order founded at Marseilles, France; active among Salish from the 1840s to today

1818 Spain gives up claim to NW

1821 Hudson Bay and Northwest Company merge

1825 Fort Vancouver on the Columbia River

1827 Fort Langley on the Fraser River

1833 Fort Nisqually founded on Puget Sound

1836 *Beaver*, HBC steamship begins traffic along the coast; Protestant missions

1836-41 Captain George Wilkes and US Exploring Expedition, sailing around the world, maps Puget Sound

1841 Catholic missionaries arrive from eastern Canada

1843 Fort Victoria founded

1846   Oregon Treaty ends joint use of NW by British and Americans, "shared" from 1818

1846-48   Paul Kane (1810-1871) toured, sketched, and painted the Northwest

Eugène-Casimir Chirouse OMI, born near Lyons, France in 1821, when his mother died so he was raised by a grandmother, inspired by Bishop Rosati of St. Louis report of Northwest Indians seeking Catholic missions, 1844, at the age of 23, he took perpetual vows, assigned to Northwest by Oblates founder Bishop Eugene de Mazenod, traveled with Charles Pandosy and Bishop A.M.A. Blanchet to Walla Walla in 1847, ordained 2 January 1848 with Pandosy in the tense days following the Whitman massacre, sent to Yakamas, during Treaty War reassigned to Tulalip until reassigned 1878 to St Mary's in BC, died 28 May 1892, buried without grave marker at St Mary's on the Fraser. Author of A short method to learn the Snohomish Indian language in 14 lessons, UC Berkeley Bancroft Library, ms., [undated], 139 pages 12 x 20 cm. OCLC 26525748, Author's name incorrect in binder's title: P. Chirouze. Prepared for the use of missionaries to the Indians. Includes grammar rules, some vocabulary, and prayers.   http://www.seattlearchdiocese.org/Assets/Archives/5948 _7ThuribleofFatherChirouse.pdf

Nephew = Eugène-Casimir Chirouse OMI, Roman Catholic priest and missionary, Oblate of Mary Immaculate; b.15 June 1854 in Hostun, Bourg-de-Péage, France, assigned to BC missions and St Mary's mission and school, d. 3 Feb. 1927 in Vancouver, buried with grave marker at St Mary's. Famously implicated in the whipping of a young woman for immorality and sentenced to jail until pardoned. http://www.biographi.ca/en/bio/chirouse_eugene_casimir_15E.html

1850-54 Governor James Douglas signs treaties on Vancouver Island

1851 Alki/Seattle founded by Denny Party

1853 Washington Territory created

1854-55   Governor Isaac Stevens signs treaties in Washington; with a separate clause to free Natives held as slaves by these tribes; Treat War 1855-7 ensues (with Seattle attacked January 26, 1856); Leschi unfairly hanged in 1858; treaties ratified by US Congress 1859

1857 Bishop Paul Durieu, OMI, imposed a native leadership system at Salish missions

Pierre-Paul Durieu OMI, was a Roman Catholic missionary and the first Bishop of New Westminster, in British Columbia, Canada; born 4 December 1830, Saint-Pal-de-Mons, France, Consecration 24 October 1845, Ordination 11 March 1854, assisted Chirouse at Tulalip, Died 1 June 1899, New Westminster, Canada. Famous for his "Durieu System" of Catholic village control, relying on officers keeping order and reporting misdeeds to the priest. Author of Chinook Vocabulary, Chinook-English: From the Original of Rt. Rev. Bishop Durieu, O.M.I., with the Chinook Words in Phonography.

Marie-Angèle Gauthier, Sister of St Anne, teacher, superior, and author; b. 9 Feb. 1828 in Vaudreuil, Lower Canada, d. 25 May 1898 in Duncan, B.C., founded and taught in Catholic schools for native girls, mostly Coast Salish.

1859 Pig War between the US and Britain in the San Juan Islands leaves unsettled the last of the international boundary through the Salish Sea until it was set as Haro (not Rosario) Strait by the 1872 binding decision of Kaiser Wilhelm I of Germany

1858 Fraser gold rush devastates Sto:lo communities

1862   massive regional smallpox epidemic erupts after natives are driven from camps at Victoria, BC, founded in 1843

Thomas Crosby (21 June 1840 – 13 January 1914), born Pickering, Yorkshire, at 16 emigrated with his parents to Woodstock, Ontario, work at a tannery until 1861 answering a newspaper call for Methodist missionaries to go to British Columbia, arriving in 1863 he taught Salish kids at Nanaimo, BC, became itinerant preacher 1866 through Vancouver Island, Gulf Islands, and city of Vancouver, until appointed to preach and teach at Chilliwack, BC, where David Sallosalton missionized American Nooksacks; ordained 1871; at an 1873 revival in Victoria, converted Elizabeth Diex, a Tsimshian matriarch from Lax Kw'alaams (Port Simpson) and later her son Chief Alfred Dudoward and his wife Kate Dudoward, beginning a Tsimishian mission with his wife Emma in 1874 until his death.

1864 first US Salmon cannery in California, soon in NW

1867 Joseph Trutch diminishes size of BC Salish reserves and denies their right to preempt homesteads

1868 Emancipation Proclamation frees African slaves but denies US Natives the right to vote

1871 British Columbia (BC) joins Canada's confederation, becoming a province: US Congress rejects treaties for "agreements" with tribes

1874 BC Natives denied the right to vote

1875 US law allows Indians to homestead; Catholic Passion Play becomes a Fraser Salish refuge after they are denied the right of public assembly

1876 Indian Act sets a uniform if harsh national policy in Canada

1882 John and Mary Slocum found the Indian Shaker Church near Olympia

1884 Louie Sam, fourteen-years-old, is lynched by Americans near Sumas; his village flees and their ancestral stone image ends up at to the Burke Museum in Seattle, later repatriated to the Fraser

1886 Revised Indian Act makes potlatching and religious events criminal offenses

1887 Dawes Allotment Act carves up and sells off US reservations

1889 Washington statehood

1900

1910 Indian Shaker Church is incorporated under Washington State Law, protecting it from religious prosecution

1912 McKenna McBride (Royal Commission on Indian Affairs in BC) debates Native land questions

1918 Southern 2/3rds of the Nisqually reservation is dispossessed for an army base

1924 All Indiens made US citizens in recognition of Native service during World War I

1931 Native Brotherhood of British Columbia forms

1934 US Indian Reorganization Act restores self determination

1936 BC reserves are placed in Federal trust

1946 Indian Claims Commission begins to settle Native land claims in the US

1951 Indian Act removes criminal ban on potlatch and ceremony

1972-85 Alkali Lake, a Shuswap reserve in British Columbia went from total alcoholism to 95% sobriety

1974 Boldt decision upholds salmon treaty right

1975 Sto:lo Declaration drafted

1978 American Indian Religious Freedom Act and Indian Child Welfare Act passes; US Supreme Court decrees, in *Oliphant v Suquamish Indian Tribe*, based on an arrest during Chief Seattle Days, that tribes do not have jurisdiction over non-natives living on the reservation

1985 Bill C-31 allows Canadian bands to determine their own membership, returning many Native women to these band rolls

1988 Indian Gaming Regulatory Act

1989 Paddle to Seattle to mark Washington centennial; canoe journeys resume, helping revive native language usage to ask permission to land and untie

1990 American Grave Protection and Repatriation Act (NAGPRA); Sparrow Decision protects the aboriginal rights in salmon fishery; Elijah Harper, a Cree member of the Manitoba legislature, kept ratification of Canadian federal-provincial Accord because full standing of First Nations was not recognized

1992 BC Treaty Commission resumed treaty negations after a century and a half

1994 Judge Edward Refeedie decision affirms US treaty right to shellfish

2005 Contemporary Coast Salish Art show at Stonington Gallery in Seattle, with a catalog

2008 *S'badəb ~ The Gifts*: *Pacific Coast Salish Art and Artists* at Seattle Art Museum, with a catalog

2009 First conference hosted by the president of Seattle University bringing together Lushootseed teachers and supporters in honor of Vi Hilbert.

2019 Licton Spings, long sacred to the Duwamish, becomes first official native landmark in Seattle.

finale

Salish is uniquely Northwest, as are its solutions. In a rich and diverse habitat, their societies are equally open and flexible in terms of genders, roles, and blood lines. At the crux of these societies are inherited names, such as *kʷəskadəb* and *ləxalbid*, which emerge from the land itself, often spoken inside someone's head, and granted by its spirits along with specific and abundant resource areas. Martin Sampson is especially qualified by family and education to mention their own alliances with a spirit Grizzly dwelling across from Hamilton, along with bears, "alligators", actually horned snakes, and, particularly, Thunderbird whose power enabled his son Ben to succeed as an electrical engineer. Susie, his mother, contacted her spirits near Day Creek, Jarman Prairie, and Hamilton, and these converted along with her when she later joined the Indian Shaker Church, also unique to the Northwest.

The Swinomish ~ Samish pole, carved as a 1940s WPA project, gives graphic representation to these cultural traditions, and, indeed, these same family emblems are repeated in the Smokehouse used for public and private ceremonies today. Similarly, the drawing of their ancestral house at Slox visually and vividly explains its historic activities in a bilingual text.

The Lushootseed language, like other Salish examples, emerged from the land and many of its words mimic the talk of animals, plants, and places. Indeed, as Andrew "Span" Joe noted, Robe Boy made the "brains" of his revived people from the very earth of Swiomish. Among Salish, as most other native peoples, the mind is located at the heart not the head of a person, at the very center of being, so these brains involve the core of a person.

Links with locales were always quite narrow in terms of economic considerations, expanding outward through kinship and political intermarriages into the the cosmos populated by spirits, songs, and powers. The chart of tribes and trade goods illustrates these basics, ushering us into the Plateau, where animal stories prove to have totemic aspects for Colvilles.

We end in southwest Washington near the Columbia and coast, where the role of many languages and multilingualism pervades these societies, whose world history embraces five ages.

In addition to general information, there is also the personal, especially important in native accounts. Martin mentions wealthy *sxaxaləbqid*, but does not explain, that he had many wives because he wanted to be immortal and realized that only many descendants would keep his name and fame alive. Martin says Scha-ha-lab-ki had eleven wives, but the Lushootseed dictionary say fourteen. "He has been described as being short, dark and bushy-headed in appearance. Scha-ha-lab-ki never claimed to be a chief. He said that [24 b] he just became wealthy and wealth brought in the women."

Indeed, by comparing the works of academics with native scholars like Martin and elders like Susie, a more complete understanding emerges, and with it a better solution for their Northwest vitality.

Works Cited

Adamson, Thelma
  1927 Unarranged Sources of Chehalis Ethnography. Seattle: Melville Jacobs Collection,
    University of Washington, Special Collections.
  1934 *Folktales of the Coast Salish.* Memoirs of the American Folklore Society 27.
  2009 *Folktales of the Coast Salish.* William Seaburg and Laurel Sercombe, eds. Lincoln:
    University of Nebraska Press.
Ballard, Arthur C.
  1927 Some Tales of the Southern Puget Sound Salish. University of Washington Publications
    in Anthropology 2 (3): 57-81.
  1929 Mythology of Southern Puget Sound. University of Washington Publications in
    Anthropology 3 (2): 31-150.
  1999 Mythology of Southern Puget Sound. Kenneth (Greg) Watson, ed. North Bend, WA:
    Snoqualmie Valley Historical Museum.
Barnett, Homer
  1957 *Indian Shakers, A Messianic Cult of the Pacific Northwest.* Carbondale: Southern
    Illinois University Press.
Bent, AC
  1919 Life Histories of Diving Birds. US Nat Mus 107
  1925 Life Histories of North American Wild Fowl. USNM 130, part 2.
Blukis Onat, Astrida, James Phipps, Karen James. Kathryn Bernick, Timothy Cowan, and
    Lacosta Browning Lykowski
  2007 Cultural Resource Study Report of the Port of Grays Harbor Industrial Development
    District Parcel Number 1, Hoquiam Washington. BOAS, Inc: Report No 200511.03.
Boas, Franz
  2002 Indian Myths and Legends of the North Pacific Coast. Victoria: Talonbooks. Randy
    Bouchard and Dorothy Kennedy, eds. Dietrich Bertz, translator. Originally Indianishe
    Sagen von der Nord-Padifischen Küste Amerikas. Sonder-Abdruck aus den
    Verlandlungen der Berliner Gesellschaft fur Anthropologie, Ethnologie und Urgeschichte.
    Berlin: Verlag von A Asher. 1895.
Bright, William, ed.
  2004 *Native American Placenames of the United States.* Norman: University of Oklahoma
    Press.
Collins, June
  1952 The Mythological Basis For Attitudes Toward Animals Among Salish-Speaking Indians.
    Journal of American Folklore 65 (258): 353-359.
Elmendorf, William
  1961a Skokomish and Other Coast Salish Tales. Washington State University Research
    Studies 29 (1): 1-37; (2): 84-117; (3): 119-150.
  1993 *Twana Narratives.* Native Historical Accounts of a Coast Salish People. Seattle:
    University of Washington Press.

Farrand, Livingston
1902 Traditions of the Quinault Indians. With assistance by WS Kahnweiler. NY: Memoirs of the American Museum of Natural History IV, Publications of the Jesup North Pacific Expedition III: 77-132.

Gibbs, George
1855 Report on the Indian Tribes of Washington Territory. Pacific Railroad Report 1: 402-36.
1877 Tribes of Western Washington and Northwestern Oregon. Washington: Department of the Interior, United States Geographical and Geological Survey of the Rocky Mountain Region, Part II: 157-241.
1970 Dictionary of the Niskwalli (Nisqually) Indian Language - Western Washington. Extract from 1877 Contributions to North American Ethnology 1: 285-361. Seattle: The Shorey Book Store Facsimile Reproduction.

Gill, John
1909 *Gill's Chinook Dictionary.* Portland: JK Gill Company.

Gunther, Erna
1925 Klallam Folk Tales. University of Washington Publications in Anthropology 1 (4): 113-170.

Haeberlin, Herman
1916-17 Puget Salish, 42 Notebooks. DC: National Anthropological Archives. # 2965.
1918 "SbEtEtda'q: A Shamanic Performance of the Coast Salish." *American Anthropologist* 20 (3), 249-257.
1924 "Mythology of Puget Sound." *Journal of American Folklore* 37 (143-144): 371-438.

Haeberlin, Herman, and Erna Gunther
1930 The Indians of Puget Sound. University of Washington Publications in Anthropology 4 (1): 1-84.

Harrington, John Peabody
1981 The Papers of John Peabody Harrington in the Smithsonian Institution, 1907-1957. Elaine Mills, ed. 30 reels. Millwood, NY: Krause International Publications.

Hymes, Dell
1981 "In Vain I Tried to Tell You:" Essays in Native American Ethnopoetics. Philadelphia: University of Pennsylvania Press.
1987 Anthologies and Narrators: *Recovering the Word: Essays on Native American Literature.* Brian Swan and Arnold Krupat, eds. Berkeley: University of California Press.

Jacobs, Melville
1959 *The Content and Style of an Oral Literature.* NY: Viking Fund Publications in Anthropology 26.
1960 *The People Are Coming Soon.* Analysis of Clackamas Chinook Myths and Texts. Seattle: University of Washington Press.

James, Justine E., Jr., with Leilani Chubby
2002 Quinault: 99-117. *Native Peoples of the Olympic Peninsula ~ Who We Are.* Jacilee Wray, ed. Norman: University of Oklahoma Press.

Kinkade, Dale
1983 Daughters of Fire: Verse Analysis of an Upper Chehalis Folktale: 267-278 of Thayer, ed.

1984 Bear and Bee: Narrative Verse Analysis of an Upper Chehalis Folktale: 246-261 of Rood (ed.) 1984.

1987 Bluejay and His Sister: 255-296. *Recovering the Word: Essays on Native American Literature.* Brian Swann & Arnold Krupat, eds. Berkeley: University of California Press.

1990a Prehistory of Salishan Languages. *International Conference on Salish and Neighboring Languages* 25: 197-208, Vancouver, B.C.

1990b Prehistory of the Native Languages of the Northwest Coast. Paper presented at The Great Ocean: International Conference on the North Pacific to 1600, Portland, Oregon. Published as Kinkade 1991b.

1991a *Upper Chehalis Dictionary.* Missoula: University of Montana Occasional Papers in Linguistics 7.

1992 Translating Pentlatch: 163-175. *On the Translation of Native American Literatures.* Brian Swann, ed. Washington: Smithsonian Institution Press.

Lane, Barbara

1973 Political and Economic Aspects of Indian-White Culture Contact in Western Washington in the Mid-19th Century. May 10. United States v. Washington.

Lang, George

2008 *Making Wawa. The Genesis of Chinook Jargon.* Vancouver: UBC Press.

McAtee, WL

1955 folk names of NE birds

Matson, Emerson

1968 *Longhouse Legends.* Camden, NJ: Thomas Nelson and Sons.

1972 *Legends of the Great Chiefs.* Tacoma: Storypole Press.

Meany, Edmond

1905 Washington Redmen Who Helped Palefaces in War: Chehalis Tribe of Twenty-Five Braves Who Fought For Whites. 15 October: 6. *Seattle Post-Intelligencer.*

Miller, Jay, and Vi Hilbert

1993 Caring for Control: A Pivot of Salishan Language and Culture. *American Indian Linguistics and Ethnography in Honor of Laurence C. Thompson.* University of Montana, Occasional Papers in Linguistics 10: 237-239.

1996 Lushootseed Animal People: Mediation and Transformation from Myth to History. pp. 138-156 in *Monsters, Tricksters, and Sacred Cows*: Animal Tales and American Identities. A. James Arnold, ed. New World Studies. Charlottesville: University of Virginia Press.

2004 "That Salish Feeling..." *Studies in Salish Linguistics in Honor of M. Dale Kinkade.* Donna B. Gerdts and Lisa Matthewson, eds. University of Montana, Occasional Papers In Linguistics No. 17: 197-210. (Vi Hilbert first author)

Norton, Helen H.

1979 The Association between Anthropogenic Prairies and Important Food Plans in Western Washington. *Northwest Anthropological Research Notes* (NARN) 13 (20): 434-449.

1980 Evidence for Bracken Fern as a food for Aboriginal Peoples of Western Washington. *Economic Botany* 33 (4): 384-396.

1985 Women and Resources of the Northwest Coast: Documentation from the 18th and Early 19th Century. University of Washington, Anthropology, PhD Dissertation.

Olson, Ronald
   1936 The Quinault Indians. University of Washington Publications in Anthropology 6 (1): 1-190.
Seaburg, William
   1999 Whatever Happened to Thelma Adamson? A Footnote in the History of Northwest Anthropological Research. *Northwest Anthropological Research Notes* 33 (1): 73-83.
Swan, James
   20 July 1855 letter from James Swan at Shoalwater to George Gibbs at Steilacoom. NAA
Terres, John
   1980 The Audubon Society Encyclopedia of North American Birds. NY: Alfred Knopf.
Thompson, Laurence, and Dale Kinkade
   1990 Languages. *Northwest Coast.* Wayne Suttles, ed. Smithsonian Institution Press: Handbook of North American Indians #7: 30-51.
Thompson, M. Terry, and Steven Egesdal
   2008 *Salish Myths and Legends. One People's Stories.* Lincoln: University of Nebraska Press.
Walls, Robert
   1987 *Bibliography Of Washington State Folklore And Folklife.* Seattle: University of Washington Press.
Wickersham, James
   1898 Nisqually Mythology, Studies of the Washington Indians. *Overland Monthly* 32: 345-51.

A

Adamson, Thelma, 12f, 146
Algic, 5
Alki Point, 106, 151
Allied Tribes of the Upper Skagit, 30
Alligator, 53
Always Tears Prairie, 16
American Hall, 39
Andrews, LZ, 53
Astoria, 18, 150
Auburn, 108

B

Baker Lake, 25, 33; Mt 130; Baker River,
    21, 28f, 126f
Ballard, Arthur, 3, 12, 108f
Barkhousen, Julie, 32
Bay Center, 18
Bayview, 22, 31f
Bedal, WA, 22
Bedal, Edith, 30
Belfast, 22, 32f
Be-lole ~Swinomish chief, 33f
Bible, 111
Big Bend, 5, 143
Big Lake, 21f, 55
Big Rock, 25
-bix^w ~ bunch, 114
Bluejay, 6, 14f, 80, 145
Boas, Franz, 12f, 146
Bob, Tommy, 37, 42
Bow Hill, 31f
Brains ~ dirt, 120, 128
Bridgeport, 138
Brown, Leo, 29f, 35
Brown's Point, 32
-bsh ~ bunch, 114
Burlington, 20f

C

Campbell, Alice, 21f, 118, 126
Campbell, Johnny, 29
Campbell, Joseph, 20, 30
Campbell, Pete, 30
Cape Mudge, 131
Capitol Peak, 145
Captain Camel Campbell, 118
Carlyle, 17
Carrier, 135f
Cascades, 3f, 22, 30f, 120
Cascade Passes, 133
Cascade River, 22
Chadas-kadim, 31f
Charles, Jimmy, 31, 36
Charles, Peter, 35, 44
Chehalis, 3f, 12f, 117, 123, 140f
Chehalis River funnel, 140
Chelan, 4f, 27, 133f
Chicago, 3
Chilcotin, 135f
Chimakuan, 145
Chimakuans, 140f
Chimakums, 5
Chinoose Creek, 19
Chinuk Wawa, 123, 140*
Chirouse, Fr Eugene Casimir, 140, 151
chorus, 16
Cladoosby's father, 105
Cladoosby, Henry, 35
Cladoosby, Marian, 37
Clangula hyemalis, 13, 19
Claquato, 145
Clatsops, 18
Clear Lake, 21f, 45f, 55
Collins, June, 3, 7, 12, 60, 118, 126
Columbia River, 12f, 18, 134f, 140f, 150
Colville, 3f, 134f
Concrete, 21, 30, 118f, 126f
Copalis, 17, 142
Coupeville, 117f, 127f
Cowichan, 4f, 118, 125, 131
crabs, 17f
crow, 136; GM, 43
Curtis, Edward, 3, 106
Cuthbert, Alice, 30
Cypress Island, 35f

D

Day Creek, 21, 31f, 61f
Daybreak ~ *ləx̱albid*, 120, 128
Daylight ~ tuxʷiqədəb, 10, 128
Deception Pass, 34, 41f, 52f, 107
Diaper boy, 120, 129, 145
dicta, 16, 112f, 119f, 129f
Diobsud Creek, 22
dipper, 7
Ditidat, 5, 140
Doctor Bailey ~ Sba-qua-blth, 28
Dr. Dan, 52
Dry Slough, 24, 33
ducks, 7, 12f, 19, 54, 57, 76, 106
Dudowards, 152
Dugualla Bay, 33f
Dungeness, 118, 123

E

Eagle, 5, 54, 120, 127, 135f
Eagle Harbor, 106
Eagle's Landing, 3
eating, 14, 81, 103, 113f, 124f
Edison Slough, 31
effigy, 117, 123
Egesdal, Steven, 146
Eld Inlet, 142
Ellensburg, 138
Emancipation Proclamation, 153
Eyley, Mary, 146

F

Farrand, Livingston, 12
Fidalgo Island, 34f, 120, 128
First Daylight, 128
First Light, 120
Flood, 123f, 130, 145f
Fornsby, John, 7, 60, 117; Fornsby, Johnny,
    123, 127; General, 53
Fort Astoria, 150
Fort Casey, 120, 127
Fort Columbia, 18
Fort Langley, 118, 125
Fort Nisqually, 117, 123

Fort Vancouver, 150
Fort Victoria, 150
forts, 32f, 117, 120f, 128
Fraser, 3, 36, 118, 125, 135, 140, 149, 153
Friday ~ Dr Pliday, 33
Friday Creek, 31f

G

General Pierce ~ Kwal-lat-sum, 33
Gibbs, George, 12, 144
Glacier Peak, 120
Golden-Mantled Ground Squirrel, 146
Goliah, 117f, 127
Grand Mound, 142f
Grandson of Dog, 145f
Grays Harbor, 12f, 144
Greenbanks, 119, 126
grizzly bear, 39, 51*, 135f, 161
Guemes Channel, 35f, 42

H

Hail, 40, 50*
Hair, 14f, 41f, 68, 110, 123, 47, 48, 73, 112,
    127; goat, 7, 123
Hamilton, 21, 26f, 39, 57f, 61, 125, 161
Hat Island, 34
Hawaii, 140f
Heck, Lucy, 12, 14f
hikʷ siʔab, 126; *hikʷ si'ab*, 118
Hilbert, Vi, 3, 10, 60f, 117f, 147, 155
Hill-Tout, Charles, 112
Holmes Harbor, 26
Honne, 146f
Hoquiam, 19
Hozomeen, 129
Huah-le-tsa, 34
Humptulips, 17f
Humptulips City, 15f

I

Illabot Creek, 28f
Indian Shaker Church, 61, 72f, 113f, 120,
    130, 153, 161
Iroquoian, 5

Iroquois, 118, 136

J

Jackman Creek, 21
Jacobs, Melville, 12, 122, 147
James Rock, 19
James, Justine, 13
Jarman Prairie, 31f, 61, 75
Jenness, Diamond, 122, 131f
Jones, Jimmie, 50
Joshua, 118, 125
Joshua, Mrs, 39
Junco, 145f

K

Kamilche, 142
Kane, Paul, 118, 125, 151
Katzie, 4, 129 #7
KeKedab, 119f; KeKedəb, 118, 126
Kəmol, 14; Kmol, 16; Kumol 12; Kom-mol-
   owish, 13
Kettle Falls, 137
Klallam, 4f, 118, 123f, 140f
Klickitat Academy, 108
Kootenay, 3, 140
Kwaliokwa, 140
kʷałqədəb, 124f

L

LaConner, 25f, 34f, 52, 120f
ləx̣albid ~ Daybreak > La-hail-by, 34; La-
   Qual-by, 43
Lamprey > silver, 145
Lice > head, 17
Longtail duck, 19
Lummi, 4f, 36, 98f, 117f, 123, 140
Lyman, WA, 21f, 46, 57f, 92
Lyons, John, 24, 42

M

Makah, 5, 13, 36, 117f, 140
Malecite, 136
Maury, 117
McLeod, Jim, 52

Meany, Edmond, 13
Metcalf, Leon, 3, 61, 72, 105
Milky Way, 49
Minter, 3
Miqmaq, 136; Micmac, 136
-mish, 114
Mitchell, Dewey, 47, 60
Model Village, 34
Moon, 45f, 108, 112, 120, 145
Moore, Jack, 88
Moses Ti-a-tmus, 29f
Mount Vernon, 20, 24f, 30, 34, 125
Mowitch Man, 33
Mt Baker, see Baker
Mulla, WA, 19

N

Naches, 8, 133
Nanaimo, 125, 152
nasals, 5, 140
nets, 5, 13, 17f, 117f; reef, 5, 129, 140;
   trawl, 129; weir, 129
Newhalem, 22f
Nisqually, 4f, 12, 22, 114f, 124f, 151, 155
nobility, 116, 124, 132
nodal kindred, 114
Nookachamps, 21f, 24*, 54*, 30
Northwest Federation of Indians, 30
Nuchahnulth, 133
Nuxalk, 4f, 141

O

Oak Harbor, 120, 128
ƛ̓əlax̣ədbid, 90
Old Man House, 107
old sqwawk duck, 12, 19
Old Toke, 12
Olson, Ronald, 12
Olympia, 28, 117, 143, 154
Olympic Marsh, 24f
Olympics, 5, 14, 142f, 153, 163
Orondo, 139
Otter, 137f
Ozette, 18

P

Padilla Bay, 22, 34
Palmer, Andie, 106 #2
Panama, 109
Passamaquoddy, 137
Patch-kanam, 24
Pat-teh-us, 30, 33
Penn Cove, 118, 123, 128
Penobscot, 137
Peters, Susie Sampson, 3, 26f, 32, 62
pilot bread, 81; puck, 103
pitch, 8f, 98
Plidy ~ Friday, 33
Point Elliott Treaty, 25f, 35f, 118, 124
Point No Point, 106
Pope, Bob, 12
potatoes, 76, 80, 83, 108, 116
prairie, 5, 13f, 22f, 28f, 35f, 45, 61f, 75,
    113, 120, 128, 141, 146
Pressentins; Charles von, 27
property, 61, 108, 114, 125, 131f
Proto-Penutian, 142
Proto-Salishans, 142
Proto-Tsamosan, 141
Psk^waws ~ Wenatchi, 4f
puberty, 115, 130
Puyallup, 4f, 31, 79, 113, 128

Q

Quarry Hill, 109f
Qued-el-ich ~ *sg^wədilič*, 54f
Quileutes, 13f, 142f

R

ramages, 115, 133
Raven, 8, 46f, 136f
red star, 45
Robe Boy, 121f, 128f, 150, 162
Rockport, 21f, 30
Roosevelt, Franklin, 54
Rosario Beach, 41, 153

S

Saanich, 4f, 32, 123 132

sadᶻəhəbixʷ, 118
Saghalie Tyee, 29
Salishan Funnel, 141f
Sally Bailey, 28
Samish ~ *sabš*, 4f, 22, 30f, 35f*, 41f, 103,
    120f, 141
Samish Lake, 22
Sampson, Alfanso, 24; Alfonso
Sampson, Alfred, 32
Sampson, Benedict, 28
Sampson, Joseph, 25
Sampson, Martin, 3f, 38, 47, 73, 86, 131
Sampson (Peters), Susan, 3, 26f, 32, 62
San Juans, 36, 153
Sanders, George, 147
Satsop, 5, 143
Sauk, 5, 21f, 28f*, 46, 134
Scha-ha-lab-ki ~ s*xaxaləbqid*, 11-14 wives,
    24
Secena, Jonas, 13, 147
Sedro Woolley, 20f, 30, 46, 162
Sercombe, Laurel, 148
sg^wədilič, 3, 7*f, 24, 54, 60, 121f, 130
sg^wig^wi, 124 #6
Shelton, WA, 143
Shelton, Ruth, 32, 76
Shoalwater, 12
Shoemaker Jim, 25f, 60
Shuswap, 4f, 135f, 154
Sieous ~ *su'yius*, Charles, 28
Skagit City, 60, 86f, 117, 123f
Skagit Falls, 8f
sƛ' abəbtikəd, 22
Smith, Marian, 113, 128, 131
snakes, 18; rattle, 51
Sneatlam ~ s*niƛəb*, 26, 53, 123f; Sneatlum,
    117f, 130
Snee-osh Point, 120, 128
Snohomish, 4f, 24f, 36f, 114, 151
Snohomish, James, 37; Jimmy, 88
Snyder, Sally, 9, 60, 118, 122f
Sta-ba-but-kin, 28f
Starchild, 129, 129, 145

stem kindred, 114
Stillaguamish, 4f, 79, 120f
su?yius, 60, 90
Suiattle, 4f, 22, 29f
Sullivan Slough, 34, 120, 128
Swaal, 140
Swan, 145f
Swan, James, 12

T

Tacoma Narrows, 3
Taholah, 18
taktəd, 96, 100
Tantaquidgeon, 136
taqʷoba, 5
Teit, James, 135
Telegraph, 36, 39
Telegraph Slough, 31f
Thunderbird, 12, 31f, 135, 161
tidišə?~ widow, 61f, 96f
tiułəbaxad, 126
Tom, Isadore ~ pətius, 10
Too-whl-kadim, 34
tsi? əgʷał, 127
Tsimshian, 112, 122, 135, 152
Twana, 4f, 140f
Twu-whil-Kadim, 43
Twu-yalets-sa, 43f

U

Uto-Aztecan, 5

V

Vashon, 117
Victoria, BC, 76, 102, 114, 150f

W

Wabanaki, 136f
Wakashans, 114, 140f, 149
Warner Prairie, 23, 31f
wawa, 140
Waw-wit-kin, 28f
Wenatchi ~ Psqʷaws, 4f, 133f, 138
Whale House ~ *sałułtxʷ*, 131
Whatcom, Betsy, 108
Whidbey Island, 24f, 33f, 107, 117f
Whitworth College, 108
Wilbur, Laura, 44
Willapa Bay, 12
Williams Lucy, 8f
Wolves, 17, 106
woodrats, 18
Word Tabu, 141 #8

X

xa?xa, 134; *xaxa*, 72; *xa'xa*, 10, 112
xʷdik, 114
xʷac'al'al, 25
Xʷane, 145;
Xʷani Xʷani, 13, 18

Y

Yala-haut-so, 51
yədwas-ta, 25
yəhaw', 6f

Z

Zephyr, 108

Please help zap out typo-gnomes

Report Correction & Comments

www.ingramcontent.com/pod-product-compliance
Lightning Source LLC
Chambersburg PA
CBHW081951260726
48657CB00009BA/2562